The Trifle Bowl and Other Tales

Lindsey Bareham

BANTAM PRESS

LONDON · TORONTO · SYDNEY · AUCKLAND · JOHANNESBURG

TRANSWORLD PUBLISHERS
61–63 Uxbridge Road, London W5 5SA
A Random House Group Company
www.transworldbooks.co.uk

First published in Great Britain
in 2013 by Bantam Press
an imprint of Transworld Publishers

A CIP catalogue record for this book
is available from the British Library.

ISBN 9780593069417

Addresses for Random House Group Ltd companies outside the UK
can be found at: www.randomhouse.co.uk
The Random House Group Ltd Reg. No. 954009

The Random House Group Limited supports the Forest Stewardship Council ®
(FSC®), the leading international forest-certification organisation. Our books carrying
the FSC label are printed on FSC®-certified paper. FSC is the only forest-certification
scheme supported by the leading environmental organisations, including Greenpeace.
Our paper procurement policy can be found at www.randomhouse.co.uk/environment

Photography: Chris Terry
Design: MortonStudio
Illustrations: Martin Haake
Food styling: Katie Giovanni
Props styling: Cynthia Inions

Typeset in Romain
Printed and bound in Great Britain by Butler, Tanner & Dennis Ltd, Frome.

2 4 6 8 10 9 7 5 3 1

To Jonathan, my big brother

SMITH & STEVENSON
BUTCHERS' COMPLETE
OUTFITTERS
107 GALLOWGATE
GLASGOW.

Contents

In My Kitchen

'The perfect kitchen, for me, would really be more like a painter's studio furnished with cooking equipment than anything conventionally accepted as a kitchen.'

ELIZABETH DAVID, *PETITS PROPOS CULINAIRES*, 1992

It's Sunday morning and I've just come back from a walk in the rain with my puppy. She's had a bath and is asleep, wrapped in a towel snuggled next to me on the sofa opposite the faux dresser in my kitchen. I'm splattered with dog shampoo, sprawled out next to her with a restorative cup of coffee. Desert Island Discs is on the radio and the haunting voice of Sandy Denny wafts round the room. My eyes turn away from the rain spattering down the French windows towards the radio, lingering on a cut glass trifle bowl that used to belong to my mother and her mother before her. 'Who knows where the time goes . . .' sings Sandy, and before I know it I'm jerked back to days gone by, remembering trifles my mum used to make and occasions when we ate them.

There used to be two identical trifle bowls and I'm ashamed to say it was me that broke the other one. They were stashed away in a cupboard under the stairs and came out for special occasions, birthdays and Christmas. Mum's trifles were made with jelly and tinned fruit, thick Bird's custard that set very hard, topped with swirls of whipped cream decorated with glacé cherries and silver balls. One trifle came with us to Westcliff-on-Sea on Boxing Day, for the annual Christmas leftovers lunch at Mum's sister's house. Eight children and five adults would be squashed round a long table in the cousins' playroom and afterwards there would be the inevitable squabble over who could read what from the cousins' collection of Broons and Oor Wullie annuals. One particular year, when I was given Rosebud, the doll I'd longed to own, the day ended with Dad getting into a scary burn-up with another car on the way home. As I linger over these memories, it suddenly hits me. Practical cooking mementos like this trifle bowl are far more of a repository of memories, and of course recipes, than you might expect.

Other people's kitchens are a bit like other people's wardrobes, full of surprises and endlessly fascinating. Mine is at the rear of a typical Victorian two-up-two-down terrace house with a back extension and postage stamp

London garden. I bought the house as a wreck after my marriage broke down and have subsequently lived through all sorts of ups and downs, some good, some bad, but my one constant has been my kitchen. Twenty years later I have brought up two sons, fed and watered their army of friends and entertained according to the vicissitudes of a freelance lifestyle, keeping afloat by writing about food, first as a restaurant critic and then as a cook.

Even though the original kitchen was gloomy and unloved, it wasn't difficult to see its potential. Over the years the room has evolved from its original and necessarily parsimonious makeover. Essentially, though, it's the same. Walls have come down and more space has been created but this kitchen has always been more than a place to cook. One wall is a huge bookcase holding the ingredient-led part of my extensive cookery book collection. Art, some of food, by Henry, my artist son, hangs on other walls. There are three tables, all with different functions. We eat at a long, pine refectory table (made by Clive who rebuilt the kitchen, twice) and sit on well-polished ladder-back chairs that were once round the dining table in my childhood home. Books pile up on a little pine table where a young Henry used to do his homework. Sometimes it's used to extend the main table or carried next door for a dinner à deux in front of the fire in the sitting room. A long, low table sits opposite the faux dresser in front of a not very squashy sofa (there used to be a TV in one of the cupboards), laid with a huge platter of constantly replenished fresh fruit. I often put my feet up here, gazing through the French windows that open on to our back yard. In summer the pergola is covered by a surprisingly prolific vine, the leaves used for dolmades, to wrap little quail and fillets of salmon with Serrano ham. By July or early August there will be big bunches of small luminescent pale green grapes dangling enticingly, almost ready for fruit salads or the jam jar. A bay tree grows with wild abandon next to the vine, and big pots of rosemary, various types of thyme, chives and a clump of mint transplanted from the allotment inform my cooking most days. An olive tree and a fig tree are on the point of producing fruit.

On warm evenings the French windows are flung open and we live and cook outside. I have two barbecues, one a neatly designed portable box and the other a handsome party size wheelie drum, a gift from one of my sons. They both get fired up all year round and so too does the gas-fuelled paella ring, which can also be used inside the house. Tucked around the corner in the alley running alongside the kitchen sits my wood-burning beehive oven, really an inverted tandoor. This wonderful River Café-style oven is great on winter nights for pizza and roast chicken and the embers of the fire are perfect for slow-roasting a large joint of pork that will be meltingly soft in the morning and still hot at lunchtime. The garden table is hidden from view to all neighbours and at night is lit with candles in hanging Moroccan lanterns. Bigger lanterns and a couple of spotlights shoot up the honeysuckle, giving the garden parameters an eerie glow. Jasmine and clematis intertwine with the vine and branches from a gnarled laburnum weave over this part of the pergola to give shade, shelter and privacy. When we hold a party, the table is moved to make way for kelims laid over the paving stones and a sound system is set up in the shed. Food could be a Moroccan-style feast with lamb and green olive tagine, couscous with spinach and almonds, chicken kebabs and Magreb roast vegetables. If it is a birthday party for one of my sons, they get to choose the food.

As I glance around my kitchen now, taking in its distinctive custard and cream colour scheme and black and white chequered tile floor, I see everything more or less as I like it. Like all kitchens, there is never enough work surface but my pride and joy is two thick marble worktops rescued

from *Le Coq d'Or* before it became *Langan's Brasserie* in *Mayfair*, on which chefs rolled pastry and pummelled bread dough. Overall, though, I love this sunny L-shaped room. The way it is dressed with food is constantly changing but it is my extensive collection of bowls and platters, knives and favourite bits of kitchen kit that I use over and over again that makes it feel like home. At the moment there are fresh cobnuts in a small cazuela waiting to be pounded for meringue. A second pomegranate sits on the window ledge – the other is half-eaten, in a plastic box in the fridge, ready to be sprinkled on garlicky, home-made hummus and moutabal. Next to the pomegranate squats a small golden pumpkin awaiting inspiration. There are downy quince and big blowsy Bramley cooking apples in a window basket and packets of polenta, pasta and noodles waiting to be put away.

On another window ledge, a glass nutmeg grater sits next to three different types of salt and my new battery-lit pepper grinder. Next to them sit fresh ginger, bright red chillies and loose cloves of garlic ready to be pounded in my black granite pestle and mortar for a spicy sambal. There is Greek olive oil, two types of Italian olive oil, several vinegars and a Japanese bowl filled with lemons and limes. A humungous coil of Greek garlic hangs from a curtain rail above the French windows, next to dried orange peel, a bunch of bay tree clippings and sage from the allotment. An artichoke soup made with home-grown vegetables bubbles away on the hob, its intriguing scent wafting around the kitchen. Big bunches of flat-leaf parsley, coriander and a pot of basil are always somewhere in this kitchen.

There is much to see in this fusion of life and work and my eyes flit over an idiosyncratic treasure trove. A collection of well-used tequila sunrise-coloured Le Creuset pans is lined up on a shelf above my cooker – to many I am in loco parentis as they really belong to my best friend Tessa, now living in Sydney. Each is a favourite for particular soups and stews. Next to them sit my extra large casserole dishes for party daube, fish pie and moussaka. The top shelves of a deceptively authentic-looking faux kitchen dresser are lined with platters that have carried more meals than I can remember. One, a blue and white Chinese plate with an old man with sleeves that cover his hands, used to reside on the oak dresser that once belonged to my maternal grandmother. It makes me think of Energen rolls (which she kept in their big box in her kitchen pantry) and Jacobs High Baked biscuits piled with grated Cheddar laid out for tea on one of her Chinese plates. Various big white platters are a favourite way of presenting food, particularly when there are lots of people around the table or for parties, piled with food like grilled aubergine with feta and parsley, couscous salads, roasted red peppers and herby stuffed courgettes. There is a teetering tower of scallop shells ready for the scallop season. A pasta machine waits patiently for its next outing. Certain ceramics prompt certain dishes. My mother's cut glass trifle bowl is used for only one thing (plus the occasional fool and fruit salad), while my Greek earthenware soup bowls with a hole for your thumb are the perfect depth for pâté and two-person hachis Parmentier. I always serve Moroccan tagines in a large earthenware cazuela, preferring my collection of different-sized white ceramic gratin dishes for pommes Dauphinoise, lasagne, cauliflower cheese and fruit crumbles.

When I look at my distinctively dark, oblong breadboard, I can almost see my father standing tall and erect as he sliced our daily wholemeal loaf in thick, neat slices. Its horizons have broadened since living with me; pugliese, campillou, *pitta*, fougasse, *rye bread*, pain de campagne, *challah and bagels*, this breadboard has seen it all. It sits next to my faithful Dualit toaster, the last in a long line of toasters after numerous catastrophes. Every time I reach for a jar of spices to season a tagine or make a curry, I think of my former husband. He, an accomplished cook fond of claiming he taught me 'everything', made my spice rack from old wine crates not long before he died. Over there hangs my first paella pan, a gift many years ago from my older brother who lived in Spain.

I sometimes think I could live in this room. Everything I need is here, even a sofa to sleep on. I feel enriched by what I see around me and can conjure up evocative memories as I cook. It's the paraphernalia of cooking, the favourite and often random items I choose to cook with that have inspired the recipes in this book. They reflect my style of informal but imaginative cooking and eating. I love making something delicious to eat from an unpromising selection of ingredients and am always on the lookout for inexpensive seasonal and sustainable food. I aim to give simple but explicit real-time instructions that make cooking and eating well accessible to the most inexperienced cook, as I was when I started cooking for myself. There is a mix of quick and more leisurely recipes inspired by all the food that has touched my life, from my grandmother's steamed sponge puddings to the tagines and curries I learnt to make during my years as a restaurant critic. You will find quick family suppers and easy seafood surprises, slow-cook dishes and other one-pot soups and stews, teatime treats and foolproof puddings, party food and barbecue feasts. Apart from recording some of the memories that ricochet around my kitchen, the book offers practical help too, as well as tips on what to buy and where to find some of the items I mention. It is larded with cookery tricks of the trade, anecdote and history, all built up from years of cooking for a living.

Although all the recipes in this book are associated with my kitchen and my memories, I hope some of the stories and all the dishes will become favourites with your friends and family.

Lindsey Bareham
JULY 2012

A Aluminium Foil

When Simon Hopkinson and I were working on *Roast Chicken and Other Stories*, our favourite lunch was baked potatoes, hummus and a jar of fearsomely hot chilli sauce. For speed, the potatoes were halved, the cut side dipped into Maldon salt flakes, laid on a foil-lined roasting tin and put in the oven before it came up to temperature. Cooking them like this, at the highest temperature my ailing little oven could muster, we weren't subject to tantalizing cooking smells for more than 30 minutes. It is the foil, always laid shiny side up, that speeds up the cooking.

Barely a day goes by without me using foil for something in my kitchen and I don't give it a second thought. Curious, then, to realize that it's been around for centuries, made initially from solid metal beaten or rolled to paper thinness. It gets the name tinfoil because the first mass-produced stuff was made from tin, later replaced by aluminium. Swiss aluminium manufacturers built the first foil rolling plant in 1910 in response to the discovery that aluminium foil could be used as a protective barrier, initially for packaging chocolate bars and tobacco.

In the kitchen, it is essential for wrapping food to exclude air but its other invaluable use is conducting heat. Apart from speeding up baked potatoes, foil has taken over from parchment for what the French call cooking *en papillote*. One of my quick and easy standbys for my sons when they were growing up and needing meals at different times was foil-wrapped parcels of fish with sliced courgettes or other juicy, fast-cooking vegetables. Foil is also useful for wrapping awkward shapes, say a roast chicken for a picnic, or keeping the remains of a packet of biscuits airtight.

I love BacoFoil foil sheets. There is something so pampered about having the foil neatly trimmed and just the right size for wrapping sandwiches, lining the grill pan or bundling food for the fridge. I fold it into strips for makeshift flan rings or cake or muffin hoops; if you put your mind to it, any shape is possible, even hearts and numbers, thus saving pounds on special tins. Look out, too, for parchment-lined foil (from Lakeland, see page 275) – a deluxe foil that promotes even heating with a non-stick lining, it is also extremely easy to fold into shapes.

Souffléd Jacket Potatoes

SERVES 8–10

Bonfire night, for me, is forever associated with jacket potatoes, big ones with thick, crusty skins, piled with ice-cold chunks of butter and overflowing with grated Cheddar. My mum used to pre-cook enough potatoes for a small army earlier in the day, leaving them to go cold and saggy. Magically, after a quick blast in a hot oven, the flaccid skin would crisp to perfection. It's a tip I came across years later in Édouard de Pomiane's seminal Cooking in Ten Minutes. *He advises never to chuck out leftover baked potatoes and it's an excellent tip. It means that a makeshift supper, adding cheese with a poached egg and bacon, or crisply fried strips of Spam, is on the table in less time than it takes to heat up a ready meal.*

Stuffing them is another way of getting ahead with jacket potatoes. Once baked, the potatoes are halved and the fluffy potato is dug out of the shell and mixed with almost anything you fancy, say chopped ham and spinach, Parmesan and buttery leeks, or a crumble of feta with mint. My special favourite is inspired by purée de pommes de terre à l'ail, *from my battered copy of* Mastering the Art of French Cooking *by Simone Beck, Louisette Bertholle and Julia Child. Two heads of garlic, they concur, seems like a horrifying amount but the result is mellow and creamy, and a huge amount of parsley sweetens the mouth. Potatoes, sauce and the final assembly can all be done in advance. Terrific on their own, they go with everything from sausages to salad.*

10 baking potatoes, approx 200g each	300ml boiling milk
2 heads of garlic (approx 25 cloves)	50g flat-leaf parsley leaves
40g butter	2 tbsp thick cream
40g flour	freshly grated Parmesan

Heat the oven to 220°C/gas mark 7. Scrub the potatoes and run a sharp knife lengthways round their middles, just etching the surface. Place on a foil-lined roasting tin and position near the top of the oven without waiting for it to come to temperature. Cook for 45 minutes, or until the skin is beginning to brown and crisp and the flesh is tender when pierced with a sharp knife.

Make the sauce while the potatoes bake. Separate the garlic cloves, bang them with your fist and flake away the papery skin. Place in a small pan, cover with boiling water and boil for 2 minutes. Drain. Melt the butter in the pan, return the garlic, cover and cook, on a very low heat, for 15–20 minutes, until soft but hardly coloured. Stir in the flour, then, off the heat, stir in the boiling milk. Stir constantly for 1 minute. Season with salt and pepper, then liquidize or pass through a sieve to make a smooth, thick sauce. Cook, stirring often, over a low heat for 5 minutes. Cover with a plate or a stretch of clingfilm (to avoid a skin forming) and leave to cool. Finely chop the parsley.

Halve the potatoes through the etched line, scrape the flesh into a bowl and line up the 'boats' in the roasting tin. Stir the cream into the potato flesh, season with salt and pepper, then add the garlic sauce and chopped parsley. Stir to mix, then spoon back into the potato halves and dredge with Parmesan. Return to a top oven shelf and cook for 15–20 minutes, slightly longer if cooking from cold, until the top is golden, the potato slightly bouffant and the skin crisp.

B Baking Sheets

These are sometimes called roasting trays. Their point is to be flat and rigid, made of heavy-duty steel, usually hard-anodized aluminium, so they conduct heat evenly and slide easily in and out of the oven. Some have slightly sloping edges but mine have one turned-up end, which is useful for getting a grip. They are used for baking meringues, biscuits, pasties and other pastries, bread and pies shaped by hand, and as a base for flan rings and cake hoops. They are useful in the same way for loose-bottomed tart and flan tins, and for pizza. I tend to slide one into the oven when I am cooking a pie or tart that isn't blind-baked first. The heat of the pre-heated baking sheet helps to cook the base layer of pastry. It's a false economy to buy cheap, usually flimsy, baking sheets, as they buckle in a hot oven and often turn rusty. Also see Roasting Tins (page 192) and Swiss Roll Tins (page 28).

Cheese and Onion Empanadas

MAKES 10–12

In the summer of 2010 I gave a Cornish pasty cookery demo at the Port Eliot festival. As a bit of light relief after the exactitudes of making authentic pasties I made these extremely simple but utterly delicious little empanadas. They are an unashamed cheat's recipe using ready-made puff pastry, tinned fried onions and ready-grated Cheddar cheese. They are glazed with beaten egg and finished with a choice of seeds. My favourite is fennel, but poppy and sesame seeds are good too, although a mixture is possibly even better. I made batch after batch before I set off so that I could give them away to friends and everyone who came to the demonstration. They were such a hit that I think it's worth passing on the recipe.

Serve them with drinks or reheat them as a snack. With a home-made tomato sauce or a big crunchy salad, say green beans, red onion and tomato, they make a delicious light meal. They are perfect, too, to have at the ready for that lull around the barbecue before anything is ready to eat. Tinned fried onions don't sound very appetizing but you will have to trust me. Eazy onions are imported from Spain, where they are cooked in olive oil. I rate them highly and always have a couple of tins in my cupboard.

375g all-butter puff pastry	300g grated Cheddar cheese
flour, for dusting	1 tbsp fennel seeds
400g tin of Eazy fried onions	1 tbsp poppy seeds
1 egg	1 tbsp sesame seeds

Cut the pastry into 9 equal pieces and roll them lightly on a floured surface until you can cut out 10.5cm circles. I use a cookie cutter. Gather up the trimmings and roll out one or two more circles. Tip the onions into a sieve to drain. Whisk the egg in a small bowl and have some water ready in a ramekin. You will also need a pastry brush, a parchment-lined baking sheet and the seeds accessible.

Hold a circle of pastry on the flat of your left hand (if you are right-handed). Paint a 1cm border with water. Place a scant dessertspoon of onion in the middle and top with a similar amount of grated cheese. Cup your hand so the pastry closes slightly, then, working from one end to the other, pinch the edges to seal. Be quite aggressive about this, poking any trailing cheese back inside the border. After one or two attempts you will work out exactly how much filling the pastry circle can take. Seal the edge with the tines of a fork and lay out on a plate as you go. When you have done all the empanadas, paint them with egg wash and sprinkle the top with seeds. Make a few steam holes with the fork. Arrange, not too close, on the baking sheet(s). Heat the oven to 200°C/gas mark 6 and bake for 15–20 minutes, checking after 15. They will puff and turn golden. Let them rest for a few minutes before eating.

B Barbecue

Two of my next-door neighbours have an Australian in their garden, not a real one, obviously, but a big gas-fuelled all-singing, all-dancing barbecue, like my sister has in Sydney and my brother used in Spain. They all cook on it all year round, but, tempting though it seems, I like the campfire spirit of an old-fashioned one. For years I've used a neatly designed small portable barbecue that lives in my shed. It gets a bit stressful cooking for more than four but the gift of a large, domed Weber from my son Zach and his wife has broadened my horizons.

I love planning a barbecue and always get carried away, making far too much food. I usually go for one centrepiece, like Moroccan-influenced lemon squid with harissa or Greek-style kofte, with a couple of no-fuss, chuck-it-on-the-barbie favourites, such as sausages, prawns, lamb chops and steaks. I always run with the theme, complementing the meat or seafood with an appropriately colourful big salad and one or two other dishes in case a vegetarian shows up.

I like the fact that all the preparation can be done in advance: the meat marinated, sausages oiled, salad dressings made, beans topped and tailed and potatoes boiled for a salad. It's vital to have a dip or two – hummus, say, or lemony smoked mackerel with creamed horseradish – and crusty bread to keep everyone occupied when there's a hiccup with the fire. No barbecue is without a glitch and it's usually caused by indecision about lighting it. I'm always worried that if I light it too soon the coals will burn down before everyone has arrived and we are ready to cook. I've come to the conclusion, though, that it always takes far

longer – probably 40 minutes – to reach the desirable red coals with white ash stage. Another important little tip is to soak wooden kebab sticks in warm water for at least an hour, preferably longer, to stop them burning.

I rarely do the actual cooking myself, as there is always someone, usually male, who enjoys it far more than I do. I've finally bought some long tongs and a gauntlet-style oven glove to avoid roasted hands. One drawback to my lovely new barbecue is that it stands alone. My little portable fire always sits on a table, so I'd never noticed how important it is to have somewhere to put things.

Persian Kebabs with Beetroot and Anchovy Salad

SERVES 4–6

It's always intriguing to come across a recipe with a seemingly random ingredient that proves to be the making of the dish. That's the case with these gorgeously meaty kebabs, and bicarbonate of soda is the curiosity. While its effect seems to encourage stickiness, you will get the best results if the mix of minced lamb and beef is quite fatty to retain moisture and juiciness. The meat is seasoned only with grated onion, salt, pepper and the bicarb. It is kneaded like dough and ends up almost like a paste that is easily formed into big, fat sausages to thread on flat stainless steel skewers. As the kebabs cook, they are basted with melted butter seasoned with crushed garlic and a hint of lime. The last of the butter is mixed with chopped parsley to give a bright green finish to the Persian-style koobideh. Serve with rice, pickled green chillies, crusty bread, hummus and this agrodolce beetroot salad livened up with anchovies. The latter is also very good with hard-boiled eggs or feta cheese.

2 medium onions
500g minced lamb, preferably shoulder
500g minced beef
2 tsp salt
1 tsp ground black pepper
½ tsp bicarbonate of soda
125g unsalted butter

2 garlic cloves, crushed
a squeeze of lime or lemon
2 tbsp chopped flat-leaf parsley leaves
For the beetroot salad:
approx 900g medium-small beetroot
1 large lemon
2 red onions, approx 200g

2 tbsp olive oil	10 pickled garlic cloves, from a jar
¼ tsp dried crushed chillies	1 tbsp capers
1 tbsp Belazu balsamic vinegar	100g Adriatic anchovy fillets
200g sun-drenched/sun-blushed tomatoes in oil	1 tbsp chopped flat-leaf parsley leaves

Peel and halve the onions. Grate on the large hole of a box grater into a mixing bowl. Add the minced meat, salt, pepper and bicarb. Mix, then knead with your hands for 5 minutes until smooth and almost like a paste. Leave for 15 minutes at room temperature, then, with damp hands, form into 10 or 12 small orange-size balls. Roll into sausage-shapes, transferring them to a plate as you go. Cover with clingfilm and chill for at least 30 minutes and up to 24 hours. Thread on to flat skewers when you are ready to cook.

Make the baste by melting the butter, then stir in the crushed garlic and a squeeze of lime. When the coals are ready (or the ridged griddle very hot), barbecue without resting the meat on the grill if possible, i.e. with one end of the skewer on the back edge and the other on the front. Baste with melted butter as you turn the kebabs, cooking until done to your liking. Mix the parsley into the last of the butter and smear the kebabs before serving.

To make the salad, cook the unpeeled beets in boiling, salted water in a covered pan for about 20 minutes, until just tender to the point of a knife. Drain, then slip into your Marigolds and rub off the skin. With fork and knife, trim away any stalk and cut the beets into kebab-size chunks. Squeeze the lemon over the top and season with salt and pepper. While the beets cook, halve, peel and finely slice the onion. Soften gently, stirring occasionally, in the olive oil in a spacious frying pan. After about 15 minutes, when slippery soft, add ½ teaspoon of salt and the chilli flakes. Cook for a couple of minutes, then remove from the heat. Add the balsamic vinegar and cook briefly until syrupy.

Tip the tomatoes into a sieve to drain. Slice the garlic into thick rounds. Add the prepared beets, tomatoes, capers and garlic. Stir, then tip on to a platter. Decorate with anchovy fillets and garnish with parsley.

B Stick Blender

I'm probably on my fourth or fifth stick blender. I tend to expect too much of them, because in theory they do everything a regular blender and liquidizer can do but are cheaper, take up less space and are easier to wash up. The truth, though, unless you buy a so-called soup blender with a powerful motor and strong blade, is that a stick blender isn't a solve-all, like a food processor. That said, I wouldn't be without mine because it is incredibly useful, particularly for small quantities. A small horizontal blade grinds nuts and spices, makes breadcrumbs, chops herbs, onions, fish and meat, and will purée cooked vegetables and blend soups and sauces in double quick time. My current blender, a mid-price Braun, now several years old, and with a 300-watt motor and 600ml beaker, is wearing well. I have learnt not to overtax it. In my experience a cheap stick blender, or one with lots of attachments, is unlikely to live up to expectations.

Tandoori Chicken with Indian Mint Sauce

SERVES 4

There was a time when I was addicted to tandoori chicken. It was a loss leader, sold for a pound a portion, at Khan's, a fashionable curry house not particularly near where I lived. If you happened to get it fresh from the tandoor, the orange gashes sagging to reveal moist, juicy meat, it was heaven on a plate. It usually came with a naff salad, a lemon wedge and a few slices of half-cooked onion but I liked it with a personal pot of their spicy yet creamy, herby green sauce, the one usually served with poppadoms. This is possibly a Desert Island supper.

6 organic chicken legs, or 12 drumsticks
2 tbsp lime or lemon juice
1 tbsp chilli powder/paprika
5 garlic cloves
40g fresh ginger

1 tbsp ground cumin
1 tbsp ground coriander
¼ tsp ground cardamom
¼ tsp ground cloves
1 tsp ground turmeric
300g thick, natural yoghurt

3 tbsp vegetable oil	20 mint leaves
50g fresh coriander	½ tsp sugar
4 green bird's-eye chillies	3 juicy limes

Joint and skin legs; skin drumsticks. Make a few diagonal slashes on both sides, cutting to the bone. Place in a shallow bowl. Rub lime juice, a pinch of salt and the chilli powder evenly into the slashes. Leave for 30 minutes.

Crush and peel the garlic. Peel and thinly slice the ginger. Place both in the stick blender beaker with the cumin, ground coriander, cardamom, cloves, turmeric, half the yoghurt and 1 tablespoon of oil. Blitz to make a smooth purée and pour over the chicken, turning to evenly coat. Chill, covered, re-anointing a couple of times, for at least 30 minutes and up to 24 hours.

Heat the oven to 200°C/gas mark 6. Lift the chicken out of the marinade, shaking off the excess, then arrange on a cake rack over a foil-lined roasting tin. Brush with oil and roast for 25–35 minutes, turning once, until the chicken is crusty at the edges and the juices run clear when pierced near the bone with a sharp, pointed knife. Set aside a few sprigs of coriander. Trim and split the chillies and scrape away the seeds. Liquidize the remaining yoghurt with the bulk of the coriander, the chilli, mint, sugar, a pinch of salt and the juice from 1 lime until smooth. Arrange the chicken on a platter with the reserved sprigs of coriander, lime wedges and the sauce in ramekins for portion control dipping.

B Blini Pan

I remember thinking I was a very grown-up cook when I bought my blini pan. It's such an endearing little frying pan, measuring only 12cm, with distinctive curved sides and a long handle quite out of proportion to its size. The rounded sides encourage the yeast-leavened blini batter to rise evenly and the long handle keeps you at a distance from the heat. Mine is made from cast iron and over the years has become reliably non-stick, but a lightweight cast-aluminium version coated with a durable non-stick surface is probably cheaper. I use it for frying lone eggs but it has all sorts of uses, particularly for home-alone meals or using up leftovers, turning that spoonful of cold mash into latkes or the last egg in the fridge into a spectacular souffléd mini-omelette. It's perfect for a Tom Thumb fry-up with quail's eggs and pancetta, or for anything you want neatly round, like drop scones or pancakes.

Surprisingly, the capacity of a blini pan is 200ml, so it holds far more than you might expect. It is not necessary, though, to own a blini pan to make blinis. The batter, traditionally made with buckwheat flour, is thick and sets the minute it hits the pan, so free-style blinis, of any size you like, will cook perfectly in a hot, oiled frying pan or flat griddle. If, though, you want perfect *round* blinis, use metal food rings, sometimes sold as muffin rings, oiling them thoroughly first.

Russian Blinis with Salmon Caviar, Soured Cream and Chives

MAKES 6–8 LARGE OR 25–30 SMALL BLINIS

Home-made blinis are puffy, soft pancakes with a gently chewy texture and mild yeasty flavour. They are usually served with a dollop of soured cream and a fold of smoked salmon, sometimes with caviar too, with chives or dill. Smoked fish and something creamy works well with blinis. Try creamed horseradish with smoked mackerel or eel, or guacamole with white crabmeat and a dribble of sweet chilli sauce. Another good topping is soured cream with orange-red salmon eggs that pop like giant space dust in the mouth.

Blinis can be made in advance and kept covered in the fridge for up to 48 hours, or frozen (layered between greaseproof paper) then defrosted and warmed through in a warm low oven before serving. Share them across the table or prepare small, bite-size blinis canapé-style. Either way, chilled vodka – the glasses frosted in the freezer – or a glass of champagne is a classy accompaniment whatever the topping. Leftover blinis are delicious scone-style, topped with clotted cream and jam.

5g fresh or dried yeast
50ml warm water
100g buckwheat or strong white
    flour, or half and half

a pinch of salt
a pinch of sugar
100ml milk
2 eggs, separated

vegetable oil for frying
150g soured cream
100g jar of salmon eggs

fresh chives
lemon wedges, to serve

Stir the yeast into the warm water and leave for a few minutes to go frothy. Sift the flour into a mixing bowl. Add the salt and sugar, milk, yeast mixture and egg yolks. Stir smooth with a metal spoon. Cover the bowl with a stretch of clingfilm and leave somewhere warm for an hour, no longer, until the surface is popping with bubbles and the mix is slightly risen, looking spongy and smelling yeasty. Whisk the egg whites until firm and holding peaks. Gently fold the whites into the mix.

Heat about a teaspoon of oil in the blini pan over a medium heat, swirl it around, then add 3 tablespoons of batter to the pan. Cook for about 20 seconds, until the surface is covered with tiny bubbles and the undersides are golden brown. Turn with a palette knife or fish slice and cook for a further 20 seconds, until firm and golden. Transfer to a serving platter or parchment-lined tray if reheating or freezing. If using metal food rings, oil and arrange in a flat griddle or frying pan, and proceed as above. If making mini, free-form blinis, drop 4 tablespoons of batter into the pan, each spaced slightly apart, and cook as above.

To serve, top the blinis with a spoonful of soured cream, add salmon eggs and top with a few finely snipped chives. Serve with lemon wedges.

B Boxes, Bags and Jars

This might seem an eccentric inclusion, but I use plastic food boxes, plastic bags and glass jars in my kitchen for something or other every day. It could be marinating meat, hydrating couscous, stashing food or storing stock. I have all sizes and shapes of box, from catering to dolly's tea-party size. Keeping them neat and tidy drives me mad. Lids mysteriously disappear or no longer fit their box and stacks implode and multiply. They are the kitchen equivalent of pairs of socks that emerge singletons after a spin in the washing machine. I once read that

Paul McCartney is very particular about and addicted to new black socks – well, I'm the same about plastic boxes.

I have two favourite shapes and sizes that cope with most of my day-to-day needs. I discovered the perfect 500ml and 750ml oblong boxes thanks to my local Indian takeaway. They are popular too, I've noticed, with Thai restaurants. These boxes are light yet firm and are made of thin, clear polypropylene. Empty, they stack perfectly with the lids on top, and full, they don't leak and are freezer, dishwasher and microwave safe, although they will eventually wear out. They, and others, can be bought online for a snip in sets of 50 (see page 275) but you might find smaller packs in your local hardware or houseware shop. I use them for storing everything and anything, from homemade hummus to pomegranate seeds, roasted peppers and tomato halves, opened packs of feta cheese, leftover cold cuts and cooked dishes that I'm taking to friends or my sons. The larger boxes are also perfect for making fruit or aspic terrines and layered jellies.

The other favourite is far sturdier and is cylinder-shaped. I bought four in a hurry from my local cook's shop when I was after something reliably airtight and a decent size, to transport soups to a *Woman's Hour* interview. 700ml is a useful capacity and they will probably last for ever. Irritatingly, they don't stack well and the Lock&Lock snap-on lids with their blue plastic seals play hide and seek in my cupboard, but I love using them for storing and transporting soups, sauces, stews and bean dishes. I often chill stock in them – their relatively narrow diameter means there is a thick layer of consolidated fat that is easy to remove. If my fridge was bigger with greater space between the shelves, I'd chill stock in kilner jars before freezing it in those brilliant flat-packing, self-standing resealable Pour&Store plastic pouches. I wash mine in the dishwasher and balance them over my extra long jam-making wooden spoon to dry.

I can't bear disorder in my fridge, although I often end up with it. I also like to see what I've got in there. So I border on the obsessive in getting rid of excessive packaging and transferring food into my plastic boxes, but most often I use bags. Herbs and salad keep better in sealed polythene food bags, but spring onions and leeks, carrots, beetroot and spinach, beans, peppers and mushrooms need air to breathe, so are better in open-ended bags.

Years ago when my step-children were young and I was in super-step-mum mode, making jams, chutneys and marmalade ad infinitum, they would paint the lids and some still survive, the jars rotating between my sons and me. I save jars of all sizes and friends collect them for me, as these days I make preserves from fruit and veg grown at my allotment. I have quite a collection of different-sized glass preserving jars built up over the years. Some are designated for pickled onions – used repeatedly the glass and lids develop a distinctive smell – but larger ones are used for preserving fruit in alcohol. A very old French jar with a wide mouth and tapering shape is constantly replenished with home-made granola.

See page 274 for an inexpensive source of Le Parfait preserving jars and separate rubber seals. The point about these jars is that they are airtight, so smaller ones are useful for glacé cherries and angelica, herbs and spices, larger ones for nuts and seeds, dried fruit, coffee and tea.

A kitchen funnel goes hand in hand with filling jars and it isn't normally an item to get excited about but I absolutely love Architec's multi-purpose Prepsfunnel (see page 274). It clicks apart and can be used separately or together. The rigid nylon base has a wide rim and large hole, perfect for jam and chutney bottling or for decanting pastas and granola, and the smaller, flexible silicone funnel directs dry foods like flour or hot wet ingredients like gravy and syrup with precision. Mine is two-tone green, but it comes in a choice of bright, cheerful two-tone colourways. It's dishwasher safe and pleasant to use.

Honey and Apple Granola

MAKES 10–12 GENEROUS SERVINGS/FILLS A 1.5 LITRE JAR

Granola is crisp and crumbly, nutty cooked muesli. It becomes addictive once you start making your own, controlling what goes into it. I make it every week, changing the recipe slightly all the time, using different honey and oil, seeds and nuts. Sometimes I make it with organic barley and rye flakes but other times I use brown rice flakes or rolled oats. Millet and spelt flakes are worth trying too. I use apple juice and honey to sweeten it and a mixture of seeds and almonds, but you can tailor the add-ons to your taste and diet. Dried fruits, such as cranberries, blueberries, figs, apricots and mango, even chocolate, can be added once the mix is cold, but I don't bother. Buying the ingredients by weight or in large bags from health food shops and Middle Eastern shops, and stores like Nuts About Nuts, Nuts, and The Nut Tree (see page 276) keeps the prices down. Granola makes a great gift, tied prettily Sally Clarke-style, in cellophane bags with a handwritten label. It keeps in an airtight container for up to three months but is unlikely to sit around that long.

- 150ml apple juice
- 2 tbsp runny honey, such as Ogilvy's Himalayan Highland
- 4 tbsp groundnut or grapeseed oil
- 300g rolled oats, or 150g organic rye flakes plus 150g organic barley flakes
- 75g blanched almonds
- 75g sunflower seeds
- 1 tbsp oat bran
- 2 tbsp sesame seeds
- 3 tbsp organic linseed
- dried fruit of choice

Heat the oven to 160°C/gas mark 3. Mix the first three ingredients; you may need to heat them together to blend properly. Place all the ingredients in a mixing bowl and mix thoroughly, not worrying if the mix clumps because that's what you want.

Spread it out in a large, shallow, heavy-duty roasting tin; mine is 28 × 48cm; it is important that the mix isn't too thick. Bake on a middle shelf for an hour, turning every 20 minutes, tossing thoroughly so it bakes evenly, continuing for a further 10 minutes if necessary, until dark, golden brown, dry and nutty. Cool in the tin before adding any dried fruit – I rarely bother, as I eat the granola over fresh fruit with yoghurt – then transfer to jars/bags, whatever.

C Cake Tins

Napoleon called us a nation of shopkeepers but these days we are a nation of bakers and the choice of cake tins on sale is mind-boggling. Shallow round tins, deep round tins, springform tins with a clasp that holds the cake ring in place and tins with a loose base, square tins and deep square tins, single tins, sets of tins, non-stick tins, light tins made of aluminium and heavy-duty tins made of tin or thick, hard-anodized aluminium to prevent warping. It is a minefield.

I tend to buy a new cake tin when the recipe I want to make requires a different size of tin to anything remotely similar in my cupboard. Over the years I've accumulated a reasonable collection, partly because I inherited all my mother's bakeware and she baked every week all her life. These tins have built up their own non-stick patina, while newer non-stick tins need careful handling to avoid scratching. I never quite trust non-stick, so I always lightly butter cake tins and unless I'm making a shallow sponge I line the tin – the butter makes it stay put – with baking parchment. I tend, too, to make the lining stand several centimetres proud of the lip to avoid the top scorching and encourage the cake to rise. I also prefer to use cake rings or hoops with a separate base – either springform or so-called loose-base. If you want to make a square cake recipe using a round tin or vice versa, remember that square cake tins are one size bigger than round; so a 20cm (8inch) square tin and a 23cm (9inch) round tin of the same depth have the same capacity. Square tins make cakes that are easy to slice neatly, wrap and store.

To make a Victoria sponge, or similar sandwich cake, you will need two identical, shallow tins and I'd recommend getting loose-base ones. They can double as flan tins. For a dense fruit cake that needs long baking, a deep tin made of heavy-gauge steel will prevent scorching. Amazon and John Lewis are good places to browse what's out there, but Lakeland excel at bakeware (see page 274 for all these). I recommend the Lakeland PushPan range with a heavy-gauge anodized aluminium base for even heat distribution. It is adjustable with a silicone seal that means the tins can be used for shallow and deep cakes.

Most tins need to be washed by hand and are easy to keep clean and in good condition if you soak them first. Never scour non-stick pans.

Orange Almond Cake

SERVES 10–12

I absolutely love this cake. It is exceptionally light and moist, and very, very easy to make. It contains no butter or flour and is the perfect pudding cake. I have made it with oranges, mandarins and tangerines, with limes and lemons. The latter two need more sugar to avoid bitterness. If you are a lime lover, it is the cake for you; if not, I'd stick with the other citrus fruit. Serve with crème fraîche. It keeps for several days, covered, in the fridge.

4 medium oranges, 7 mandarins or tangerines, 6 Amalfi lemons or 6 perfect limes

6 eggs

250g caster sugar, plus extra 100g for lemon and lime cakes

250g ground almonds

1 tsp baking powder

a knob of butter

icing sugar for dusting

You will need a 23 x 7cm springform or loose-base tin

Wash and simmer the whole, unpeeled oranges or other citrus fruit in just sufficient water to cover, in a lidded pan for 2 hours. When cool enough to handle, cut them open and remove the pips. Tear the orange into the bowl of a food processor and blitz to a purée with no more than 6 tablespoons of the cooking water. This could be done 24 hours in advance. Heat the oven to 180°C/gas mark 5. Using a hand-held electric whisk or a processor with a whisk attachment, whisk the eggs with the sugar for several minutes until pale, fluffy and thick. Stir in the almonds, baking powder and citrus purée to make a stiff batter.

Lightly butter a 23cm springform cake tin, or one with a removable base. If using the latter, cut out a circle of baking parchment to fit the base and a long strip that will stand 8cm proud to cover the sides. If using a springform, cut out a circle to fit the base. Spoon in the batter and smooth the top. Bake for 45–60 minutes, checking after 45, until the cake is risen and just firm to a flat hand. Cool in the tin before releasing the clip to reveal a perfect cake. If using a loose-base tin, trim the baking parchment to the rim. Cover with an inverted plate, then deftly invert, reversing the cake so the bottom becomes the top. Carefully slide a palette knife between the base and circle of baking parchment, so you can lift off the base and then the paper. The cake will be pale, smooth and golden. Dust with icing sugar before serving.

Annie's Chocolate and Raspberry Birthday Cake

SERVES 12

Every year since they were born, I've made a birthday cake for my two sons in the shape of the numbers of their age. They have been covered with Smarties, edible snakes and worms, silver and gold balls, Maltesers, sugar prawns and chocolate drops, chocolate flakes, fresh strawberries and truffles. I've dyed the icing vivid colours but pure white was the choice for the first cake for my new grandchild.

Occasionally I make birthday and celebration cakes for friends but it's rare that I actually bake the cake. I cheat, buying round cakes for curly numbers and Swiss rolls for straight ones, then I set to slicing them up to make the numbers. I wrap them in very thin sheets of marzipan painted with melted jam. Then the fun begins. The icing and the decorating are always different and the cakes always look stunning.

I went the whole hog with this cake, to celebrate the sixtieth birthday of my friend Annie Hanson. She loves chocolate and I wanted it to be pretty and feminine and very chocolatey. The recipe could be adapted for other numbers and if you don't want to bother with a numerical cake, simply fill and cover the top of the cake with chocolate paste and raspberries.

For the almond chocolate cake:
200g butter, plus an extra knob
200g best quality dark chocolate
a pinch of Maldon sea salt
4 medium eggs
100g caster sugar
150g self-raising flour
100g ground almonds
For the filling:
100g best quality dark chocolate
50g butter
100ml whipping cream
apricot jam

icing sugar
500g ready-rolled marzipan
edible rice paper
300g firm raspberries
For the icing and decoration:
250g white icing sugar
approx 3 tbsp lemon juice
silver balls
angelica or dried apricot
crystallized rose petals
candles
You will need a round 20 x 7cm
    springform or loose-base tin

Heat the oven to 150°C/gas mark 2. Smear the base of a 20cm non-stick springform cake tin with the knob of butter and line with baking parchment. Chop 200g of butter and break 200g of chocolate into a metal bowl, then place over a half-filled pan of simmering water. Add a pinch of salt and stir occasionally as the butter and chocolate melt. When smooth and amalgamated, allow to cool.

Beat the eggs and sugar for several minutes, until pale and fluffy. Beat in the cooled chocolate mixture – it will deflate the mixture slightly – then gradually fold in the flour and almonds. Pour the thick, creamy mixture into the prepared cake tin. Bake for 45–50 minutes, until firm and risen and a skewer inserted in the centre comes out clean. Leave in the tin for 10 minutes before turning out on to a wire rack.

To make the chocolate filling, melt 100g of chocolate and 50g of butter as before and remove from the heat. Lightly whip the cream and stir into the chocolate butter. It will immediately thicken. Set aside until required. Mix 2 tablespoons of boiling water into 4 tablespoons of jam.

As soon as the cake is cool, slice it in half horizontally. Place it back together. Place a 12cm saucer at the edge of one side of the cake and cut out a circle. This is going to be the nought. Cut out a 4cm central circle. If you want to increase the size of the nought, cut it in half and use trimmings to plug the gap. Use the remaining cake to fashion the six; I followed the curve of the cake to make the curve of the six and leftovers to make the circle. Don't worry if it looks like a terrible mess; this is a very forgiving recipe. Dust a work surface, your hands and a rolling pin with icing sugar and roll out about a quarter of the marzipan very thinly to 3–4 times its original size. Use a pastry brush to paint the marzipan with apricot jam. Place the nought on the marzipan, spread the cut surfaces with chocolate paste, top the base with raspberries and carefully fit the lid. Entirely cover the nought with jam-smeared marzipan, cutting and pasting as neatly as you can. Carefully lift on to lightly moistened rice paper (to make it stick). Repeat with the six. Carefully transfer to a cake board.

Mix the lemon juice into the sifted icing sugar to make a simple sugar icing. Use a palette knife to smear it all over the cake. Decorate the cake immediately before the icing sets. I chucked handfuls of silver balls at the cake and made flowers with crystallized rose petals and strips of angelica. Add the candles last. Leave the icing to dry in a cool place, not the fridge.

Strawberry Pavlova Roulade

SERVES 6

A Swiss roll tin is an incredibly useful little baking tin. The last thing I use it for is making Swiss roll but the name immediately conjures up its shape, size and depth (approximately 30 × 20 × 2cm deep). I have several, of various grades of aluminium and quality of non-stick coating. My favourite is made of anodized aluminium without a non-stick coating and that is ageing the best. As I tend to line it with foil whenever I'm roasting vegetables and with parchment if I'm baking, the non-stick aspect is irrelevant. I like the fact that it is so strong there is no risk of buckling even at very high temperatures.

Here's an impressively delicious way of serving strawberries and cream rolled up in soft, springy meringue. Making it is great fun, a tad messy but quite magical. The meringue billows like a goose-down pillow during its brief high-temperature baking but quickly deflates as it cools, ending up like a pale, puffy bath mat.

Once cooled, the meringue is spread with whipped cream stirred with chopped strawberries and then the fun begins. To make the rolling easier, the meringue is turned out on to a tea towel, avoiding the need to touch the squishy plump roll. It doesn't matter how messy the result is because it can be tidied up by pushing extra strawberries into the ends. It's served with a thick, smooth cooked strawberry sauce to swirl over the slices. This sort of meringue is silky soft and vaguely creamy, so quite different in taste and texture to crisp meringue nests or chewy pavlova. For the perfect summer meal, use the leftover yolks to make hollandaise sauce to serve with poached salmon and asparagus.

4 large egg whites	2 tbsp icing sugar
1 tsp cornflour	300ml whipping cream
1 tsp white wine vinegar	800g British strawberries
½ tsp vanilla extract	2 tbsp caster sugar
150g caster sugar	1 tbsp lime juice

Heat the oven to 190°C/gas mark 5. Whisk the egg whites to stiff peaks, using a scrupulously clean electric whisk and bowl. Mix together the cornflour, vinegar and vanilla. With the machine running, add 1 tablespoon of sugar at a time, adding the cornflour mix halfway through, until the mixture is glossy and stiff.

Line a Swiss roll tin approx 30 × 20cm with baking parchment, leaving a 1cm collar. Spread the bouncy meringue smooth and even to the edge. Bake for 8 minutes, until bouffant and lightly golden. Dust the surface of the deflating meringue with sifted icing sugar. Lay a clean tea towel over the top and deftly invert. Carefully remove the baking parchment and leave to cool.

Whip the cream until it holds soft peaks. Set aside 8 perfect strawberries. Hull the rest. Halve half the strawbs and briefly soften in a pan over a low heat with 2 tablespoons of caster sugar and the lime juice. Blitz, then pass through a sieve to catch the pips into a jug to cool. Chop the other half and fold into the cream.

Spread the strawberry-laced cream over the cooled meringue and use the tea towel to help roll the meringue forward, ending with the seam underneath. Use a metal spatula to carefully lift it on to a platter. Halve the perfect fruit and decorate the ends of the roulade. Serve in thick slices, with a swirl of sauce.

C Casserole Dishes

It's thanks to my friend Tessa, who decided not to take her Le Creuset pans with her when she emigrated to Australia, that I have such an enviable collection. They are the backbone of my kitchen and I use one or other of them several times a week, always for soups, *daubes* and stews, for curries, chili con carne and cassoulet, whole chicken pot roasts, and anything that requires long, slow cooking. I've noticed that different pots and pans react differently to cooking certain things, particularly onions, but I can always rely on these heavy, enamel-lined cast-iron pans. Buying one, particularly a family-size pot, is a serious investment but treated properly, it will last a lifetime.

The Le Creuset company was founded in 1925, in Fresnoy-le-Grand in northern France, by two Belgian industrialists, a casting specialist and an enamelling specialist. The cocotte, a straight-sided, round pan, was their first design and flame or orange, now known as 'volcanic', the original colour. The foundry still uses standard sand-casting methods, and after hand finishing the pans are sprayed with two coats of enamel, each fired at 800°C. According to their website (see page 274), the pans require a twelve-step finishing process, facilitated by fifteen different pairs of hands to ensure there are no flaws or imperfections. Unlike most cooking pans, Le Creuset improve with age, building up a reliable non-stick surface and a patina of dishes past.

Over the years there have been minor changes to the classic design. The current logo was introduced in 1970 and pots have a number cast into the base. These numbers refer to the metric size of the pot. My favourites, the ones I use the most, are oval-shaped 22cm, 26cm and 27cm. A 22cm pot with a lid that doubles as a frying pan – perfect for tarte Tatin for four – is rarely far from the hob. But my cute 15cm pot is a rarity.

Poulet Antiboise

SERVES 4–6

This is one of the simplest and most delicious ways of cooking a whole chicken. Whenever I make it, everyone wants the recipe. It's known as buried chicken in my house and I learnt to cook this Niçoise dish from Elizabeth David's A Book of Mediterranean Food. *The bird nestles upside down in a deep casserole on an impossibly large mound of finely sliced onions. The only seasonings are olive oil, salt and a pinch of cayenne pepper. After about an hour and a half in a moderate oven, the onions flop down to a purée imbued with chicken juices and olive oil. This sweet sauce is served over or surrounded by the jointed bird, with a few stoned black olives and triangles of parsley-edged fried bread. I tend to serve it with mashed potato.*

6 or 7 large onions, approx 900g	12–18 small black olives
1.7kg organic or free-range chicken	4 slices of dense-textured bread
6 tbsp olive oil	3 tbsp finely chopped flat-leaf
a pinch of cayenne pepper	parsley leaves

Heat the oven to 180°C/gas mark 4. Peel, halve and finely slice the onions. Remove any flaps of fat just inside the chicken cavity and season inside with salt and black pepper.

Pour 2 tablespoons of oil into a large Le Creuset-style, deep, lidded casserole that can just accommodate the onions and chicken. Pile the sliced onions into the pan. Season lavishly with salt and a pinch of cayenne pepper. Pour 2 tablespoons of olive oil over the onions. Place the chicken, breast side down, on top of the onions, pressing it down firmly. Pour the remaining olive oil over the chicken. Cover – you may find the lid won't fit, so use baking parchment or foil and perch the lid on top; as the onions melt, the lid will position itself properly. Cook in the middle of the oven for 90 minutes.

Remove from the oven. Leave covered for 10 minutes before lifting the chicken on to a board for carving. Carve into pieces rather than slices, discarding the now flabby skin, and arrange on a platter covered with or surrounded by onions. Garnish with olives and fried bread. To make the fried bread, cut the crusts off the bread, slice in quarters and fry until golden in some of the oil from the casserole. Dip one edge of the fried bread into the onion juices, then into the parsley so it sticks.

Chicken with Forty Cloves of Garlic

SERVES 6

One of the happiest outcomes for an excess of garlic is this recipe. It's a Provençal dish, from the land where garlic and olive oil dominate the diet, and utterly beguiling. It will convert the garlic wary.

It is very simple to make, but like all simple dishes, it pays to take care with the ingredients. Choose a top-notch chicken, one that has run around and eaten well, developing plenty of muscle and flavour. Alternatively, and I often scale down the recipe for an easy after-work supper, it can be made very successfully with organic chicken legs. Allow one per person but add a few extra to satisfy the inevitable cries for more. To be authentic, this homely but classy dish should be made with fruity Provençal olive oil. The quantity to add is a matter of choice. For a taste of the hills of Provence, you will need dried herbes de Provence, although a fresh bouquet garni of rosemary, thyme and bay is a reasonable alternative that flavours the oil deliciously well.

Although this dish is cooked in a sealed casserole – an oval Le Creuset is perfect – the most delicious aromas will begin to percolate through the house after about thirty minutes. Traditionally the pot is sealed with pastry and the seal cracked at the table to release the genie for all to savour. I prefer to serve it on a platter so the vast quantity of garlic and limpid green, herb-scented 'gravy' can be contemplated in all its glory, so I cheat with kitchen foil.

Whole, unpeeled garlic stewed gently in olive oil ends up as soft as butter, with a rich, mellow flavour. I often tuck cloves around a joint of meat, so the soft, sweet paste can be squashed into the gravy. In this dish it becomes a vegetable, squeezed on to the chicken and the olive oil slurped like gravy. If that sounds impossibly rich, it isn't. The dish is surprisingly light and is best served with boiled potatoes to mash into the 'gravy'. You will not be left with garlic breath.

If by any strange chance there is garlic left over, try it squeezed on to hot toast and top with whatever you fancy; goat's cheese and roasted peppers are particularly good. Leftover olive oil makes terrific vinaigrette and the carcass will make exceptional stock.

1.8kg organic, free-range chicken
Maldon sea salt flakes
freshly ground black pepper
1 tbsp dried *herbes de Provence*, or
  6 sprigs of fresh rosemary, 6 sprigs
  of fresh thyme and 2 bay leaves

2 strips lemon zest
4 garlic bulbs (40 large cloves)
250–500ml fruity olive oil
You will also need a large sheet of
  aluminium foil

Heat the oven to 200°C/gas mark 6. Untruss the chicken. Often there are big lumps of fat just inside the cavity entrance, one on either side. I freeze these to render for Jewish chopped liver (see page 52). Lavishly season inside the cavity with salt and pepper. If using *herbes de Provence*, sprinkle ¼ tablespoon in the cavity with the lemon zest. Or place 2 sprigs of rosemary and thyme inside the cavity with the lemon zest. Place the chicken, breast side uppermost, in a large, lidded casserole dish that holds the chicken snugly. Separate the garlic cloves; there are an average 10 cloves per bulb or head, as it's often called, sometimes more. Flake away the excessive papery skin but do not peel the cloves. Scatter the cloves around the chicken. Pour the olive oil over the chicken so it trickles down to more or less cover the garlic. Sprinkle with the reserved *herbes de Provence* (or tuck the remaining rosemary and thyme, and the bay leaves, over and around bird and garlic). Season with salt and pepper. Place a double fold of foil over the dish with a generous overhang. Position the lid and use the foil overhang to thoroughly seal.

Place the dish in the middle of the oven and turn the temperature down to 180°C/gas mark 4. Cook for 90 minutes. Remove from the oven. Rest for at least 10 minutes – it will keep without harming for 30 minutes – before transferring to a warmed platter. Spoon the olive oil and garlic over the top, so they tumble down the bird. Serve with a share of the garlic and olive oil, with boiled potatoes and a green vegetable such as chard on the side.

c Charlotte Mould

This is one of those bits of kit you don't know you want until you are introduced to the dish it was designed for. Apple charlotte is a sublime English pudding that was probably created as a convenient way of eating up gluts of windfall apples and stale bread. The combination of naturally creamy puréed apple held inside a buttery crisp bread shell is something my mother made with windfall apples from orchards behind the firemen's hut near my childhood home in Kent. It manages to be both homely and rather special and is usually eaten hot, with a dusting of caster sugar and thick cream.

The dish is often attributed to Queen Charlotte, wife of George III, the patron of apple growers, but it is possible we have the celebrated French-born British chef Auguste Escoffier – 'the king of chefs and chef of kings' – to thank. He includes a simple but explicit recipe for *Charlotte de Pommes* in his *Guide Culinaire*, published in 1903. He specifies large Pippin apples (Cox's Orange Pippins were a popular eating apple at the turn of the century) and a little apricot jam stirred into the soft purée. He served it with a kirsch-flavoured stewed apricot sauce. The inspiration for the dish was almost certainly *Charlotte Russe*, a fancy cold dessert invented by Antoine Carême, the great French chef, after a visit to Russia. This French dish is quite different and is best described as an inside-out trifle lined with ladies' finger or boudoir biscuits, filled with gelatine-set custard and sometimes layered with raspberries or pineapple, peaches or banana, or scraps of *marrons glacés* and a little rum or kirsch.

Both puddings are prepared in a charlotte mould. This is a bit like a deep cake tin with seamless sloping sides to ensure the pudding can be turned out without disaster. A bag of autumn windfalls, just like my mother might have used, prompted my first attempt at making apple charlotte. Unfortunately, I didn't inherit my mother's mould. Casting around my kitchen for a suitable alternative, my eyes alighted on the dog's metal water bowl. It is almost perfect but not quite deep enough. A china pudding bowl is an acceptable alternative, but the real McCoy is made of anodized aluminium alloy, a particularly good heat conductor, or Pyrex glass bakeware. Both ensure the bread gets a good crisp finish.

Depending on the design, the charlotte mould has a special lip or small lugs to help with the lifting and tipping. For a family pudding, you want one with a 1.8 litre capacity and 18cm diameter. Alan Silverwood make excellent inexpensive aluminium moulds (see page 274). Now that I own one and am an aficionado of apple charlotte, I've made many different variations on the theme, adding aromatic quince to the apple purée and mixing apple varieties.

It's a simple dish to master but an important point is making sure the apple filling is thick and dry. I love the fluffy texture and tart flavour of cooking apples but however dry they are cooked, the essential sugar will slacken the pulp. Adding a couple of spoonfuls of breadcrumbs will help soak up the juices, successfully making a mixture that includes cooking apples that bit firmer.

The bread for a charlotte is cut into wide soldiers and it's a good idea to have a run through first with unbuttered bread, to ensure you have enough and to plan the 'layout'. Cooks in a hurry can butter both sides of the bread but it's worth clarifying the butter first and painting it on to the bread. This ensures a buttery taste without risk of burning.

The mould is useful too for cakes, mousses and timbales or variations on *Charlotte Russe.*

Apple Charlotte with Apricot Sauce

SERVES 6

When turned out, this pudding looks stunning in a homespun way, rather like a golden, crusty hot summer pudding (in fact, a charlotte mould is a good receptacle for making summer pudding). The skill is ensuring that the butter-soaked bread wall holds the apple securely, stemming it like a dam, so it's sensible to overlap the slices. Once the first cut is made, the pudding is likely to collapse in an aromatic flop. This doesn't matter a jot, in fact it's all part of the fun of apple charlotte.

1 lemon	*For the apricot sauce:*
12 large Cox or Russet apples	200g very ripe or stewed dried
2 tbsp caster sugar	apricots
¼ tsp freshly grated nutmeg or	2 tbsp honey or sugar
cinnamon	150ml fresh orange juice or water
100g unsalted butter	1–2 tbsp kirsch
1 day-old loaf of white bread, about	You will need a 1.2 litre capacity /
10 slices, crusts removed	18cm charlotte mould

Squeeze the lemon juice into a mixing bowl. Add 4 tablespoons of water. Peel, quarter and core the apples, one at a time, thinly slicing into the bowl. Stir the apples through the acidulated water as you add them. Tip the whole lot into a suitable saucepan, cover and cook over a low heat, stirring occasionally, for about 20 minutes, until the apples are tender and beginning to break down. Add the sugar, stirring with a wooden spoon as it dissolves whilst working the apples into a soft pulp. Simmer, uncovered, for 10–15 minutes, until the pulp is smooth, thick and dry. Stir in the nutmeg or cinnamon.

    While the apple cooks, cut the butter in chunks into a small saucepan and melt over a low heat. Cut the bread into slices about 5mm thick and remove the crusts. Cut into strips slightly taller than the mould and 3–4cm wide. Cut out a circle for the base and keep back a couple of slices for the lid. Have a dry run to check how many pieces you will need, then brush the inside of the tin with melted butter. Place a circle of baking parchment in the buttered base and butter that too. This is a belt-and-braces security measure to avoid the base sticking when the pudding is turned out. Quickly brush both sides of the bread with butter and line the tin, slightly overlapping the slices. Butter the base circle as before and fit snugly. Fill with apple pulp. Butter the lid on both sides and fit over the apple, abutting the lid. Trim the slices so they line up neatly. Cut a circle of baking parchment and lay it on top of the bread lid.

Heat the oven to 200°C/gas mark 6. Place the mould on a baking sheet and cook for 35–40 minutes. For the sauce, simmer the apricots with the honey and orange juice until soft. Liquidize, then dilute with water, if necessary, simmering until the sauce coats the back of a spoon. Stir in the kirsch. Transfer to a jug. Remove the cooked charlotte from the oven. Discard the paper, cover the mould with a plate and invert. Allow to rest for 5–10 minutes before removing the mould. Serve with the cooled apricot sauce.

C Clay Chicken Brick

In 1964, in the early days of Habitat, Terence Conran introduced Britain to the chicken brick. It looked like a giant unglazed terracotta acorn with a wavy join, lifting apart to make a chicken-size clay coffin. Once placed in the oven, the chicken cooked in its own juices without butter or oil to emerge moist, the skin crisp and golden.

It was an incredibly exciting concept, novel and mad and very trendy. The brick can, of course, be used for other meats, even stews and root vegetables like potatoes, beetroot and carrots, or for fruit – anything except fish or curries, which will irretrievably scent the terracotta. The brick goes into a cold oven turned to the required temperature, so food takes slightly longer than normal. The idea is based on ancient cooking methods of placing food in earthenware containers over fire, sealing in air and moisture, so the food cooks naturally in its own juices. There are two schools of thought about whether or not the brick needs to be soaked in cold water for 30 minutes or so first. It certainly helps prevent the crock from cracking. As the brick ages, it will absorb flavours and turn darker in colour but that is quite normal. One very important point: a chicken brick should be washed in hot water with a little salt or vinegar but never with detergent.

Habitat discontinued the chicken brick in 2008 but brought it back by popular demand. (To buy one, see page 274.)

Pot-roast Chicken with Black Garlic

SERVES 4–6

I heard about black garlic (see page 276) on the Isle of Wight from sailing friends who divide their time between Cowes and the British Virgin Islands in the Caribbean. 'It's as black as liquorice,' said my friend, 'with a texture like dried fruit with a sweet, almost balsamic flavour.' It's an American idea, treating (mainly Korean) garlic for a month in special high-humidity ovens. Apart from turning the garlic black, the process concentrates its amino acids, increasing the antioxidant count and removing its lingering smell.

So far it's been hailed mainly as a health benefit, but it's interesting to cook with. By sliding slivers under the chicken skin and filling the cavity with more, the chicken ends up intensely juicy, with a subtle, haunting, slightly sweet garlicky flavour.

1.4kg free-range chicken	a few sprigs of fresh thyme or
50g black garlic cloves	tarragon, or a mixture of the two
1 lemon	

Season inside the cavity of the chicken with salt and pepper. Loosen the skin over the breast and legs by carefully but firmly slipping your fingers under the skin and working sideways. Thinly slice the garlic and spread slices from a couple of cloves over each thigh and breast. Smooth the skin back in place. Halve the lemon and squeeze over the bird. Pop the squeezed lemon halves in the cavity with the herbs. Add the remaining whole garlic cloves.

Place the bird in the bottom section of the chicken brick. Add the lid and place the brick on a middle shelf in a cold oven. Turn the temperature gauge to 200°C/gas mark 6. Cook for 2 hours. Remove from the oven and leave for 15 minutes before transferring to a warmed serving plate.

Carve the bird chunkily, ensuring that everyone gets some of the crisp skin with black garlic underneath. Pour the bird juices into a small jug, and don't forget the garlic in the cavity.

C Crab Crackers

Like many specialist tools, crab and lobster crackers aren't essential equipment. Traditionally they're made in the shape of a lobster's claws but they are virtually interchangeable with hinged nutcrackers. The inside edges of crab crackers are similarly ridged, but straight instead of nut-shaped, so hard, slippery claws can't slip before they are cracked. They tend to be made of aluminium, sometimes stainless steel, and are sold singly or in a set, usually called a seafood tool set or crustacean set, comprising two crackers and six picks. If the claws are big, it is easier to crack them with a small wooden mallet but it takes practice to gauge sufficient control to avoid crushing the meat inside. Crackers are invaluable, though, for accessing the silkiest white meat in the spindly legs and the joints of the claws closest to the body. The meat is winkled out with a pick: a long, thin fork, possibly more useful than the crackers. (See page 274 for *pink* crab crackers.)

The average yield of meat from a crab will be one-third of its whole weight, and about two-thirds of it will be brown meat. Male crabs – cocks – have larger claws than females – hens – and as it's the claws and legs that contain most of the white meat, males are generally thought to be the best buy. The tail, curled under the body, determines the sex of a crab. The female tail is broad and round while the male is narrow and pointed.

Cracking the legs and claws is only part of dealing with a cooked crab. Begin by placing the boiled crab on its back and twisting the claws from the body. Twist off the bony tail flap and discard. Prise the body from the main shell by pressing hard with the full weight of your thumb opposite the eyes where the carcass obviously dovetails into the shell. Remove the stomach bag and the grey, crêpey 'dead man's fingers'. Remove the legs and cut the body in two. Cut each half in two again, cutting across to expose the meat in the leg chambers. Scrape the firm creamy meat round the edge of the shell and then the brown meat and slush in the middle into a small bowl. The latter is extremely rich and tasty and might be a bit watery. If so, drain the liquid off or into the stockpot. Season with a little salt and pepper and a splash of wine vinegar or lemon juice – not too much, just enough to season the meat

– and stir thoroughly. Pick the white meat from the body cavities and stir it into the seasoned brown meat. Crack the claws and legs gently in a few places, taking care not to crush the meat inside. Arrange on a platter and serve the brown meat separately. Serve with crab crackers and pickers. With mayo and chips this is a favourite family treat.

I have been known to cheat when I make crab recipes, not picking the crab myself but using 100g packs of handpicked white and brown Cornish crabmeat (see page 276).

Crab, Saffron and Leek Tart

SERVES 6

This tart is forever associated with hot sunny days at the Fish Store, the family home in Mousehole, Cornwall. I would make it with freshly picked crab, but in London I often cheat with ready picked Newlyn crab from the fishmonger (from Waitrose, see page 276). Serve the tart hot or cold, with new potatoes or green beans, or a simple green salad.

200g flour, plus a little extra	3 large eggs
125g butter, plus a little extra	200g thick cream or crème fraîche
2–3 tbsp natural yoghurt	2 tsp Grey Poupon mustard
4 trimmed leeks, approx 400g	350g brown and white crabmeat
a pinch of saffron stamens	100g Gruyère cheese, grated

Sift the flour into a mixing bowl. Add 100g of butter in chunks and rub into the flour until it resembles breadcrumbs. Add 2 tablespoons, possibly 3, of yoghurt and quickly work into the flour mixture, forming it into a soft ball. Cover and chill for 30 minutes.

Heat the oven to 200°C/gas mark 6. Butter a 23cm flan tin with a removable base and dust with flour, tipping out the excess. Roll out the pastry to fit, pressing it down gently into the base edges and trimming with a bit of an overhang to avoid shrinkage. Cover loosely with foil. Line the base with baking beans or rice and bake for 10 minutes. Remove the foil and cook pale golden for a further 5–10 minutes.

Split the leeks lengthways and slice into half-moons. Rinse thoroughly and shake dry. Melt 25g of butter in a spacious, lidded frying or sauté pan. Stir in the leeks, cover and cook, stirring occasionally, for about 10 minutes, until juicy and wilted. Stir in the saffron, season with salt and pepper and cook uncovered for a few minutes to drive off the liquid. Set aside to cool. Whisk the eggs in a mixing bowl and stir in the cream and mustard, then the crab, breaking up any big pieces. Stir the cooled leeks into the egg mixture. Sprinkle two-thirds of the cheese across the base of the pastry case. Place on a baking sheet. Spoon the crab mixture into the case; it should fit exactly, going right up to the top. Scatter over the remaining cheese. Bake for 35 minutes, or until the top is golden and billowing and feels firm but springy. Cool for 10 minutes before removing the collar. Serve hot, warm or cold.

D Dariole Moulds

Dariole moulds look like small metal flowerpots with straight or slightly curved sides, the base always narrower than the top. They are very similar to but usually slighter larger than popover pans. Both are made of aluminium. Confusingly, they are also known as madeleine tins – not to be confused with the baking tins for French madeleines, the paw-shaped, fluted sponges so popular in France. Our madeleine is an English sponge dipped in red jam, rolled through coconut, with a cherry on top. The moulds are sold singly or in sets and are used for sweet and savoury mousses and jellies, sponges and custards and creamy puds like panna cotta. Their varied use means they tend to be oven and freezer proof, and range in capacity from 95 to 200ml, but they are always approximately 7cm tall.

In the early fifteenth century, the name dariole referred to meat-filled pastry cooked in such a mould. Later the filling changed to custard, but the derivation of dariole comes from *daurar*, meaning 'to turn golden' and probably referring to the golden crust of the original pie.

For silicone moulds, sold singly or in sets for stability, see page 274.

Chocolate Fondant Puddings

SERVES 6

For me this is possibly the ultimate chocolate pudding; a dark, light sponge with a soft gooey middle that oozes forth as the spoon strikes home.

150g butter, plus a little extra
50g self-raising flour, plus extra for
  dusting
150g dark chocolate (minimum

70% cocoa solids)
4 large eggs
75g caster sugar
crème fraîche, to serve

Use the extra butter to smear six 175ml metal dariole moulds. Dust with flour and shake/tap out the excess. Put the moulds on a baking sheet and place in the freezer. Break the chocolate into a bowl that can fit over a half-filled pan of simmering water without touching the water. Cut 150g of butter over the chocolate and stir occasionally as the two melt and merge. Crack the eggs into the bowl of an electric mixer, add the sugar and whisk at high speed for several minutes, until thick, mousse-like and doubled in volume. Using a metal spoon, gradually fold the chocolate sauce into the mousse until smooth and slackened, then sift the flour over the top and quickly fold until smooth. Don't overdo it or you will knock all the air out of the mixture.

Three-quarters fill the prepared moulds. Cover the puddings with clingfilm and chill until required. Heat the oven to 200°C/gas mark 6. Bake the puddings for 8–9 minutes until risen and set. Rest for 2 minutes, then run a knife round the inside edge of each dariole and deftly turn on to a plate. Serve with crème fraîche.

D Deep Fryer

It seems inconceivable now but my mother used to cook fish and chips for six every Friday, using nothing but a frying pan. Perhaps that's why one of my first cookery purchases, second to an all-purpose Dutch oven and later a wok, was a chip pan. It's nothing special, but it's big, holding over two litres and made of dark enamelled steel. The enamel makes the pan easy to clean and prevents it absorbing smells. The pan has small side handles and a well-fitting lid with slots for the basket handles. The handles have extensions that fold out to rest on the rim, enabling the basket to drain back into the pan. I've never been tempted by a more sophisticated pan, perhaps with a deodorizing filter fitted into the lid, or a thermostatically controlled electric deep fryer. I don't own a deep-frying thermometer either, instead rather foolishly relishing the trial and error of testing the temperature with scraps of bread.

Successful deep-frying, I've discovered by trial and error, is an imprecise style of cooking affected by many variables. I'm always mindful of the risk of fat fires so I only ever half-fill the pan with oil. I tend to use fresh oil every time, except for chips, when I drain and strain the oil, and I rarely use anything other than groundnut or sunflower oil. Both have a high smoke point, which means the oil can be heated to a higher temperature than many other oils without decomposing or burning, or bursting into flames.

Greek Fried Fish with Vinegar and Beetroot

SERVES 4

Here's a clever trick picked up in Greece for giving fish a batter effect without making batter. It is perfect for whole little fish, like sprats and sardines or small red mullet, but almost any white fish fillets, particularly sole and plaice and other un-bony flat fish, are suitable. The fish is briefly marinated in cider or wine vinegar, then given a double-dusting of flour before being quickly fried in hot oil. The vinegar gives the fish a surprising amount of tart yet interesting flavour, while the flour and a quick dip in water create a faux batter. I like this with a variation on mushy peas made by liquidizing 300g of boiled petits pois with a teaspoon of English mint sauce and a tablespoon of Greek yoghurt, but in Greece it is often eaten with beetroot cooked in this exceptional way.

6 fillets sole or plaice, skinned	*For the beetroot:*
3 tbsp cider vinegar	2 bunches of beetroot with leaves,
flour, for dusting	minimum 500g
groundnut or sunflower oil, for	1 tbsp lemon juice or wine vinegar
deep-frying	4 tbsp Greek olive oil
lemon wedges	

Prepare the beetroot first; it can be kept waiting without spoiling. Cut the stems close to the root. Discard any withered or yellowing leaves, then wash the rest and shake dry. Wash the beetroots without breaking the skin, leaving the roots intact. Boil the beets in plenty of salted water for about 30 minutes, until tender to the point of the knife. Rub away the skin (wearing Marigolds) and trim the ends. Boil the stems and leaves in a separate pan of salted water for about 5 minutes, until tender. Drain. Coil the drained stems and leaves into a serving bowl and cover with big chunks of beetroot, leaving smaller beets whole. Whisk the lemon juice or vinegar and olive oil briefly and pour over the top.

Split the fish fillets lengthways, following the natural line of the fish. Pour the cider vinegar into a dish and wipe the fish through the vinegar to smear all over. Leave piled up in the dish while you prepare everything else. Spread about 4 big spoonfuls of flour on a large dinner plate. Half-fill a mixing bowl with water. Heat the oil to 180°C (when it takes a scrap of bread about 6 seconds to turn golden). Arrange 4 or 5 sheets of kitchen paper on a plate and have warmed dinner plates at the ready. Using tongs, lift one fillet of fish, shake off excess vinegar and wipe through the flour. Shake off excess, then quickly dip the fish in the water, give it another shake and wipe through the flour a second time. Give it a final shake and arrange on a plate while you do the rest. Fry in batches in the hot oil, so the batter quickly crisps and turns golden brown; it should take no longer than a couple of minutes. Rest on the kitchen paper before plating each fillet with a lemon wedge. Serve with the beetroot.

Thai Quail Scotch Eggs

MAKES 12

Home-made Scotch eggs are a revelation. They look wonderful, all plump and wonky and far bigger than you'd expect. Their link with Scotland is tenuous to say the least, in fact 'Scottish' eggs, made with highly seasoned sausage meat and a pullet's egg, are the invention of a chef at Fortnum & Mason in 1738, devised as a natty way of presenting eggs and sausages for their luxurious hampers.

The recipe was probably inspired by a Moghul dish called nargisi kofta (Narcissus meatballs) and is an idea to play around with. Scotch eggs made with quail's eggs end up about the size of a hen's egg and are surprisingly substantial. Instead of sausage meat, this recipe uses minced chicken flavoured South East Asian style, with chilli and coriander. The eggs are at their best warm but will keep, covered, in the fridge, overnight. Bring them back to room temperature before serving so all the flavours can shine through.

100g sourdough-style bread
   with crust
12 quail's eggs
flour, for dusting
2 medium eggs
1 red bird's-eye chilli
25g bunch coriander

300g minced chicken
groundnut or sunflower oil, for
   deep frying
To serve:
curls of iceberg lettuce
Thai sweet chilli dipping sauce

Tear the bread into pieces and blitz into fine crumbs. Spread out on a large plate or small tray until required. Place the quail's eggs in a pan of cold water, bring to the boil and boil for 2 minutes. Drain, then refresh under cold running water for a couple of minutes. Gently crack the shells and use a small, sharp knife to nick the surprisingly thick, rubbery membrane under the shell, then carefully peel the eggs. Pat dry on kitchen paper.

Sift 4 tablespoons of flour into a cereal bowl. Roll the eggs through the flour. Whisk the hen's eggs in a shallow bowl. Trim and split the chilli. Scrape away the seeds and chop very finely. Set aside a few coriander sprigs and finely chop the rest.

Place the chicken in a mixing bowl. Scatter the chilli, chopped coriander and a little salt and pepper over the top, then mix thoroughly with a fork. Divide the mixture in half and form each half into 6 balls. Working on one Scotch egg at a time, flatten a ball of sausage meat on your hand. Paint it with beaten egg and place a floured quail's egg in the middle. Form the sausage meat around the egg, pressing together to seal and evenly cover. To encourage a snug fit, roll in a square of clingfilm and twist tight. Repeat with the other eggs.

Finalize the preparations by dipping each egg (discarding the clingfilm first) in flour, then in beaten egg and finally in the crumbs, placing on a plate as you complete the remaining eggs.

Heat sufficient oil in a fryer to completely immerse the eggs; don't be mean about this, more is better than less. Test for readiness (180°C) by dropping a scrap of bread into the oil; it will turn golden after about 6 seconds. Depending on the size of your pan, cook the eggs in uncrowded batches for 4–8 minutes, until evenly crisp and pale golden. Drain on kitchen paper. Eat warm or cold, with a curl of crisp lettuce, sprigs of coriander and Thai sweet chilli dipping sauce.

D Dough Hook

I'd never heard of a dough hook until it arrived as part of a retro-style American KitchenAid stand mixer, sent by the PR company hired in 1995 to publicize its launch in the UK. The hook looks like a misshapen C, made of strong metal capable of pounding bread dough, simulating in five or six minutes what it takes a strong hand to knead in double the time. I was slow to experiment, but once I did I became addicted to this easy way of making bread. In fact, I rave about it so much that the heavy machine sometimes goes on loan to friends and family for breadmaking sessions. The design was inspired by an engineer who by chance noticed a commercial baker using a heavy iron spoon to mix dough, and was initially launched industrially in 1908, with a home version in 1919. The hook has limited use in my kitchen but I would hate to be without it, particularly as I use the other KitchenAid attachments – a flat beater and large globe whisk – almost every day.

No-fuss White Loaf

MAKES 2 x 500G LOAVES

This is the bread I make most often with my dough hook. It relies on easy-blend yeast, which doesn't need to be dissolved in warm water and produces a good everyday loaf with an even crumb and decent crust. It slices well and toasts relatively quickly, and is perfect for sandwiches. The recipe makes two loaves; I tend to eat one and freeze the other. Use this recipe as a template; try half or all strong wholemeal or stoneground bread flour, or add wheatgerm (50g). For a mixed seed loaf, add 1 tablespoon each of sesame, linseed, poppy and sunflower seeds, and for a sweeter, softer loaf use milk instead of water. Try different oils - rapeseed is a good choice - or melted butter. (See also Loaf Tin, page 126.)

10g butter	1 tsp salt
flour, for dusting	1 tsp sugar
650g strong white bread flour	1 tbsp olive oil, plus extra splash
1 sachet easy-blend yeast	400ml warm water

Boil the kettle. Butter two 500g loaf tins. Dust with flour and shake out excess. Rinse the mixer bowl with boiling water and quickly dry. Place the 650g of flour in the warm bowl with the yeast, salt and sugar. Fit the flat beater and mix briefly on speed 2. Stop the machine and change to the dough hook. Add 1 tablespoon of olive oil to the water. Turn the machine to speed 1, add the water gradually at the edge, then change to speed 2 and continue for 5–6 minutes, until the mixture has formed into soft and elastic dough. Use the extra splash of olive oil to smear a mixing bowl. Place the dough in the bowl, cover with a stretch of clingfilm and place somewhere warm for 1–1½ hours to double in size.

Punch the dough down with your fist and knead a few times. Cut the dough in half and shape into loaves, pushing the dough down into the tins. Cover with clingfilm again and leave for about 30 minutes, or until doubled in size. Heat the oven to 220°C/gas mark 7. Make two or three quick slashes with a sharp knife across the width of the dough or one long slash down the length, dust with flour and bake on a middle shelf for 25–35 minutes until risen and golden. Turn out and tap the bottom – it should sound hollow. If not, return it to the oven for a few more minutes. Cool on a cake rack before slicing.

E Earthenware Pots

Earthenware pots have a distinctive rustic charm. They tend to be made by hand or from moulds in classic shapes and a wide range of sizes, usually gratin-style, but bulbous bean pots with a narrower opening or straight-sided marmites and cocottes are designed for particular dishes requiring long, slow cooking. Earthenware, like stoneware and porcelain, is made of clay. Of the three, it is fired at the lowest temperature, making it the most breakable and the cheapest. With care, earthenware pots can be used over direct heat – I always use a heat diffuser – but they are best suited to oven cooking. Some pots are unglazed, others only glazed on the inside, but both are the original oven-to-table or cook-and-serve ware.

Earthenware was my first cooking crush; I wanted the whole range and I wanted at least two of each size. There is something very pleasing about making two cauliflower cheese or potato gratins in identical dishes or complementing a large earthenware dish with a smaller version. I went through crazes of preferring oblong shapes to round ones but loved, always, the oval dishes with fluted handles and sloping sides. I am seduced, too, by the subtle difference in colour of the clay used to make earthenware. The glaze applied to make the pot non-porous, is often slapdash, adding to the charm of the pot. My favourite is probably the pale, sandy colour of the clay used by one French pottery I discovered on holiday in Brittany, its glaze bringing another hue to the pot. I built up quite a collection of clay pots from potteries such as that one but temptation lurked at Habitat, in Elizabeth David's shop in Pimlico, and in the cavernous French Kitchenware and Tableware Supply Co. on Westbourne Grove, near Whiteleys.

In those days it was rare to own a dishwasher, so dishes were soaked after use in cold water and scrubbed with a scourer. This probably prolonged their life because earthenware doesn't take well to extremes of heat. It is, though, a great cooking medium, particularly for long, slow oven dishes, its porous nature keeping the food moist. Earthenware dishes mature as they age, the unglazed part growing darker and ingrained with a patina of past meals, taking on a distinctive personality.

Many earthenware pots have come and gone in my kitchen but a hardcore have survived and newer ones join them from time to time. One particular favourite, a slightly tapered, unglazed round bowl about 6cm deep with a 15cm diameter and a hole fashioned out of the rim to hang it by, is Greek. It comes from a small family taverna on the road out of Agios Nikolaos, on the north-eastern coast of Crete, taking the road that passes the island of Spinalonga, the deserted leper colony brought to life in Victoria Hislop's book *The Island*. My husband and I found the place by chance and stayed three weeks while we explored Crete by bike, scooter and car. Later we went back with our baby and much to their delight named him Zachary, derived from the Greek word for sugar.

Every day we ate from these unusual dishes and I fell in love with them. I still have three; the fourth is in Stan Hey's kitchen in Bradford-on-Avon, where it was taken one Christmas full of chicken liver pâté. The dishes hold 900ml, making them perfect for two-portion dishes like shepherd's pie and chicken pie, plum crumble and gooseberry cobbler, but I particularly like them for pâté and hummus.

Another favourite, shaped like an elongated Norman window, might be Italian and originally used for making bread. It must be quite old. It comes from Elizabeth David's kitchen, a treasured gift from her nephew, who inherited her house in Halsey Street and its contents. I'd got to know Elizabeth quite well over the last few years of her life and it's thanks to Jill Norman, her literary executor, that I was on a list of beneficiaries. This unusual dish is a pretty golden honey colour and its deep shape and large size make it perfect for a family shepherd's pie, lasagne or gratin.

The other dish I use repeatedly for all sorts of things, particularly couscous and rice salads, vegetable salads and tagines, is a large *cazuela*, a gift from Spain from my ex-boyfriend, Andrew Payne. It has a small relative, which I use for nuts and olives. At the bottom of the pile is a huge, incredibly thick and heavy oval-shaped dish that comes into its own when I'm feeding the five thousand. Perfect for party fish pie, lasagne or mousakka.

Chopped Liver with Toasted Bagels

SERVES 4

Jewish chopped liver is very similar to chicken liver pâté but made with lots of slippery soft onion and hard-boiled egg. A crucial ingredient is melted chicken fat, or schmaltz, nuggets of fat tucked inside the neck of a chicken's cavity (I freeze them) – your butcher will oblige. It's important, incidentally, not to over-blend the mixture because chopped liver isn't supposed to be a smooth paste like pâté. It is particularly good with a minimal garnish of minced raw onion and finely grated hard-boiled egg to offset the rich creaminess of the liver. I like to make a meal of it, serving thinly sliced toasted bagels rather than the usual matzos, but crusty bread and butter is good too.

2–3 nuggets of chicken fat
1 large onion, approx 175g
250g chicken livers
2 hard-boiled eggs

1 shallot or small onion
12 cornichons or 3 Mrs Elswood sweet-sour pickled cucumbers
4 bagels, at least

Place the chicken fat in a small pan over a low heat. Leave to melt into *schmaltz*; the process takes about 10 minutes and you need 3 strained tablespoons. Peel, halve and finely chop the onion. Pick over the livers, separating the lobes and discarding any stringy bits. Pat dry and season with salt. Pour the *schmaltz* into a frying pan, stir in the onion, cover and cook, stirring occasionally, over a low heat until melting soft and pale in colour. Tip into a sieve over a bowl, return the drained *schmaltz* to the frying pan and cook the livers for 2–3 minutes a side until firm but bouncy and still pink inside. Return the onions and leave, covered, to cool.

Coarsely chop one egg. When the livers have cooled, tip the contents of the pan into the bowl of a food processor. Season with freshly ground black pepper and add the coarsely chopped egg. Pulse to mix and chop but don't overdo it. Transfer to a serving dish. Cover with clingfilm and chill until required. Serve a scoop of chopped liver garnished with minced raw onion and finely grated egg. Accompany with cornichons or slices of pickled cucumber, and thinly sliced toasted bagels.

Old-fashioned Shepherd's Pie with Lemon Mash

SERVES 4–6

The smell of shepherd's pie cooking is overlaid with memories, wafting me back to my own and my children's childhood suppers. This version is pretty much my mum's recipe made with the remains of a roast lamb joint instead of fresh minced lamb. Traditionally it's a plain dish, the minced or chopped meat stirred into fried onion with carrot and leftover gravy, or liquid from cooking the carrots, salt and pepper the only seasoning. The amount of meat can be eked out with extra vegetables like celery and the flavour perked up with fresh herbs, although all sorts of other ingredients find their way into shepherd's pie. I always add tomato ketchup if I am making it with fresh mince, my sister likes Lea & Perrins, but mushrooms or peas, tomatoes and wine, even haggis or black pudding, morcilla or boudin noir, turn up in shepherd's pie. I like plenty of butter in the soft, fluffy mashed potato topping but another reinvention is to use sweet potato or other root vegetable mash. My job when Mum made shepherd's pie was ploughing the mash with a fork to get a good crusty, golden finish. It looks stupendous if the mash has been beaten with egg and then piped.

1 large onion	1 tbsp chopped fresh flat-leaf
2–3 tbsp dripping or vegetable oil	parsley
2 sprigs of fresh thyme	1kg boiling potatoes
1 large carrot	50g butter
500–750g leftover roast lamb	150ml milk
1 tbsp flour	3 tbsp freshly grated Parmesan
1 lemon	3 tbsp fine breadcrumbs

Peel and finely chop or grate the onion. Heat the dripping or oil in a spacious frying or sauté pan and cook the onion until soft and golden, stirring in the thyme. Scrape the carrot and slice thinly. Boil in 250ml salted water until just tender. Drain and save 175ml of the water.

While the onion cooks, slice the meat off the bone in big pieces, pick over and remove fat and sinew. Chop into small pieces. Season with salt and pepper. Stir the meat and carrot into the softened onion, discarding the thyme sprig – most of the leaves will have fallen off. Sift the flour over the top and stir until disappeared. Add the carrot water, and any leftover meat juices or gravy. Simmer, stirring, for a few minutes until thick. Stir in the juice from half the lemon and the chopped parsley.

Pile into a 2 litre capacity, 4cm deep earthenware, ceramic or glass dish.

Heat the oven to 200°C/gas mark 6. Peel and rinse the potatoes and boil in salted water until tender. Drain. Melt most of the butter with the milk in the potato pan. Return the potatoes, mash smooth, then add the juice from the remaining lemon half. Beat with a wooden spoon until light and fluffy. Top the cooled pie filling with the mash, making swirls with a fork. Dot with the last of the butter and dredge with Parmesan mixed with breadcrumbs. Bake for 30 minutes, or until the top is crusty and golden.

South African Lamb Bobotie

SERVES 4–6

It's always helpful to know a few interesting dishes made with inexpensive minced meat. Bobotie, declared South Africa's national dish by the United Nations Women's Organisation in 1954, is one such. It is a curious combination of flavours – minced lamb or beef with curry, chutney and raisins, topped off by egg custard – but is surprisingly elegant and interesting to eat. In South Africa it is often served with mashed potato or rice coloured with turmeric and sweetened with more raisins.

1 thick slice of white bread	50g raisins
250ml milk	25g flaked almonds
1 large onion	2 tbsp Mrs Ball's chutney or apricot
2 garlic cloves	jam
2 tbsp vegetable oil	1 tbsp sugar
2 bay leaves	1 tbsp red wine vinegar
500g minced lamb or beef	3 eggs
1 tbsp curry powder	

Remove the crusts from the bread. Tear into a bowl with 50ml of milk and leave to soak. Peel and finely chop the onion and garlic. Heat the oil in a spacious sauté pan and stir in the onion with the bay leaves. Cook, stirring often, for 10–15 minutes, until beginning to soften. Add the finely chopped garlic and cook, stirring often, for 5 more minutes. Scoop on to a plate.

Return the pan to the heat. Crumble the minced meat into the hot pan and brown thoroughly. Add the curry powder, stirring to amalgamate. Return the onion, garlic and bay leaves, add the raisins and almonds, chutney, sugar, 1 teaspoon of salt, the vinegar and the squeezed bread (saving the squeezed milk, covered, in the fridge). Stir thoroughly to mix. Tip into a 1.5 litre capacity gratin-style earthenware or ceramic dish and press down with the back of a spoon to make a flat, firm surface. Leave to go cold, preferably chilled, covered, overnight.

Heat the oven to 200°C/gas mark 6. Whisk together both lots of milk and the eggs. Pour the eggy milk over the top of the mixture and bake for 35–40 minutes, until the custard is puffed and golden. Serve with extra chutney.

Classic Fish Pie with Egg and Parsley Sauce

SERVES 10–12

If you are wondering what to cook for a casual lunch party, one of the best solutions is fish pie. Everyone always loves fish pie and if it's made carefully, doing your best to ensure no bones are left in the fish and the sauce is well flavoured, thick and creamy, and there's plenty of it, it is always a huge success. From the cook's point of view, not only can the shopping be done gradually, stashing the fish in the freezer, but the cooking can be leisurely and finished 24 hours in advance. Serving is easy, eating only requires a fork, and fish pie doesn't slide about on the plate so it can be done perched on the corner of the sofa.

Fish pie can be as elaborate or as simple as you like. It is always tastier if it includes a fair proportion of naturally smoked haddock. Smoked pollack is a new idea, certainly new to me, discovered at Turner's, up the Coombe in Newlyn (see page 276), one of my favourite fish shops. Any member of the cod family – particularly cod, pollack and haddock, which have relatively big, dense flakes – is perfect for the main quantity of fish. Ling, whiting and coley, also called pollack and colin, are cheaper, but the flesh is far softer, so bear that in mind with the initial cooking times. Some people add salmon for colour and prawns for luxury, but it's a matter of taste. I like plenty of coarsely chopped hard-boiled egg and humungous amounts of chopped parsley. Spinach, first blanched in boiling water and squeezed dry, is a great thing to add to fish pie, as are leeks or spring onions, sliced and softened in butter.

Apart from all the obvious points, like plenty of fish and taking care to remove all the bones, it's a well-seasoned sauce that really makes fish pie. Unless you are putting the fish into the dish raw, which I rarely do, the sauce is always made from the liquid the fish is poached in. It could be water or milk or half and half, adding cream later to make the sauce really luxurious. A finely chopped onion, bay leaves and peppercorns in the poaching liquid make a terrific difference to the flavour. Salt is rarely necessary if you include smoked fish but a dab of anchovy paste (from a tube) is a good way to sharpen up the seasoning. Normally, when I make a family fish pie, I fold the fish and other ingredients into the sauce. For a party, when there is so much more of everything, it is easier to pour the sauce over the filling. One very good tip is to let the sauce and filling go completely cold before the mash is added, otherwise the mash will sink and be difficult to spread evenly. It is also important to make the mash stiffer than usual, so it doesn't melt into a soft cream. Duchesse-style mash made with beaten egg will stay forked into lovely ridges that end up a like a crusty, golden furrowed field. Extra crunch and a final salty seasoning come from a lavish dusting of Parmesan.

I particularly like peas – frozen petits pois – with fish pie and if they're mixed with lightly cooked green beans and peeled cucumber half-moons, they become a bit smarter. I always cut the beans in half to make serving and eating easier. One final tip: it takes a surprisingly long time to boil sufficient water to cook the accompanying vegetables. Get ahead just before guests arrive (I use the kettle) to avoid being greeted in a sea of steam. For 10–12 people you will need 1kg of frozen petits pois, 450g of halved fine green beans, and 2 small peeled, seeded cucumbers (halved lengthways and cut into thick half-moons). Cook them separately in the same water, transferring them to a separate large lidded pan as you go. Toss thoroughly with a huge knob of butter and leave covered. They'll stay hot for ages, just toss again before serving.

5 large eggs
1.5kg white fish fillets, such as
  pollack, cod, haddock, ling or
  whiting, or a mixture
1kg naturally smoked haddock
1 litre milk
1 small onion
6 black peppercorns
2 bay leaves
400g fresh or frozen cooked and
  peeled prawns

75g butter
75g flour
50g flat-leaf parsley leaves
For the topping:
2kg large 'old' potatoes
50g melted butter
100ml hot milk
1 large egg, beaten
50g freshly grated Parmesan

Heat the oven to 200°C/gas mark 6. Boil the eggs for 9 minutes. Drain, crack all over, then return to the pan and cover with cold water. Peel the eggs in between other jobs.

Lay the fish in a roasting pan and add the milk. Peel and chop the onion and add to the pan together with the peppercorns and bay leaves. Cook in the oven for 10 minutes, so the fish is almost but not quite cooked. Remove from the oven and leave to cool in the milk. If using frozen prawns, slip them into a bowl of warm water and leave for 5 minutes to defrost. Drain and pat dry with kitchen paper. Have ready the dish or dishes you plan to cook the pies in. I use two large gratin dishes with a total capacity of 6 litres, but deeper dishes would be fine.

Run a finger over the fish and carefully remove any stray bones. Peel the fish off the skin, if necessary, and break into bite-size chunks directly into the dish or dishes, sharing the smoked haddock evenly. Carefully strain the milk into a jug. Scatter the prawns over the fish. Coarsely chop the peeled eggs and scatter over the top.

To make the sauce, melt 75g of butter in a suitable pan. Off the heat, briskly stir in the flour until incorporated. Return to the heat and gradually incorporate the milk, stirring constantly to ensure a smooth sauce. Continue stirring as the sauce comes slowly to the boil, using a globe whisk if it turns lumpy. Immediately reduce the heat and simmer, still stirring constantly to avoid sticking and burning, for 5 minutes, to cook the flour. Taste to be sure, seasoning to taste. Cover the pan to avoid a skin forming. Chop the parsley leaves. Stir the parsley into the sauce and spoon it over the fish mixture. Leave to get cold.

Peel the potatoes, chop into large, even-sized pieces, rinse and cook in boiling salted water. Drain and mash (or pass through a

Mouli-Légumes or ricer; do not use a food processor) with the melted butter and hot milk. Beat in the egg. Start by placing 4 big spoonfuls of mash strategically around the edge of the cold pie or pies, and add the rest in the middle. Use a fork to carefully spread the mash over the fish. Smooth, then fluff the surface. Dredge with grated Parmesan. Chill, covered, until ready to cook.

Remove from the fridge 3 hours before cooking. Heat the oven to 180°C/gas mark 4 and cook for 35–45 minutes, until crusty, bubbling and golden. Depending on your oven, you may need to alternate oven shelves or cook in rotation.

F Fish Kettle

I'm one of the many people who own a fish kettle because it was a gift. To buy, they can be relatively inexpensive or astronomically priced. Mine has a stellar position on a shelf above the kitchen sink window next to the pasta-making machine. I don't use it that often, and there have been big gaps in my life when I've got by without one, borrowing or making do with a deep oven pan and foil, but there is no denying that using a fish kettle is a great way to cook a large round fish. It's associated with salmon, and to cook a cleaned and trimmed whole salmon, lower the fish into just-boiled court-bouillon or water – it will take several minutes to return to a simmer – and poach gently for 16–18 minutes. A few minutes either way won't harm the texture of the fish. If the salmon is being served cold, it can be left in the liquid until required for skinning, etc.

It's thought the kettle or poacher – pun intended – originated in Scotland, designed for cooking just-caught fish at the river's edge. The long, deep oblong metal pan comes in various sizes but the most common is 60cm. The finest are made of copper and stainless steel but most, like mine, are made of aluminium with a stainless steel perforated poaching rack. Most racks come with hooked handles at either end so the fish is easily lowered and lifted in and out of the pan. Mine, though, is slatted without handles, so I have to go a bit Heath Robinson with tongs if I want to remove the fish while still hot. The kettle straddles two burners or can be used in the oven or over a barbecue. See page 274 for suppliers.

Le Grand Aioli and a Little One

SERVES 6–8 AND 2

Le Grand Aioli *is a spectacular Provençal dish, made by poaching a whole cod and serving it surrounded by young seasonal Mediterranean vegetables, arranged attractively in clumps of colour, interspersed with hard-boiled eggs, maybe snails, and wedges of lemon. A bowl of garlicky aioli goes with the fish and a bottle of olive oil, ideally the same one used to make the aioli, seasons the vegetables.*

It is very straightforward to make, with much of the preparation done in advance, and suits being served hot or tepid, so is ideal whatever the weather. This particular version is made with a couple of British seaside ingredients – samphire and winkles, or periwinkles to give them their full name – both bought from my fishmonger. If you prefer, leave them out.

Le Grand Aioli *is often made with salt cod and I sometimes make a speeded-up portion-control version inspired by the way they do it at La Colombe d'Or, St Paul de Vence, just outside Nice. A thick fillet of pearly white cod is served topped with a plump black snail, surrounded by a soft-boiled egg, a few potatoes, a chunky cauliflower floret, a pile of bright green samphire and a couple of beautifully turned carrots and courgettes. A jug of very garlicky aioli brings every mouthful to life.*

This way of making the dish is as uncomplicated for one as it is for a party, particularly if you cheat with the aioli, stirring crushed garlic into Hellmann's. Six or more fillets of fish could be cooked in the fish kettle; just follow the instructions for the court-bouillon in the main recipe.

8 large eggs	*For the court-bouillon:*
500g fresh or frozen winkles	3 large carrots
400g fine green beans	1 large onion
24 young carrots	2 celery sticks
24 bulbous spring onions	1 lemon
400g samphire	4 cloves
1kg small new potatoes	6 black peppercorns
approx 2kg cod, hake or pollack,	3 bay leaves
trimmed and descaled	a sprig of fresh thyme
50g bunch flat-leaf parsley	3.5 litres water
bottle of olive oil and Maldon sea	*For the aioli:*
salt, to serve	3 large garlic cloves

3 large egg yolks
400ml decent olive oil
2 tbsp lemon juice
3 lemons, cut into wedges

For the 'Little One':
2 thick fillets of cod
1 tbsp Maldon sea salt
8 new potatoes

1 large carrot
1 medium courgette
4 tbsp Hellmann's mayonnaise
2 garlic cloves
1 lemon
2 cloves
2 large cauliflower florets
50g samphire
2 fresh eggs

Begin by preparing the court-bouillon. Trim, scrape and chunk the carrots. Peel and slice the onion, chop the celery and slice the lemon. Pile the vegetables, lemon, cloves, peppercorns, bay and thyme into the fish kettle with 1 teaspoon of salt and 3.5 litres cold water. Bring to the boil, then simmer for 20 minutes.

Meanwhile make the aioli. Ensure all the ingredients are at room temperature. Peel and finely chop the garlic. Sprinkle with a little salt and crush to a smooth, juicy paste. Beat the egg yolks smooth, stir in the garlic and gradually beat in the oil in a thin stream, beating continuously, adding a little lemon juice and then more oil until it is used up and the mayonnaise is thick and glossy.

Bring a large pan of water to the boil. Meanwhile, boil the eggs in a small pan of water for 5 minutes. Scoop out of the pan. Crack the shells all over. If using fresh winkles, wash in several changes of water then, using the egg water, add 2 teaspoons of salt and boil for 2 minutes. Drain.

Top and tail the beans. Trim the carrots. Trim the spring onions. Rinse the samphire. Scrape the potatoes. Add 2 teaspoons of salt to the big pan of boiling water. Add the beans, return to the boil and boil for 3 minutes. Scoop into a basin of ice-cold water. Drain. Boil the carrots for 3 minutes. Scoop into a colander to drain. Repeat with the spring onions and samphire, draining as before. Boil the potatoes until tender in the same water. Lift out and reserve. If serving the vegetables hot, keep the water hot, ready for reheating the vegetables in the colander.

Bring the court-bouillon to the boil and slip in the fish. Return to the boil, reduce the heat and simmer for 5 minutes. Turn off the heat, cover with the lid and leave for 30 minutes.

Lift the fish on to a large, white platter that can hold fish and vegetables and peel away the exposed skin. Cover with foil to keep warm while you reheat the vegetables. Arrange the vegetables, winkles, peeled, halved eggs and lemon wedges in clumps around the fish, adding small bunches of parsley. Serve with the bottle of oil, aioli, sea salt and a cork stuck with pins for winkling (behind their black trapdoor).

For the 'Little One', place the fish on a plate and sprinkle the skinned side with salt. Leave for 20 minutes. Scrape the potatoes and place in a pan with 1 teaspoon of salt. Scrape and trim the carrot. Cut in half and then halve the pieces lengthways. Repeat with the courgette but remove a 1cm strip of skin from the sides to give a professional 'turned' look.

Place the mayo in a small bowl. Crack the garlic, peel away the skin, chop then crush to a juicy paste with a pinch of salt. Stir into the mayo.

Slice 2 cheeks off the lemon to serve with the fish and add a squeeze of the remaining lemon to the mayo. Boil the kettle. Half-fill a medium-sized saucepan with boiling water, squeeze in the last of the lemon juice, and add 2 cloves. Simmer for 5 minutes. Rinse the salt off the fish and slip into the liquid. Return to the boil, remove from the heat, cover and leave for 10 minutes while you cook the vegetables.

Boil the potatoes until tender, and use remaining boiling water from the kettle to boil the carrots, courgette, cauliflower and samphire until al dente. Drain.

Place the eggs in a small pan and cover with cold water. Bring to the boil and boil for 5 minutes. Drain but leave the pan under a cold running tap to cool. Crack the shells and remove.

Lift the fish on to a fold of kitchen paper to drain, peel off the skin and serve surrounded by piles of vegetables, a lengthways-halved egg, the mayo and a lemon wedge.

F Fondue Set

I've always liked the *idea* of a fondue meal more than the actual dish. I remember fondue parties the first time around more for the hangover the next day than the pleasure of hot bread and cheese. I still have my original fondue set, tucked up in its bright yellow Habitat box at the back of a rarely disturbed cupboard. It came out a lot when Simon and I were writing *The Prawn Cocktail Years*, but dipping crusts of bread in melted Gruyère with kirsch isn't a meal I want to eat too often. My dentist told me that on his skiing holiday, people were ordering it as a starter, rounding it off by cracking an egg or two per person into the last scrapings of the pot.

Fondue cooking originates in Switzerland and caught on when skiing holidays started to be fashionable in the sixties and seventies. Fondue dinner parties swept the land and a fondue set became the must-have cooking pot, top of the wedding list. Habitat was the place to buy one and still is. So-called fondue is actually an ancient style of cooking, invented out of necessity in the eighteenth century by Swiss villages, cut off from large towns during the long winters. They had to rely on foods like cheese and bread made in the spring and summer to last through the winter months. Villagers found that if they melted the hard, dry cheese it tasted far better. Dipping chunks of stale bread into the melted cheese, a bite-size cheese on toast, made both ingredients palatable. Enterprising villagers added wine and other seasonings to improve the flavour and texture, while stale and oven-dried bread that won't disintegrate in the hot Vesuvial fluid remains the best option. In my flat-dwelling days I used to buy slabs of incredibly cheap fondue cheese for cheese on toast but it's possible now to buy sets of microwavable fondue in little plastic ramekins.

The traditional pot is usually made from earthenware and called a *caquelon*. Clay (see Earthenware, page 50) has good heat retention and distribution qualities, making it perfect, but it's prone to cracking if not treated carefully. The finest pots, suitable for heating oil and cooking meat, are copper or enamelled iron, which have even better heat absorption and distribution properties. Most though, like mine, are made of stainless steel. They come with six matching long, spear-like forks with resistant handles to prevent them getting too hot to hold. Some handles are coloured – mine have hoops – to avoid spear confusion. The set comes with a stand and tray for the burner, with a snuffer to put it out. The Aladdin's-lamp-like burner is fuelled by methylated spirits and is highly flammable. The stand comes in handy when the dining table is heavily loaded with food, saving space and lifting dishes. Ideal for *plateau de fruits de mer*.

For suppliers, see page 274. Amazingly, there is even a book devoted to the fondue. A hundred recipes; who'd have thought it possible?

Beef Shabu Shabu and Zosui

SERVES 2

Since I have learnt this healthy, fun way of sharing steak and vegetables, my fondue set is back in business. With true Japanese style, everything is prepared in advance and thoughtfully arranged on a platter for cooking at the table in the fondue pot. Traditionally it is cooked in a shallow cast-iron sukiyaki pan over a special burner or electric hotplate, but the fondue set is perfect. I have even bought special Hakuji white porcelain square plates and bowls for serving it.

The best beef in Japan is wagyu beef from the Kobe region. Its fat-marbled character has earned it the name shimofuri, *or frost-covered, and that would be the ultimate treat for shabu shabu (your butcher may be able to order it for you, otherwise see page 276). Japanese cooks buy their beef ready sliced for shabu shabu and it needs to be paper-thin, so that it is ready to eat after a quick swish in the stock. To the Japanese ear, this sounds like 'shabu shabu'. It is dipped into two sauces to season and cool it down before being eaten in rotation with the vegetables, although some people prefer to eat all the meat and then all the vegetables. Rump steak is a good wagyu alternative. Ask your butcher to slice it on the bacon-slicer. To do it at home, freeze the trimmed steak for an hour before slicing with a thin-bladed, very sharp knife. When all the meat and vegetables have been eaten, rather than drink the stock as soup, it can be turned into a more filling finale, by either adding ready-prepared noodles or making zosui. The latter is the Japanese equivalent of congee or rice soup with egg, soy and spring onion.*

300g rump steak

1 leek, trimmed

4 fresh shiitake mushrooms

2 baby bok choi

80g enoki mushrooms

1.2 litres water and 2 x 10 x 10cm pieces of kombu seaweed, or 1.2 litres light chicken stock

50ml sake

For the ponzu sauce:

3 tbsp fresh lime juice

3 tbsp Kikkoman soy sauce

100g daikon, very, very finely grated

2 spring onions

For the sesame sauce:
3 tbsp sesame paste
1 tbsp Kikkoman soy sauce
2 tbsp Thai fish sauce (nam pla)
1 tbsp rice vinegar
2 tbsp water
1 tsp sugar
½ garlic clove

For the zosui:
200g hot steamed rice
soy sauce
2 spring onions
2 eggs

If you are slicing the beef yourself, freeze it for about an hour until stiff and easier to deal with. Next make the sauces. For the ponzu, mix the lime and soy. Just before you are ready to serve (in individual bowls), stir in the daikon and finely sliced spring onions. For the sesame sauce, mix the sesame paste, soy, fish sauce, vinegar and water, then add the sugar. Peel, finely chop and crush the garlic, and stir into the sauce.

Now prepare the vegetables. Slice the leek diagonally to make 7cm lengths, approximately 1cm wide. Remove the stalks from the shiitake. Cut a star-cum-cross in the top of the mushrooms by tilting the knife slightly, making three cuts. Separate the leaves of the bok choi. Break the enoki into small clumps. Either arrange everything on one platter, or divide between two. Arrange the vegetables by type on one side of the plate and lay out the beef on the other. To slice the beef, use a very sharp, thin-bladed knife to trim away the thick fat running down one side of the steak. Stand the steak on this end and very carefully slice into paper-thin sheets, laying them out in overlapping slices on a platter. Decant the sauces into individual saucers/bowls, and make place settings with chopsticks, plates and bowls for the zosui.

When you are ready to cook, simmer the water with the kombu for 10 minutes. Remove the kombu and add the sake and a generous pinch of salt. If using stock, heat it before adding sake and salt. To cook and eat, use chopsticks to wave a piece of beef through the stock, just long enough for the colour to change, then into the two sauces to cool and season. Follow with the vegetables and end by drinking the soup. To make the zosui, add the rice to the remaining hot stock with a seasoning of soy and sliced spring onions. Quickly whisk the eggs with your chopsticks and add to the pan. The dish is ready in moments when the egg is set.

F Food Processor

I can't say I was a fan of *The Crafty Cook*, Michael Barry's TV cookery show in the seventies, but a demonstration by him of a new food processor was sufficient to entice me up to Hampstead to Sheila Fitzjones's house. Sheila was at the vanguard of cookery PR, a line of business just starting to blossom, and if she represented a new product, there was every chance it was worth knowing about. The new Magimix from France was sold through Divertimenti, the domestic arm of the French Kitchenware and Tableware Supply Co. The latter had been selling the Robot-Coupe, the professional equivalent of the Magimix, for some time and fans included Robert Carrier, the Heston Blumenthal of the day.

At the time, the Swiss chef Anton Mosimann was cutting a dash at the Dorchester reinventing bread and butter pudding and introducing his version of trendy nouvelle cuisine. It was the start of our love affair with celebrity chefs and the beginning of a new-found interest in 'real' food and eating out. We had just discovered pasta, and Ann Barr and Paul Levy were on the button with their outré *Official Foodie Handbook*, subtitled *Be Modern – Worship Food*.

Every chef worth his salt already owned a Robot-Coupe. This brilliantly simple yet powerful and reliable food processor was invented over forty years ago by Pierre Verdan, a French catering company salesman, who came up with the idea after noticing how much time his clients spent in the kitchen chopping, shredding and mixing. He devised a simple but effective solution, a bowl with a revolving blade in the base. The design has hardly changed. The Magimix's square base means it tucks neatly into a spare kitchen corner; its quiet and powerful motor comes with a twelve-year guarantee. It is very simple to use, the bowl clicking into place and all functions powered by three press-button switches on the front of the machine. I use mine every day, for chopping and liquidizing, for slicing and grating when I have a quantity of fruit and vegetables to process, and sometimes to make pastry, although I tend to do that by hand. There's a neat box for keeping the accessories tidied away and it comes with a small bowl as well as the regular one and both are made of shatterproof lexan plastic, the same material used for riot shields and aircraft windows.

I still own an early model, now consigned to the family house in Cornwall, but it's useful to know that spares for all models can be bought (see page 274).

Avgolemono with Chicken Rissoles

SERVES 4

This lovely dish is all about leftovers. You will need the concentrated broth from poaching a chicken and the pickings from the carcass. The result, based on Greek avgolemono (egg and lemon) soup, is thickened with rice and bobs with parsley-flecked chicken and rice dumplings. With a squeeze of lemon, leftovers have rarely tasted better.

approx 2 litres fresh chicken stock

100g basmati rice

1 new season garlic clove

1 medium onion

150g leftover poached chicken

1 large beaten egg

50g fresh breadcrumbs

4 tbsp finely chopped flat-leaf
  parsley leaves

1 tbsp finely chopped mint

2 lemons

Simmer the stock until reduced by almost half; you want 1.2 litres. Wash the rice until the water runs clear. Add the rice to the stock and simmer gently for 15 minutes, or until tender. Using a slotted spoon, scoop half the rice into a mixing bowl.

Peel, chop and crush the garlic with a pinch of salt. Peel and grate the onion. Pulse chop or finely chop the chicken by hand. Add all these ingredients to the cooled rice. Season generously with black pepper and blend thoroughly, adding the (beaten) egg to bind.

Gradually incorporate the breadcrumbs to make a firm and fairly dry mixture. Form the chicken mixture into walnut-sized balls – you will be able to make at least 26. Scatter the chopped parsley and mint over a tray or work surface and gently roll the balls in it until completely covered. Bring the soup back to simmering and lower the rissoles into the broth. Simmer for 10 minutes, until firm and cooked through.

Serve immediately or, better still, leave covered and serve warm rather than hot, when the rice will have soaked up more liquid. Serve with lemon wedges to sharpen the flavours.

Turkey Tonnato

SERVES 6

A thick, creamy tuna sauce hides sliced, roast turkey, providing a canvas to decorate with strips of anchovy, sliced green olives and capers. A real show-stopper and something to remember next Christmas but also worth making at any time of the year with leftover (or bought) roast chicken.

400–600g roast turkey, preferably white meat
50g tin of anchovies in olive oil
approx 200g tin of tuna in oil
175ml Hellmann's mayonnaise

2 tsp Grey Poupon or Maille Dijon mustard
1 tbsp lemon juice
1–2 tbsp water
6 pitted green olives
2 tbsp capers

Slice the turkey and spread it out in overlapping slices on a platter. Take 3 anchovies from the tin and 1 tablespoon of its oil. Place in the food processor bowl with the drained tuna, mayo, mustard, lemon juice and water. Blitz smooth. Add extra lemon juice to taste and/or water to achieve a pouring consistency similar to custard. Spoon and spread the sauce over the turkey to completely cover.

Slice the remaining anchovies in long, thin strips, and finely slice down the olives into 6–8 thin half-moons. Give the capers a squeeze to get rid of excess liquid. Decorate the tuna 'canvas' with swirls of anchovy, olives and capers.

F Frying Pans

Both my sons have turned out to be good, natural cooks but when they were growing up, it was Henry, the younger one, who was most likely to cook for himself rather than rely on toast or cereal. His first speciality was breakfast and he ruined several frying pans as he perfected his skills. He absent-mindedly left empty pans over a high heat and on countless other occasions etched non-stick surfaces with a metal fish slice, invariably compounding the damage by washing up with a wire scourer or immediately holding the pan under a cold tap. My crêpe pan

is no longer reliably non-stick but two frying pans survive intact; one a small Le Creuset cast-iron, vitreous enamel pan, the other a French untreated steel pan, now black as ink and smooth as a baby's bottom, its non-stick surface earned over years of daily use. The latter is a classic French design, with a wide base and shallow sides, sloping outwards to make lifting and turning food easy. The handle is strong and riveted to the pan and never gets too hot to handle. It is my everyday frying pan, used for fry-ups, meatballs and browning meat for stews, steaks and escalopes. It is completely flat, so is perfect for rolled omelettes.

The little cast-iron frying pan tends to be used more in the oven than as a frying pan, although it's handy for dry-frying, often called roasting, nuts and seeds and spices for grinding. I always use it when I make tarte Tatin for four, although I have a specially designed, hard-anodized aluminium 28 x 5cm deep Tatin pan from Alan Silverwood (see page 274) that feeds 10 or 12. The little pan is perfect too for roasting garlic, shallots and onions, and a favourite choice for small game birds and quail.

More recently, my frying pan empire has expanded with three new favourites and they all involve state-of-the-art anodized aluminium. This abundant metal used to be the cheap cookware option, but fears of a possible connection between aluminium and Alzheimer's disease killed it stone dead. If you are still using ordinary aluminium pans, they are only a real health hazard if the surface is pitted but they shouldn't be used for acidic and leafy foods, like tomatoes and spinach. Anodizing effectively seals aluminium and strengthens it whilst allowing it to remain receptive to non-stick coating. Aluminium is a great cooking medium because it conducts heat fast and evenly.

Two of the new frying pans come with a lifetime guarantee and are a useful 20cm, with curved sides tapering to a 15cm thick, heavy base. The Circulon pan has a circular groove pattern on the black, non-stick cooking surface and a riveted steel handle and is safe to use with metal utensils. It can go in the dishwasher. The eco-friendly Green Pan is similarly shaped and slightly deeper, made of heavy gauge aluminium with a glossy dark grey Thermolon ceramic non-stick coating. Its stay-cool handle has to be wrapped in foil if it goes in the oven. Both pans fry food beautifully, particularly onions and breadcrumbed food, making them a treat to use.

My other 'new' favourite pan, made by Le Creuset, is such a pleasure to use that it has almost taken over from my sauté pan. Its heavy-duty, hard-anodized aluminium has been given a four-star treatment that makes it as strong and heavy as steel. A riveted steel handle and large lug opposite the handle make it easy to lift. It's 28cm x 5cm deep with curved sides, so it holds a lot and is great for risotto and other rice dishes, for chicken stews like coq au vin and for chili con carne. It has a glass lid.

I don't use my sad-looking crêpe pan that often, but despite its imperfections it still cooks good pancakes. It is very light and the sloping sides and shallow depth make it a joy to use; I even attempt tossing.

Messicana with Sweet Potato, Feta and Pine Kernels

SERVES 4

Here's a blessedly quick and simple pasta dish that looks beautiful, a lovely mix of saffron-yellow sweet potato, bright green beans, white feta cheese and golden-brown toasted pine kernels, with a generous splash of fruity olive oil to pull it all together. Instead of grassy beans it is also good made with peppery rocket or watercress which will wilt slightly against the hot pasta.

Quantities given are for four generous portions but it is child's play to scale the quantities up or down to feed more or fewer people. Any short or round pasta, from penne, fusilli and casarecce, to orecchiette, radiatori and farfalle, works best. Serve the pasta with a lemon wedge to squeeze over the top at the last moment, and the pepper grinder.

600g sweet potatoes	50g pine kernels
350g green beans	1 tbsp olive oil
400g round or short pasta	200g Greek feta cheese
3–4 tbsp best olive oil	

Peel the sweet potatoes, cut into kebab-size chunks and boil in salted water for about 5 minutes, until just tender. Drain. Top and tail the beans, snap in half and boil in a second pan of boiling, salted water for 2 minutes. Drain.

Co-ordinate the vegetable cooking with cooking the pasta – also in plenty of boiling salted water – then drain and return it to the pan with a splash of best olive oil and about 2 tablespoons of the pasta cooking water.

Quickly stir-fry the pine kernels in 1 tablespoon of olive oil until golden. Tip on to a fold of kitchen paper to drain. Tip all the cooked ingredients into a warmed serving bowl, crumble the feta over the top, add a splash of olive oil and toss before serving, before the cheese completely melts.

Creole Crab Cakes with Sweet Chilli Mayo

SERVES 4–6

Ready-picked crab is perfect for crab cakes. I love them flavoured Louisiana-style, with the Creole 'holy trinity' of green pepper, onion and celery, a hint of thyme, chilli and flat-leaf parsley. It's a simple recipe, the mixture bound, surprisingly, with mayonnaise and stiffened with breadcrumbs. I've recently come to the conclusion that crab cakes are most delicious with an escalope-style egg and breadcrumb covering. The textural contrast of biting through the crisp shell into the soft, squashy filling is orgasmic. I like them with a cheat's Creole sauce made by mixing equal quantities of tomato ketchup and mayo with a generous splash of Tabasco. Look out for 100g packs of handpicked white and brown Cornish crabmeat at Waitrose (see also page 276) and some fishmongers.

4 spring onions	4 tbsp Hellmann's mayonnaise
90g celery from the heart	25g flat-leaf parsley leaves
1 small green pepper, approx 100g	250g fresh breadcrumbs
1 tbsp vegetable oil	approx 6 tbsp flour, for dusting
1 large red chilli, approx 15g	2 eggs
1 tbsp chopped fresh thyme	vegetable oil, for frying
200g white crabmeat	4tbsp each mayonnaise, ketchup
200g brown crabmeat	and tabasco

Trim and finely chop the spring onions, celery and green pepper. Heat the oil in a frying pan, stir in the prepared veg, season with salt and pepper and gently soften, stirring often for 10 minutes until semi-soft. Finely dice the chilli. Stir the chilli and thyme into the veg and stir-fry for a further 5 minutes. Spread out on a plate to cool.

Place the crabmeat, mayo and finely chopped parsley leaves in a mixing bowl. Add 100g of breadcrumbs, then the cooled veg, and stir again thoroughly to make a stiff, soft mixture. Dust a work surface and your hands with flour. Aiming for 12 pieces and working quickly, take a couple of tablespoons of mixture and form into cakes-cum-patties, patting the tops and sides to flatten, but not worrying too much about a neat finish, transferring to a plate as you go. To finish the crab cakes, lightly whisk the eggs in a shallow bowl. Place the remaining 150g of crumbs in a second bowl and sift about 4 tablespoons of flour into a third.

Working quickly, handling the crab cakes as little as possible, dust first with flour, pass through the egg and press into the crumbs, washing your hands between each task. Arrange on a plate. Cover with clingfilm. Chill for an hour. Heat a 1cm depth of oil in a frying pan until hot enough to brown a scrap of bread in 20 seconds. Cook the crab cakes in batches of 4, for 3–4 minutes a side, just long enough to make a pale golden crust. Lift from the pan on to a double fold of absorbent kitchen paper. Mix the mayo, ketchup and tabasco to make the sauce.

Black Fig Tarte Tatin

SERVES 4

My little cast-iron Le Creuset frying pan is perfect for making tarte Tatin. For the original, made with apples, I always use Cox's apples, but of all the versions I've made – with pineapple, pears, tomatoes and beetroot – fig is the favourite. Make it when figs are glutting, as they seem to do more often these days, and serve it hot from the oven with crème fraîche.

12 black figs	150g puff pastry
100g sugar	crème fraîche, to serve
50g butter	

Heat the oven to 200°C/gas mark 6. Halve the figs lengthways. Trim the ends if they are hard. Melt the sugar and butter together, stirring as it begins to colour, continuing until the syrup turns a deep golden colour like toffee. Remove from the heat and carefully arrange the figs radiating round, overlapping slightly, cut side down, filling the gap in the centre with fruit. On a floured surface, roll the pastry to the thickness of a 50p piece and lay it over the top, pressing with a wooden spoon to cut a circle. Tuck it down inside the rim. Bake for 20–25 minutes, until the pastry is puffed and golden brown. Carefully pour off excess juices.

Now comes the tricky bit. Place a large plate over the top of the tart and quickly invert, watching out for the hot juices. Serve with crème fraîche. Use this recipe as a template for the real McCoy, using 8–12 Cox's apples, peeled, cored and quartered.

Orange and Saffron Chicken Biryani

SERVES 4

The sweet and sour tanginess of Seville orange marmalade (see page 185) adds an unconventional tang to this already choice orange and saffron, cardamom-seasoned chicken biryani. The dish smells wonderful as it cooks, sending exotic wafts of cardamom and orange mingling with chicken and rice around the kitchen. It's a usefully good-natured dish and can be kept waiting, covered, for the best part of an hour without spoiling.

1 large onion, approx 200g	1 bay leaf
50g Marcona blanched almonds	5 cardamom pods
2 tbsp vegetable oil	a generous pinch of saffron strands
4 large organic chicken thighs, approx 750g	2 tbsp raisins, preferably golden
2 juicing oranges	250g basmati rice
25g butter	600ml chicken stock
1 tbsp runny honey	3 tbsp marmalade

Peel, halve and finely slice the onion. Quickly stir-fry the almonds in a little oil in a spacious, lidded frying pan until golden. Drain on kitchen paper. Turn up the heat, add the remaining oil and stir-fry the onion until shrivelled and dark brown, adjusting the heat to avoid burning. Allow at least 20 minutes for this. Scoop on to kitchen paper to drain.

Slice the chicken into bite-size pieces. Zest the oranges. Melt the butter in the oily onion juices and gently brown the chicken. Season with salt and pepper. Add the juice from the oranges, the honey, bay leaf, lightly crushed cardamom, orange zest, saffron and raisins. Bubble up the juices, cooking for a few minutes until turning syrupy and the chicken is glossy. Stir in the washed rice. Add half the onion, most of the almonds and 450ml of stock. Bring to the boil, reduce the heat to very low, cover the pan and cook for 15 minutes. Turn off the heat and leave, covered, without removing the lid, for 15 minutes. Simmer the remaining 150ml of stock with the marmalade. Scoop out and discard the peel, then cook until syrupy and reduced to about 3 tablespoons. Swirl the pan as the sauce reduces, adjusting the heat so it doesn't burn. Turn the biryani on to a warmed platter and fork in the reserved almonds and onions. Dribble over the sauce and serve.

Rabbit with Cannellini Beans and Pears

SERVES 4

The gentle gamey flavour and lean chicken-like texture of rabbit goes very well with smoked bacon and pears in this lovely autumnal meal-in-a-bowl. Creamy cannellini beans thicken the herby juices while green beans give the dish a grassy fresh crunch. Serve it as a fork supper with crusty bread and butter or make more of a meal of it with a side dish of boiled potatoes. When you are buying pears for this recipe, choose really hard ones otherwise they will cook to a mush. Conference, which always need to ripen in the fruit bowl, are perfect.

600g diced wild rabbit
flour, for dusting
3 tbsp olive oil
70g smoked streaky bacon, chopped
1 large onion
4 small hard Conference pears

1 bay leaf, 4 sprigs of thyme and a
    small sprig of rosemary, tied with
    string
500ml chicken stock
400g tin of cannellini beans
300g green beans
25g flat-leaf parsley leaves

Pat the rabbit dry with kitchen paper and dust with flour, shaking off excess. Heat 2 tbsp oil in a spacious, lidded frying pan and quickly brown the rabbit over a high heat in several batches, transferring it to a plate as you go. Reduce the heat, add the remaining oil and bacon and cook until the fat melts and crisps. Peel, halve and finely slice the onion and stir it into the bacon. Cook, stirring occasionally, until semi-soft. Halve the pears, cut out the core, peel and lay, cut side down, amongst the onions. Cook for 2–3 minutes, then return the rabbit, the bundle of herbs and the stock. Bring slowly to the boil, stirring to agitate the flour from the rabbit to thicken the juices. Season with salt and pepper and cook, covered, over a very low heat for 45–60 minutes, until the rabbit is tender. If, incidentally, you use farmed rabbit, halve the cooking time.

Rinse and drain the cannellini beans and add to the pan. Taste and adjust the seasoning. Remove the herb bundle. Halve the trimmed green beans and boil for 2 minutes in salted water. Stir the chopped parsley into the stew, pile the drained green beans on top and serve.

Porcini, Parmesan and Lemon Pancake Gratin

SERVES 4

I used to feel sorry for my mum on Pancake Day. I'm one of four children and we were like cuckoos in the nest as she tried in vain to keep us at arm's length from the splattering frying pan. No sooner had we eaten one pancake than we demanded another. One brother liked his thick and flabby while I preferred thin and crisp, but we all loved them rolled with a dusting of caster sugar and a generous squeeze of lemon. It's that combination of hot and soft yet crisp-frilled eggy pancake, with a light surface of crunchy sugar and tart, sour lemon juice, that is so addictive whatever your age. I've done my time in the Shrove Tuesday hot spot, and it is usually a mum job, although a male friend holds a grown-up pancake party every year. His solution to being tied to the stove is a tossing competition, so those who dare cook their own pancakes and there are always plenty of show-offs happy to take over. As the drink flows and cheeks turn rosy, the tossing gets higher and a barely contained hysteria emanates from the kitchen. It is always great fun.

Another way to take the pressure off the cook is made-ahead pancakes turned into a complete dish. In the seventies, London was hit by a crêpe craze. Rose Gray, sadly no longer with us at the River Café, set up under the arches in Notting Hill's Portobello Road, but it was the French crêperie Asterix, named after the Gallic cartoon hero, which popularized stuffed pancakes. Folding soft, gooey food in a pancake envelope is my idea of heaven.

Another idea is to stack pancakes with stuffing between the layers. The woody flavour and dense chewy texture of dried porcini will bolster the flavour of button mushrooms in this gratin-cum-pie. Stewed together after the porcini have been hydrated, in buttery onions with thyme, a hint of chilli and saffron, the mushrooms are layered between pancakes with a lemon-flavoured creamy sauce. Each layer is lightly dredged with grated Parmesan, with a much thicker layer on top. As it bakes the flavours exchange and the sauce percolates through the pancakes and round the edges, filling the kitchen with delectable smells. Originally I'd thought to stuff and roll the pancakes but keeping them flat and whole works perfectly, particularly if you have a round gratin dish approximately the same size as the pancakes. Cut it like a cake and serve with green beans or a crisp green salad.

The pancake recipe, incidentally, is perfect for the classic sugar and lemon treatment.

30g dried porcini
1 large onion
50g butter
1 bay leaf
1 tsp chopped fresh thyme
a pinch of crushed chilli
a pinch of saffron strands
400g button mushrooms
25g flour
1 tsp lemon juice

300ml milk
40g freshly grated Parmesan
For the pancake batter:
75g butter
100g plain flour
a pinch of salt
1 whole egg
1 egg yolk
275ml milk

Begin by making the pancake batter. Melt 50g of butter. Sift the flour into the bowl of a blender. Add all the other pancake ingredients except the butter. Blend thoroughly, pass through a sieve if necessary, stir in the melted butter and leave to rest for at least 30 minutes. Stir before using. Melt a scrap of the remaining 25g butter in a non-stick crêpe pan. When hot and sizzling, pour in enough batter – about 4 tablespoons measured into a jug – to cover the pan base but quickly lift, tilt and swirl the batter evenly. Cook over a medium heat for a minute or so, until the surface is set, then flip over in the usual way with a palette knife. Layer up between sheets of baking parchment as you go. You want 4 decent pancakes; the first pancake is often a disaster; if so, chuck it away and start again.

Place the porcini in a bowl and cover with boiling water. Cover and leave for at least 20 minutes, preferably 30. Halve, peel and finely chop the onion. Melt half the butter in a spacious sauté pan over a medium-low heat and stir in the onion, bay leaf, thyme, chilli and saffron. Cook, stirring often, until the onion is glassy and lightly coloured, allowing about 15 minutes. While the onion cooks, wipe the mushrooms, cutting larger ones in half. Stir the mushrooms into the onion, stirring for several minutes until they look damp and slightly shrunken. Scoop the porcini out of their soaking water and add to the pan, then carefully strain the liquid into a small pan (it will contain grit).

Simmer, stirring occasionally, until a small amount of syrupy liquid remains, then add it to the mushrooms and porcini. To make the sauce, melt the remaining 25g butter in a suitable pan, stir in the flour until smooth, then stir in the lemon juice. Remove from the heat and gradually add the milk, stirring with a wooden spoon. Return to the heat and simmer, stirring constantly, for 5 minutes to make a smooth sauce. Add salt to taste. Turn off the heat and leave to cool slightly.

Heat the oven to 170°C/gas mark 3. Smear a spoonful of sauce over the base of a round gratin dish. Cover with a pancake and spread with a quarter of the mushroom mixture. Swirl a couple of tablespoons of sauce over the top and season with Parmesan. Cover with a second pancake and continue thus, finishing with mushrooms and a generous covering of sauce. Dredge lavishly with Parmesan and bake for 30–40 minutes, until crusty and bubbling round the edges.

G Graters

Graters are basically metal sheets punctured with rows of small holes and slats. Useful for grating cheese, fruit and vegetables, and slicing cucumbers and potatoes, the design is pretty basic and their use largely overtaken by food processor attachments that do the work quickly and without risk of injury. Well, that was the case until the market began to flood with Microplane graters. These also have rows of blades-cum-perforations but are razor-sharp and made in a perplexing choice of shapes and sizes. They have given a new lease of life to graters, making us want several to make different-shaped gratings. Unlike regular graters, no pressure is required and food is grated precisely without tearing or clogging. Storage, to protect fingers, rather than the blades, can be problematic.

I use graters a lot, getting pleasure from reducing a single carrot or a chunk of cheese to a pile of gratings. Graters are particularly useful for small amounts, being far easier to rinse clean than dismantling and then washing the various parts of the food processor. At the last count I own eight graters, all with slightly different-shaped punctured holes and slats. Some are flat, some are curved with slide-off containers that catch grated food, others are long and thin, or small and squat. I use them on a whim, preferring a particular shaped rasping one day and another the next. The most versatile is my mother's old box grater, stamped with 'made from stainless steel in Hong Kong', its four sides catering for most grating needs, the cutting edges now only just sharp enough. I have an updated state-of-the-art version (made by Cuisipro) with a user-friendly rubberized handle, and dangerously sharp, sleekly designed perforations. It has a clever lid-cum-base that helps contain whatever is being grated. This chunky base has a handle to make lifting and carrying comfortable and incorporates a round grater with very fine, super-sharp little teeth, in the style of a porcelain Japanese grater which renders daikon, ginger and garlic to a moist pulp. This latter type of fine grating is similar to a particular type of zester (see page 270).

Several of my graters are specifically for Parmesan, producing a wide range of different gratings, from wafer-thin, flat slices, to various sized specks and crumbs of cheese. It's often occurred to me that it would be useful to see a series of photos showing the gratings on the packaging, because they can be quite a surprise.

Courgette Pancakes with Feta and Parmesan

SERVES 4

When we first took over the allotment I share with my sons, we were a bit free and easy with the courgette seed. We ended up with about ten flourishing plants and weeks of courgettes, some with their yellow flower. If you turned your back they grew as if being pumped like balloons and if you left the plants untended for a couple of days, little courgettes turned into huge marrows. I made soup after soup, pickle and ratatouille, griddled them for salad, even made jam, but these little pancakes were the star.

The courgettes are grated and mixed into a particularly stiff eggy batter thick with freshly grated Parmesan, a crumble of feta cheese and a generous amount of finely snipped chives. The pancakes need only a few minutes in the pan. I love a big pile of them with a dollop of crème fraîche, a shower of chives and extra Parmesan but they go extremely well with all sorts of things, from lemon-grilled white fish fillets to roast chicken with a fresh tomato sauce. Try them with ribbons of chicken breast marinated for

30 minutes with a generous squeeze of lemon juice, a splash of olive oil and a crushed garlic clove. Cook the drained chicken on a hot griddle or fry in batches in a little oil.

3 medium-sized courgettes, approx 300g	a bunch of chives
2 fresh eggs	150ml crème fraîche
50g flour	50g Greek feta cheese
20g butter, melted	75g chunk of Parmesan
	1 tsp vegetable oil

Trim and wash the courgettes, then grate them on the large hole of a cheese grater. Place in a colander and sprinkle with 1 tablespoon of salt. Leave for 20 minutes. Rinse and squeeze dry. Break the eggs into a mixing bowl and whisk in the flour and melted butter until smooth. Snip 2 tablespoons of chives into the mixture. Season lightly with salt and generously with pepper. Add a dollop of crème fraîche, the crumbled feta and 50g of finely grated Parmesan. Stir in the prepared courgettes.

If you need to keep the pancakes warm before serving, which you probably will, heat the oven to a low temperature before you start cooking. Heat a smear of oil in a non-stick frying pan over a medium heat and add spoonfuls of the mixture. Cook for a couple of minutes on each side, turning when the pancakes are golden brown and slightly souffléd. Serve with a scoop of crème fraîche, extra freshly grated Parmesan and a generous garnish of chives.

G Gratin Dishes

Gratin is the name of a style of cooking and the name of the dish it is cooked in. The dishes are made of materials like enamelled cast iron, porcelain and earthenware, occasionally stoneware, that can withstand oven and grill cooking. Typical gratin shapes are round or oval, sometimes oblong, occasionally square, and they are made in a range of sizes. The gratin dish is a shallow design with straight or, better still, sloping sides to increase the surface area to give maximum amount of gratinéed topping. Gratins are always served in the dish they are cooked in. A gratinéed dish is covered with a layer of breadcrumbs, sometimes grated cheese too, that cooks to a crisp contrast with the soft food underneath. Gratins are a useful way of using up leftovers. Pickings from a roast chicken or a few sausages will transform in a creamy sauce with the characteristic crisp topping.

Elizabeth David had a beautiful armoire in her downstairs kitchen where she kept a shop's worth of gratin dishes, all piled by size and colour. I've got quite a few myself, various sized white porcelain Apilco dishes, but my favourites – I have two, one holds a litre and the other nearly 2 litres – were bought in the eighties from a shop, long gone, in the Fulham Road that specialized in well-designed cookware. Everything about these dishes, from the thickness of the porcelain to their oval shape and the slope and depth of the sides, is perfection. I didn't know at the time, but they came from a famous German porcelain manufacturer, Arzberg Tric, founded in 1887 with links to Bauhaus through its original designer Hermann Gretsch. In 1931, he created Form 1382, a range of plain yet elegant china, so stylish it is still in production and on display at the Museum of Modern Art in New York. My dishes are designed by Michael Sieger, who, like Gretsch, is a master of form, function and usefulness. You'll find details of a website where you can see the entire Form 1382 and Tric range on page 274, and there are also details of where to buy them. I do remember my dishes were very expensive but the pleasure they give more than compensates and now I wish I had bought more. Ikea do similar, far, far cheaper dishes, but they are not in the same league.

I'm also very fond of two cast-iron oval Le Creuset dishes, which are particularly suited to pasta-based gratins like cannelloni and lasagne. I always use them for poaching fish for fish pie or smoked haddock for a lone supper. I also own a couple of very large oblong porcelain dishes that are perfect for family gratins, meatloaf, stuffed aubergines and moussaka.

Pulled Ham and Spinach Gratin

SERVES 2

Spinach and ham is one of those culinary marriages made in heaven, particularly in this creamy fondue-style cheese sauce, rich with white wine and sweet, voluptuous Emmental cheese. Any decent ham could be torn or pulled into chunky scraps for this recipe but pulled ham hock is what you really want. This gratin has a thicker than usual breadcrumb and cheese topping, in perfect contrast to the soft, slippery filling.

200g organic spinach	150ml milk
35g butter	75g grated Emmental cheese
25g flour	a squeeze of lemon
1 dsp Maille or Grey Poupon grain mustard	180g pulled ham hock
	30g crustless bread
125ml white wine	2 tbsp freshly grated Parmesan

Heat the oven to 200°C/gas mark 6. Boil the kettle and use the water to half-fill a large pan. Return to the boil, add 1 teaspoon of salt and push the spinach under the water. Within seconds it will have wilted. Drain immediately and squash against the sides of the colander to extract maximum water. Leave to cool.

Melt 25g of butter in a medium pan and stir in the flour followed by the mustard. Add the wine and stir constantly to make a thick smooth sauce before adding the milk. Continue stirring, adjusting the heat so the sauce simmers gently for 5 minutes. Add 50g of Emmental, stirring until smooth. Taste and adjust the seasoning with salt and a squeeze of lemon.

Transfer the squeezed spinach to a work surface and slice through it a few times. Stir the spinach and ham into the sauce, mixing thoroughly, then tip into a 1 litre capacity gratin-style dish. Mine is 24 × 14 × 4.5cm deep.

Blitz the torn bread into coarse crumbs. Mix with the remaining Emmental and the Parmesan and scatter over the top. Dot with the reserved butter and bake for 30 minutes, or until the top is crusty and bubbling round the edge.

Paraguayan Sole and Tomato Spaghetti Gratin

SERVES 4

I came across this unlikely sounding dish when The Times *asked me to write a week of recipes to complement teams in the World Cup. Its actual name is* tallarines chalacos *and it owes its heritage to a time when Italy occupied Paraguay.*

My contribution is to add chopped tomato, giving a fresh juiciness to the baked spaghetti sandwich of quickly fried white fish with chilli-flecked, slippery-soft red pepper and onion. It is possibly the oddest sounding gratin I've come across but I cannot recommend it highly enough. Serve it with green beans.

2 medium-large onions, approx 200g each
4 tbsp olive oil
2 pointed red peppers, approx 250g
1 tsp dried crushed chillies

3 vine tomatoes, approx 250g
8 lemon sole fillets, approx 400g
300g spaghetti
4 tbsp grated Parmesan

Peel, halve and finely chop the onions. Soften in 3 tablespoons of olive oil in a sauté pan over a medium heat. Stir often so they cook evenly. Halve the peppers lengthways, slice into strips and then into small dice. Stir into the onions. Add the chilli and cook for a further 10–15 minutes, stirring occasionally, until slippery soft and thoroughly cooked. Tip into a bowl. Pour boiling water over the tomatoes, count to 30, drain, peel and halve. Scrape out the seeds and chop the flesh. Slice the fish fillets into 2 or 3 pieces. Pat dry.

Heat the remaining oil in the pan and briefly fry the fish on both sides in batches until just cooked. Cook the spaghetti in plenty of boiling, salted water. Drain. Spread two-thirds of the spaghetti in a 2 litre capacity gratin-style dish. Spread the pepper mixture over the top and arrange the fish in a single layer. Add the tomato. Arrange the remaining spaghetti over the top to make a thin layer. Dredge with Parmesan. Bake in a hot oven – 200°C/gas mark 6 – for 20–25 minutes, until the top is crusty and golden.

Thanos Moussaka

SERVES 8

Every summer for several years, my best friend Tessa and I have gone on holiday to Lemnos, a Greek island strategically close to Turkey noted for its wines, fruity rich olive oil, golden bread and pasta, abundant seafood and outstanding feta cheese. One of the reasons we keep going back is a grumpy chef called Harry who has a taverna on the beach at Thanos.

Harry's taverna sits back from the arc of Thanos bay, flanked by fields where he grows most of what he needs for his lunch menus. For two weeks each summer, we eat lunch every day at Harry's. His Greek salad is made with fresh herbs and a slab of aged feta, wafer-thin zucchini chips are scooped through garlicky tzatziki, smoky griddled squid and sardines will have been caught that morning and the pasta is silkier than anything I've eaten in Italy.

I thought I'd died and gone to heaven when I saw Harry's moussaka. He makes several huge trays at a time, lets them go cold, then cuts huge square slabs and quickly reheats them to order. It arrives beautifully presented with a swirl of olive oil and a ring of finely chopped parsley, the deep béchamel topping towering over two layers of creamy aubergine sandwiching tomato-laced minced meat and a layer of thickly sliced potatoes.

I was surprised to discover that Harry uses beef mince (always breast), not lamb, for his moussaka. Everything about the dish, he says, is better made the day before. His ragù, flavoured with fresh tomato passata and dried oregano, is cooked until almost dry. The tricky bit, we agreed, is the aubergines. Salting them is vital. Harry deep-fries his – using very, very hot oil and cooking a few slices at a time so they stay dry – instead of griddling, pan-frying or roasting, which all radically alter the finished dish.

Another neat trick of Harry's is to sprinkle breadcrumbs between the layers to avoid oiliness, and the result is a remarkably light and clean flavour and texture. Previously when I've made moussaka, I've added feta to the nutmeg-seasoned béchamel sauce that sits on the top. Harry doesn't, preferring to add grated Kephalotyri, the Greek edition of Parmesan, between the layers.

Here, then, is my version of Harry's moussaka. It's quite a mission to make but can be done in stages over a couple of days. It needs no accompaniment except, perhaps, a lettuce salad, but you might copy the Harry routine of starting with his zucchini chips (dipped in flour, deep-fried in batches) to scoop up zingy tzatziki, probably with a Greek salad on the side.

4–5 aubergines, approx 1kg

2 tbsp salt

400g large waxy potatoes, such as
  Pink Fir Apple, Anya or Charlotte

1 large onion

3 large garlic cloves

3 tbsp olive oil, plus a little extra

750g minced organic beef or lamb,
  or half-and-half

a large glass of red wine

6 vine-ripened tomatoes

4 tsp dried oregano

80g bunch flat-leaf parsley

100g sourdough-style bread

oil, for deep frying

100g Kephalotyri, Parmesan or
  Provolone cheese

75g butter

75g plain flour

750ml full-fat milk

2 egg yolks

freshly grated nutmeg

fruity olive oil, to serve

Trim the aubergines and slice lengthways, approx 5mm thick. Lay out in a clean sink, sprinkle with salt and leave for 30 minutes. Rinse off the salt and pat dry with kitchen paper. Meanwhile, boil the potatoes in their skins. When cool enough to handle, peel and thickly slice lengthways. Halve, peel and finely chop the onion. Crack the garlic, flake away the skin, chop and crush to a paste with the flat of a knife. Heat 3 tablespoons of olive oil in a spacious sauté pan and stir in the onion. Season lightly with salt, cover and cook, stirring occasionally, for 15–20 minutes until sloppy and lightly coloured. Stir in the garlic and when aromatic, crumble the meat on to the onion, breaking up the clumps with a wooden spoon. Increase the heat and keep stirring as it all turns brown, about 10 minutes. Add the wine and leave to simmer into the meat; you want it juicy rather than wet.

Cut the core out of the tomatoes in a pointed plug shape, then chop the tomatoes. Blitz in a food processor to make passata. Add 2 teaspoons of salt, 1 teaspoon of freshly grated black pepper and the oregano to the mince, then add the passata. Simmer briskly for 5 minutes while you pick all the leaves off the parsley stalks and chop. Add half the parsley to the ragù, stir well, reduce the heat and leave to simmer steadily for 40 minutes, when it should be thick and moist rather than wet. Leave to cool. Set aside 2 tablespoons of parsley and stir the rest into the cold ragù.

Tear the bread, crusts too, into the bowl of the food processor and blitz to fine crumbs. Spread out on a tray to dry slightly. Have ready a few folds of absorbent kitchen paper. Heat the oil for deep-frying and when very hot – a square of bread will brown in seconds – immerse a few aubergine slices at a time. Cook for a couple of minutes until brown and buttery-soft to the point of a knife. Rest on kitchen paper. Continue thus until all the slices are done.

Choose a metal or ceramic gratin dish approximately 32 × 34 × 7cm deep. Make a layer of sliced potato, follow with a quarter of the breadcrumbs and grate over approximately a quarter of the cheese. Top with half the aubergine, more crumbs and cheese, then all the mince, more crumbs and cheese, then the final layer of aubergine, crumbs and cheese. The dish can be cooked to this stage, covered and chilled until one or two days later.

Make the béchamel topping in the usual way: melt the butter, stir in the flour to make a thick roux, off the heat add the milk, stirring with a wooden spoon to amalgamate. Return to a gentle heat, and keep stirring – a globe whisk quickly resolves lumps – as it thickens and comes to the boil. Immediately reduce the heat and season lavishly with salt – milk is surprisingly sweet – and lashings of nutmeg. Simmer gently to cook the flour for 5 minutes or so. Remove from the heat and stir a ladleful of béchamel into the egg yolks, then return this mixture to the pan and stir vigorously. Turn into a bowl, cover with clingfilm and leave for 15 minutes to thicken and cool slightly. Spoon and spread the béchamel over the cold moussaka.

Either cook immediately in a hot oven – 200°C/gas mark 6 – for 35 minutes, until the top is golden and the sauce is bubbling round the sides, or allow to go completely cold, then cut into squares and cook individually for 15–20 minutes. Garnish, Harry-style, with a sprinkling of reserved parsley and a swirl of olive oil. Either way, moussaka is best eaten warm rather than piping hot from the oven.

G Ridged Griddle Pan

One bright sunny morning in the late eighties, in the early days of the River Café, when the open-plan kitchen was on the right by the front door, I called in for coffee with my old friend Rose Gray. Ruthie Rogers, her partner in the Café, was griddling the tiniest courgettes I'd ever seen and later we tried some with lemon, olive oil and thyme. At the time cooking on a ridged, almost barbecue hotplate was an unusual choice and the River Café was at the vanguard of making the cast-iron, ridged griddle pan a must-have bit of kitchen kit. We all wanted to make their *pugliese bruschetta* and pile it with those little zucchini. Theirs, of course, was a catering griddle and part of the hob. When I had my kitchen done, it was a toss-up whether to get one myself or go for a wok burner and I've regretted ever since that I went for the latter.

Twenty-odd years later, most people who take an interest in cooking own a griddle. I have two. I bought the first at a Spanish market without realizing how to use it, intrigued by its oblong shape, wide ridges and little drainage lips at either end. The second, which I prefer, is round with narrower, thinner ridges and sits comfortably over one burner, whereas the other, which is used only for fish, really needs two. Both have fold-down handles so no space is compromised but if I were to choose again, I'd go for Le Creuset's cast-iron giant grill (45 x 75cm) in their Grillit range. Diagonally ridged on one side and smooth on the other, it doubles as a frying-pan-cum-girdle (see page 97). These shallow cast-iron or cast-aluminium pans must sit over direct heat for several minutes to get scorchingly hot before cooking begins. It is the food, not the pan, that is oiled, sometimes heavily salted too. Food will cook quickly and evenly and in the case of meat, in particular, must form a crusty seal before moving. After cooking, once cooled, the griddle needs a good scrubbing in hot water with a lightweight scourer and washing-up liquid. Mine have built up a black coating that makes them reliably non-stick.

The essential tool for griddle cooking is a decent pair of tongs. Two identical pairs hang above my hob ready for action. I've tried several styles over the years but the most dextrous and secure have pointy, scalloped heads, a spring action joint and are made of dishwasher-safe stainless steel. See page 275 for stockists.

Grilled Polenta with Mushroom Puttanesca

SERVES 4

Grilled polenta, made from cooked polenta poured on to a chopping board or plate where it sets in a slab, is great standby food. Once cool, it keeps, covered, in the fridge for several days and is a useful start to an after-work supper. Cut into shapes and oiled, it is seared on the griddle until the outside turns crusty and nutty and the inside will be molten. It is a wonderful combination. I tend to use quick-cook polenta, which is ready in minutes. Mushrooms completely change puttanesca and make it more substantial. A soft-poached egg is a very good extra.

1 litre boiling water	½ tsp chilli flakes
250g quick-cook polenta	20 Crespo pitted dry black olives
3 tbsp olive oil	with herbs
1 onion, approx 150g	2 tbsp capers
4 garlic cloves	a knob of butter
6 vine tomatoes, approx 600g	a few fresh basil leaves, if available
200g closed-cap mushrooms	a chunk of Parmesan
2 anchovies tinned in olive oil	

Add 1 teaspoon of salt to the vigorously boiling water, then add the polenta. Using a long-handled wooden spoon, stir to disperse as it erupts, while turning the heat very low. Stir every now and again to avoid the polenta sticking and a skin forming, continuing until it is very thick and shrinking from the walls of the pan. Pour and smooth the polenta on to a flat baking sheet or plate. Leave to go cold.

Heat the griddle until very hot, allowing several minutes for this. Cut slices or triangles of polenta, smear with a little olive oil and griddle for 3–5 minutes a side, until etched with tram lines.

Make the sauce while the polenta cools. Halve, peel and finely chop the onion and finely slice the peeled garlic. Heat the oil in a sauté or spacious frying pan and gently soften the onion and garlic, stirring often. Pierce the tomatoes, place in a bowl and cover with boiling water. Count to 30, then drain, peel and chop. Wipe the mushrooms and quarter. Increase the heat slightly and stir the mushrooms into the onion. Cook, stirring often, until moist-looking, then add the tomatoes, chopped anchovies and chilli flakes. Cook briskly, stirring often, for 10–15 minutes, until the tomatoes flop and thicken. Stir in the halved olives and the capers and beat in the butter, adding the torn basil. Serve pieces of polenta with the sauce and a few basil leaves, and pass the Parmesan for grating over the top.

Figs and Duck Livers on Griddled Toast

SERVES 2

When my sons Zach and Hen were teenagers they cycled weekday mornings to Chiswick station to meet their friends and catch a train to Clapham Junction for school. They parked their bikes at the back of my friend Christian Gustin-Andrews's restaurant, Christian's. As the years rolled by and they needed extra cash to supplement their allowance, both worked for Christian as washers-up, and then as waiters. This lovely snack is something Christian cooked for me on a visit to his home in the Dordogne. Lucky chap can pick ripe figs from the tree in his garden.

2 shallots

1 garlic clove

250g duck livers

25g butter

2 tbsp olive oil

2 ripe figs

4 thick slices of brown seed bread

1 tbsp red wine vinegar

butter, for the toast

Halve, peel and finely chop the shallots. Peel the garlic, chop finely, sprinkle with a generous pinch of salt and then work to a juicy paste. Pick over the livers, discarding any sinew, fat, etc. Pat dry with kitchen paper. Melt half the butter with the oil in a frying pan and fry the livers, turning as soon as they firm up and change colour. Add the shallots and garlic, adjusting the heat so they soften without crisping.

At the same time, heat the griddle for several minutes until very hot. Slice the figs lengthways into 3 thick slices. Butter the bread on both sides and toast on the griddle. Put the figs in the pan to warm and soften slightly, then flip on to the toast. Add the vinegar and remaining butter to the pan, letting it bubble up and mingle with the pan juices. Tip livers and juices over the figgy fried toast.

Bistro Steak with Make-ahead *Pommes Frites*

SERVES 6

Hanger steak is the American name for onglet, *the French bistro steak that is always cooked rare and served with* frites. *We call it skirt, although butchers refer to it as the 'hanging tender' because it hangs below the ribs, an extension of the tenderloin, in the diaphragm of the animal. It used to be classified as offal because of its close proximity to the kidneys, which explains its rich, almost gamey, beefy flavour. It's actually two muscles divided by tough connective tissue, which must be removed, then tidied up to leave a thin, narrow boneless cut of meat with a fibrous structure, almost shaggy, falling into pleats across its width. Your butcher probably won't thank me for flagging up hanger steak but it's time to stop overlooking this extraordinary muscle, which usually ends up in pasties, pies and the mincer. When properly cooked and carved, it is tender and full of flavour, with a silky texture, although it requires a bit more chew than steaks from less-worked parts of the body.*

Bavette is another loose-textured flank steak much prized in France but remaining one of the least appreciated cuts of meat here. It's a wide flat abdominal muscle, shaped a bit like a stingray, which is butchered into strips, which can then be cut into individual steaks.

Frites should be part-cooked and ready for the final few minutes in very hot oil before the steak is cooked.

*For hanger/*onglet *steak:*
700g trimmed hanger/*onglet*/skirt
  steak
Maldon sea salt
2 tbsp groundnut oil

For bavette *steak:*
2 x 250g trimmed *bavette*/flank
  steaks
Maldon sea salt
2 tbsp groundnut oil
For pommes frites:
6 large floury potatoes
groundnut oil for deep-frying

Take the steak out of the fridge an hour before you plan to cook it. Prepare everything else – *frites* and watercress or garlicky green salad – to co-ordinate with cooking the steak. The second stage of cooking the *frites* can start while the steak rests.

Both steaks are prepared and cooked in exactly the same way, although *bavette* takes marginally longer. Although the cooking time seems ludicrously short, you will have to trust me. It is vital to rest the meat for double the cooking time before slicing across the grain. Use oil with a high burning temperature like groundnut or rapeseed, not olive.

Pat the meat dry with kitchen paper. Smear with oil and season generously with sea salt, pressing it into the meat. Heat the griddle pan over a high heat for several minutes until scorchingly hot. Lay out the steak or steaks, pressing down with a spatula. Leave untouched for 2 minutes, the *bavette* for 2½ minutes, then turn and repeat. Remove to a board and leave to rest for 8 minutes, 10 minutes for the *bavette*. Slice the hanger across the grain, cutting thin, long slices, spreading them across the board or a warmed serving plate. Slice the *bavette* across the grain, making a cross with the grain, in slightly thicker slices, laying out as before. Don't miss out on the juices. You won't need salt but a squeeze of lemon points up the flavours and you will need freshly ground black pepper.

For the *frites*, cut the potatoes lengthways into your preferred thinness. Wash under cold running water until the water is clear and rid of starch. Drain in a colander and wrap in a tea towel to dry.

Half-fill a suitable pan or electric deep-fat fryer with oil and heat to 130°C (when a scrap of bread takes about 30 seconds to colour). Cook the *frites* in batches so as not to overcrowd the pan and fry for about 5 minutes, until cooked through but only lightly coloured. Lift out of the basket and allow to drain. This stage could be done in boiling water. The *frites* can be held in this state for a few hours, but allow to go cold.

For the final crisping, increase the temperature of the oil to 180°C (when a scrap of bread crisps in a few seconds) and cook in batches for between 5 and 15 minutes until crisp and golden. This time variance depends on the type of potato available at different times of the year. If, and it happens occasionally, the potatoes refuse to crisp, remove the basket from the oil, raise the temperature and cook for a third time. Drain on absorbent kitchen paper, sprinkle with salt and serve soonest. I tend to transfer the batches to a paper napkin-lined bowl and keep them warm in a low oven, then toss with salt at the last moment.

G Smooth Griddle Pan, Girdle or Bakestone

I bought my griddle, or girdle as my Scottish great-aunt would have called it, to make crumpets but she was famous for her Scotch pancakes. Great-Aunt Meg's pan was flat and smooth, made of cast iron, although I have seen similar pans with four perfect circular indentations. Once upon a time these pans were used over an open fire for cooking drop scones, crumpets and oatcakes and other foods that require minimal fat. Some have a handle that hoops over the top, others a hand-size slit on one side, also useful for hanging it away. Mine, made by Swift and a pricey fifty quid (available from Lakeland, see page 274), has handles at both sides, riveted on to the deep, down-sloping lip of the sturdily non-stick coated surface. The lip curves to the base, sloping slightly to give a 25cm cooking area, although the actual size of the pan is 34cm. Made of stainless steel with a Teflon non-stick surface, it has a thick base that makes the pan very heavy but ensures even heat distribution. I love this pan and get my money's worth out of it. It is great for family fry-ups, for potato cakes and meatballs, anything that doesn't require much fat or liquid. It is ovenproof, so is also good for large pies and ensures the base pastry is properly cooked.

Like the ridged griddle, it must be searingly hot before cooking begins. Test by flicking it with a little water; it will seize and sizzle if it is hot enough.

Great-Aunt Meg's Drop Scones with Fresh Strawberry Jam

MAKES ABOUT 12

I have vivid memories of being taken as a small child to visit Great-Aunt Meg in Edinburgh. There was an aspidistra on a stand in the hall and sugared almonds in a bowl. Antimacassars hung over the backs of the chairs in the front room where we took tea. It was high tea in the Scottish fashion and sandwiches had to be eaten before cake. Confusingly, there was another

Scottish Great-Aunt Meg, who lived up-country at Stenton, and both of them made drop scones which they called Scotch pancakes. Their lives were far more intertwined with my cousins' family than mine, because their mum, Margaret, my mother's sister, was educated in Scotland and stayed at Balerno with Meg (as she was always known; there were even more than two Megs in the extended Sanderson family) when she was at Edinburgh University. When Great-Aunt Meg from Stenton was too frail to care for herself, she went to live with the cousins, by now firmly established in Westcliff-on-Sea. Drop scones were a favourite teatime treat and all us children were taught to make them. My eldest cousin Liz remembers pouring the batter in the shape of our initials but mostly they were vaguely round and puffy, a pale golden colour. This tea-time treat was quickly whipped up whenever anyone came to tea, and eaten with butter and jam. The pancakes are also delicious for pudding with stewed fruit and crème fraîche or Greek yoghurt. Liz describes the mix as Yorkshire pudding with sugar.

Her daughter, Frances, remembers being allowed to pick big fat loganberries from the garden to eat with them but I remember strawberry jam.

Fresh strawberry jam is a cross between jam and compote but the relatively low sugar content means it doesn't set hard or last long and must be kept in the fridge. Lemon juice helps the setting and balsamic vinegar adds a hint of peppery sweetness. The jam is also good with crumpets and scones, over yoghurt and with other creamy puddings like Caramelized Rice Pudding (see page 151).

150g plain flour
a pinch of salt
2 tbsp sugar
1 egg
150ml milk
lard or oil, for frying

For the jam:
400g strawberries
150g sugar
1 tbsp balsamic vinegar
2 tbsp lemon juice

Sieve the flour and salt into a mixing bowl and stir in the sugar. Make a well in the middle and add the egg. Gradually whisk in the milk to make a thick, smooth batter. Leave to stand for 30 minutes. Heat a griddle (or heavy frying pan) until very hot, smear with a wisp of lard or oil, and drop spoonfuls of mixture into the pan. When the surfaces are covered with tiny bubbles and the pancakes begin to rise, quickly flip with a metal spatula. Keep warm, covered with a napkin.

To make the jam, rinse the strawberries, remove stalks and leaves – quickly done with a small knife, cutting in a pointed plug shape, and turning strawberry rather than knife – and place in a medium-sized pan with all the other ingredients. Stir and leave for about 30 minutes, giving the occasional stir, until the sugar dissolves and the fruit is saturated. Place over a medium heat, stirring constantly until all the sugar has melted. Boil, stirring regularly in a figure of eight, for 10–30 minutes, until the jam looks thick and syrupy. Test by placing a teaspoonful on a saucer. Cool, then push with your finger. If it wrinkles it's done. If not, continue boiling for a few more minutes. Remove from the heat and pour into a clean jar. Cover, cool and keep in the fridge.

H Haricot Bean Pot/*Olla*

In Barcelona's famous La Boqueria food market there is a stall devoted to dried beans. White beans, black beans, kidney-shaped beans and oval beans, small beans, medium-sized beans and great big whoppas. It's hard to decide which to buy, they all look so tempting. For the cook in a hurry, they also sell cooked beans by weight, ready for the evening *olla*.

Olla has become a generic term for any Hispanic cooking pot but is particularly associated with *olla podrida*, the Spanish edition of *pot-au-feu* and the national stew of Andalucia. The real *olla* is a distinctive tall, lidded pot with curved sides, not to be confused with the more pot-bellied *puchero*. Both are made of metal or clay and have little handles at the top, close to the lip, to make lifting and carrying comfortable. Such pots date back to ancient Rome and were used to store food as well as to cook in. They are particularly rated for bean soups and stews. Some people think the shape of the pot helps to cook the beans evenly but others believe a clay *olla* builds up a bean flavour bank enriched by each batch of beans. It's also thought that trace elements in the clay, particularly zinc, filter like fairy dust into the soaking and cooking water. Some families own a clay *olla* that has been in the family for generations. They are highly prized.

I have owned a modest-sized clay *olla* for donkey's years. Amazingly it has survived the rough and tumble of various moves and the rigours of family life. For at least twenty-five years, its primary use has been for soaking and then cooking beans. It came from the market at Moraira, on the Costa Blanca, near where my brother lived.

Most dried beans, particularly haricot, which I especially like, need to be soaked overnight in plenty of water. A quicker method is to bring the washed beans slowly to the boil – this takes about an hour – leave the pot covered for a further hour, then drain and simmer gently in fresh water with seasonings until tender. Cooking the beans gently for a long time prevents the skins splitting and results in very creamy beans. The flavour of bean soups and stews will mature if left overnight before eating.

White Bean Soup, Fried Bread and Ham

SERVES 6

For this soup white beans are flavoured with caramelized onion cooked in olive oil, bay and thyme, with a back snap of paprika and a hint of lemon. Sadly the soup doesn't end up white, but a garnish of salty fried Serrano ham and garlicky fried bread packs it with flavour.

400g dried haricot beans	1 Spanish onion
a small bunch of fresh thyme	6 tbsp olive oil
2 bay leaves	2 tbsp paprika
1 small unwaxed lemon	4 slices of Serrano ham
4 large garlic cloves	2 thick slices of sourdough

Rinse the beans, discarding stones, etc. Place in an *olla* or other large, lidded pot and generously cover with water. Soak overnight. Drain, then return the beans to the *olla* with the thyme, bay leaves and a strip of lemon zest, tied in a bundle with kitchen string. Crack the garlic with your fist, flake away the skin and add 3 cloves to the pot together with 2 litres of water. Bring the liquid slowly to the boil – this takes about an hour – removing scum as it appears. Simmer, partially covered, for 30 minutes while you trim, halve and finely slice the onion.

Heat 2 tablespoons of olive oil in a spacious frying pan and cook the onion, stirring often, until glossy, floppy and taking on colour. Allow at least 20 minutes for this. Increase the heat, add the paprika, and cook briskly, stirring constantly, for a couple of minutes, then tip the contents of the pan into the beans. Add a cup of cold water and simmer, partially covered, until the beans are completely soft. Stir in 2 teaspoons of salt.

Remove the herb bundle and liquidize the contents of the pan in batches until smooth and fluffy. Pour back into the pan, heat through, taste and adjust the seasoning with salt, black pepper and lemon juice. If it seems very thick, add extra water. Chop the ham into small scraps. Finely chop the reserved garlic clove. Chop the bread into crouton-sized pieces. Heat 1 tablespoon of oil in the frying pan and fry the ham crisp. Scoop on to a fold of kitchen paper and add 2 tablespoons of oil to the pan. Quickly stir-fry the chopped garlic, adding some of the bread, tossing until crisp and golden. Tip on to a plate, and use the remaining oil to fry the bread in batches. Serve the soup with garlicky croutons and ham.

■Ice Cream Maker

There is an unremarkable, small shop on the right-hand side as you come into Newlyn in Cornwall from the Penzance direction, where they make my favourite vanilla ice cream. Between Easter and October, there are often long queues and not just of children. The parking warden might turn a blind eye to cars that pull up opposite the shop, their owners nipping in for a cornet. Only one flavour is on sale and it comes with or without a Cadbury's flake.

Jelberts was started by Jim Glover's grandfather before the Second World War and grew out of a modest dairy business. The ice cream side of things began to flourish when food rationing ended but the family recipe using local milk and clotted cream remains unchanged. Jim can remember watching the ice cream being churned by hand, his uncle, mother and grandfather taking it in turns to sit at a truncated barrel with steel paddles inside a cylinder placed over slabs of salted ice, the work getting harder and harder as the mix got stiffer and stiffer.

I often think about the early days of Jelberts when I make ice cream at home, using my plug-in Cuisinart Ice Cream Professional, which churns and chills, producing ice cream every thirty minutes, turning my kitchen into an ice cream parlour. The downside of this impressive bit of kitchen kit is that, although neatly designed, it takes up a big chunk of work space. It also means I need to make a lot of ice cream before it becomes cost-effective. Before I succumbed to the luxury of my Cuisinart, I used one of those bowl and paddle machines. It packs away in a drawer but the bowl has to be frozen for twenty-four hours before use, or kept permanently in the freezer, and can only cope with making one batch at a time. Before that, I made ice cream by hand and still have recipes I prefer to make that way.

There are two basic recipes for making ice cream. One involves an egg and cream custard, and the other, like Jelberts', is made with sugar, milk and cream. There are many variations. Some people swear by single cream, others like whipping cream and yoghurt is the 'healthy' option.

The most superior ice cream, the sort you get at serious restaurants, is made from a base of vanilla-flavoured cream, or a mixture of cream and whole milk, sugar, and an indecent number of egg yolks. The custard is cooled, then chilled, before churning and when it's almost ready, thick in a Mr Whippy sloppy kind of way, the flavouring is added. This could be anything from caramel to fresh, frozen or sugar-poached fruit; it could even be lemon curd. This style of ice cream is rich and luscious with an almost chewy texture that stretches seductively over the tongue.

The other, so-called dairy ice cream is cornet ice cream and by comparison is a breeze to make. Using part milk or all yoghurt, it can be fine-tuned with different types of cream and by using distinctively flavoured sugar. Flavourings, too, for both types of ice cream are as infinite as your imagination, but *Lola's Ice Cream & Sundaes* by Morfudd Richards (Ebury Press, 2009) is a treasure trove of ideas.

Rhubarb and Clotted Cream Ice Cream

FILLS 2 X 500G TUBS

I've often thought that top quality store-bought fresh custard could be used as an ice cream base, and it works. Here it's flavoured with rhubarb cooked with fresh orange juice, with clotted cream for extra richness.

400g rhubarb	113g Rodda's Cornish clotted cream
2 juicing oranges	500g best quality fresh vanilla
60g dark unrefined muscovado sugar	custard

Slice the rhubarb thinly, into pieces approx 3mm thick. Place in a lidded sauté pan. Squeeze over the orange juice, sprinkle with the sugar and place over a low heat. Stir until the sugar dissolves, then shake the pan to spread the fruit evenly, cover and cook for 10 minutes. Scoop the fruit into a sieve over a bowl and return the juices to the pan. Tip into a shallow container and chill in the freezer. Simmer the juices until reduced to 4 tablespoons. Tip this dark syrup over the rhubarb and continue chilling.

Meanwhile, stir the clotted cream into the custard and tip into the bowl of the ice cream maker. Churn for 20 minutes, until soft-firm, then add the chilled rhubarb and continue churning for a further 15 minutes or so, until firm. Turn into containers (I used the rinsed-out custard pot and a yoghurt pot) and freeze for at least an hour, until thoroughly firm.

J Jelly Moulds

The sight of a trembling jelly never loses its childish charm, and making it with fresh, seasonal fruit and gelatine leaves, instead of adding boiling water to squares of packet jelly, is an addictive revelation. Moulds used to be made from copper, tin, china and glass, but these days a wide range of replica Victorian shapes are made in inexpensive plastic, and original moulds are highly collectable. Sam Bompas and Harry Parr are jelly artists. They make one-off moulds to order and a limited range of moulds – Buckingham Palace, Brighton Pavilion and St Paul's Cathedral – on sale at Selfridges just before the Royal wedding (they are school contemporaries of Prince William) sold out instantly, with a promise of more to come. Their book, *Jelly with Bompas & Parr* (Pavilion, 2010), is a must for jelly lovers. *Jellies and Their Moulds* by Peter Brears (Prospect Books, 2010) traces the history of this quintessentially English tradition and includes prints of fantastical jelly moulds through the ages, including castle and turret moulds designed by Alexis Soyer, the great Reform Club chef, before 1846.

Virtually any liquid can be made into a jelly and that includes alcohol, notably champagne, perry and cider, even gin and tonic with a lime twist. Blackberry juice and freshly squeezed orange juice, particularly blood orange juice, sweetened with sugar and sharpened with a squeeze of lemon or lime, make light, elegant jellies but any fresh fruit juice, or juice combination, including store-bought juice, can be used. The only exception is pineapple, which inhibits the gelatine setting. Suspending soft fruit like raspberries, strawberries, blueberries, even grapes and stoned cherries, in jelly looks stunning and tastes delicious but to avoid the fruit rising to the surface, the jelly must be made in layers, allowing each layer to set (two hours per layer) and suspend its fruit before adding the next.

The art of a good jelly is achieving a quivering wobble and the best results come from sheet gelatine. It is a curious ingredient, usually sold in 20g/12-leaf packets, and looks like a thin sheet of plastic etched with a diamond pattern. It has no flavour and produces a very clear jelly. You need 4 leaves (approximately 8g) for every 570ml of liquid. It is softened in a little cold water then added to sweetened hot, never boiling, liquid. Turning out the jelly is the tricky part and requires strong nerves.

Blackberry Jelly

SERVES 4

My mother and her mother before her were inveterate foragers and I cannot walk past a flourishing blackberry bush without picking as many berries as I can carry. I grow them at my allotment and it doesn't take long to pick enough plump ripe berries to make a lovely jelly that tastes of pure blackberry. Apart from the berries and leaf gelatine, the only ingredients are sugar, lemon juice and water. It sets a deep, blue-black, looking as stunning as it tastes. I made mine in a small jelly mould and managed to turn it out without mishap but it's easier to portion-control if poured into small moulds or glasses. For the latter approach, I'd recommend topping the jelly with a thick layer of cold custard or softly whipped cream. Sliding the spoon through jelly is an extremely pleasurable nostalgic experience and the flavour of blackberries is shockingly intense. The downside is that this kind of grown-up jelly takes several hours to set – overnight is best. Very good with Lemon and Honey Madeleines (see page 272).

4 sheets of leaf gelatine	100g caster sugar
150ml water	1 carton of fresh vanilla custard or
300g blackberries	300ml whipping cream
2 tbsp lemon juice	

Place the gelatine in a cereal bowl and moisten with a little of the given water, just enough to cover. Leave to soften. Place the blackberries, lemon juice and remaining water in a saucepan with the sugar. Gently heat, stirring continually, for a few minutes, until the sugar is completely dissolved and the fruit is very soft and has released its juices. Place a sieve over a clean pan and tip the contents of the pan into the sieve, pressing the juices out of the fruit with the back of a spoon. Scrape underneath so nothing is wasted. Place the pan of juice over a low heat, add the slippery soft gelatine and its water and stir as it dissolves. Pour into the jelly mould or cool slightly before pouring into glasses. Cool, then chill for about 4 hours or overnight until set.

If using a mould, half-fill a mixing bowl with boiling water and carefully immerse the mould without letting the water touch the jelly. Hold for a few seconds to melt a very thin layer so the jelly will slide easily out of the mould. Cover with a plate and quickly invert. Serve custard or cream softly whipped with vanilla essence separately. If serving the jelly in glasses, fill to the top with custard or cream.

K Kettle

My maternal grandmother lived next door to us in the house my mother grew up in. It was much bigger than our house, with many old-fashioned aspects including a gas cooker with ring burners and an eye-level grill that shot out long thin flames. I remember quite clearly the click of turning on the gas, the pop as she lit the burner, and the shrill, insistent whistle from the kettle when the water was boiling. We had a silent electric kettle that turned itself off when it had built up steam. It was only used for tea and filling hot water bottles, while Granny boiled her kettle all the time for all sorts of uses. I often begin my recipes with the instruction to put the kettle on. I do so because the kettle seems to boil faster than a pan of water (putting the lid on helps), but it's Édouard de Pomiane, who wrote *Cooking in Ten Minutes* over seventy years ago, who points out that almost every meal requires boiling water, so get that organized before you do anything else.

There are a lot of very nasty electric kettles on sale these days and it's interesting that both my sons, now with their own households, have chosen the updated version of the Morphy Richards stainless steel kettle I grew up with. I, on the other hand, have a very fast kettle designed for Siemens by Porsche. Not only is it super efficient and cordless, but I like its sleek lines and brushed steel finish and the fact that it doesn't take up much space. There are other good design details but I won't bang on about them. The important point is that it can boil 1.5 litres of water in 152 seconds.

State-of-the-art kettles, though, look more like Granny's with a tea-pot style spout. Instead of blackened aluminium, though, they come in bright, shiny metallic red or glossy stainless steel. The whistling Alessi Kettle with Bird, designed in 1985, and now a modern classic, has all the nostalgia with none of the drawbacks.

Spatchcock Quail with Pancetta and Spinach Gnocchi

SERVES 2–4

Gamey little quail tick lots of boxes for a midweek treat. Cutting out their backbone is a quick and easy job and makes cooking extremely fast. Laying the spatchcocked birds on a bed of thyme with a few slices of garlic and a splash of olive oil scents the flesh and fills the kitchen with a mouth-watering aroma. While the little birds roast, there is plenty of time for cooking potato gnocchi into a variation on potsticker dumplings. After a quick dip in boiling water, the gnocchi are fried with scraps of bacon, then stirred with a handful of young spinach leaves that wilt instantly in the heat. This dish is a lovely mixture of textures and flavours, delivering all the joys of a full-on roast dinner without the hassle. Quail are surprisingly meaty. I find one is enough, but big eaters generally need two depending on what else is on offer.

4 oven-ready quail
a flourishing bunch of fresh thyme
4 garlic cloves
3 tbsp olive oil
2 lemons

500g potato gnocchi
75g chopped pancetta or smoked
   streaky bacon
200g young spinach leaves

Boil the kettle. Heat the oven to 220°C/gas mark 7. Use scissors to cut out the quail spines. Open out the birds and flatten slightly with the heel of your hand, nipping the skin at either end so they lie flat. Arrange 4 piles of thyme in a roasting tin. Peel and thinly slice the garlic and spread it over the thyme. Smear the birds with olive oil and rest, skin side up, on top. Halve the lemons and rest, cut side down, between the birds. Roast in the oven for 15 minutes. Remove from the oven and rest for 5 minutes.

   Boil the kettle again. Drop the gnocchi into a pan of salted boiling water (from the kettle). As soon as they rise to the surface, scoop them into a colander. Heat the remaining olive oil in a spacious frying pan and add the pancetta. Cook for a few minutes, then add the gnocchi, increasing the heat so they get nicely golden. Add the spinach, quickly folding it through the gnocchi and giving it just enough time to wilt. Scoop on to 2 or 4 warmed plates and top with a quail (or two), adding any juices in the pan and a roasted lemon half to squeeze over the top.

K Knives

Oh, the joy of a new knife. Nothing beats the thrill of sliding its perfectly sharp blade through an onion as if it were butter. I love kitchen knives and have far too many because I am a moth to a candle when I see the knife display cabinet at the cook's shop.

My very first knife was a carbon-steel Sabatier. For years I used it for cutting everything, from onions to meat and fish, and my bad sharpening technique has honed it to a strange wavy shape. I use it occasionally and still lament the loss of two much smaller Sabatier paring knives. As my collection of knives grew, I bought a wooden knife box to keep them out of harm's way. I never really liked it and it's long since been replaced by two magnetic knife racks. Another knife I've owned for a very long time is possibly Victorian. It has a long, thin carbon steel blade stamped with 'A. Reynolds, Sheffield, England', and like all the best knives, the handle is riveted to the steel. I've no idea what its true function is but for years it was my carving knife. I can't remember the last time I used it and it rests on my second magnetized knife rack, along with various other Sabatier, Victorinox, Opinel, Global and out-of-favour paring and cook's knives.

Also on that rack are a couple of knives I love. One is a stumpy Parmesan knife that resembles a stunted, thick but blunt-bladed scabbard. It used to belong to Elizabeth David and is always a pleasure to use. In fact I make a point of using it to break off a chunk from my wedge of Parmesan. The other came with the gift of a whole Irish smoked salmon, one of the best presents I've ever received (thanks, Pete Kane). The blade is long and thin, with short indentations lined up on either side. It always comes out when I have salmon or gravlax to slice, and is perfect, too, for smoked or poached ham on the bone.

Number one knife magnet is closer to my main work surfaces and this is where I keep my favourite knives. My filleting knife and a large cook's knife are made by Henckels. These superb knives are made of a single piece of stainless steel and go through forty stages of production. I own one Japanese knife, a small cleaver given to me by David Eyre and Michael Belben as a thank you for a review that put them on the map way back in 1992, when the Eagle opened in Farringdon Road. It rests behind my other knives and is used on a whim rather than relentlessly like my Global Yoshikin GS7 pointed cook's knife.

The knife I use the most – in fact I have several – is a small inexpensive Victorinox paring knife with a sculpted, ergonomic black handle. I've owned many over the years and they've been either lost or purloined, or left behind somewhere, but never worn out. Once one snapped in half, the blade breaking clean just above the handle when I was crushing garlic, but when queried by my local cook's shop it was replaced with no questions.

There is a vast range of cook's knives on sale and they vary in quality and durability. My advice would be to invest in one or two top quality professional standard knives and a couple of inexpensive small ones. Look after them and they will last a lifetime. Carbon steel sharpens brilliantly but needs careful looking after to avoid rusting. Other steel knives, particularly Global, which need their own special sharpener, can be problematic. A good sharpener is vital. My skills with a knife-sharpening steel leave a lot to be desired. Sometimes I can get the rhythm and do it perfectly, other times I seem to blunt the knife. I am addicted to my Chantry knife sharpener, a gift from Simon Hopkinson. It replicates a sharpening steel with two crossed steels set on springs, is small and neat, sits on a work surface and works by slicing the knife through it. I use it every day but when I travel I take my silver surface-clamping Anysharp; better known as the World's Best Knife Sharpener (from Amazon). For good places to knife recce, and for block sets of knives that afford good value, see page 275.

Orange and Apple Crumble

SERVES 4–6

It requires a bit of patience to prepare the fruit for this crumble. Slicing the segments out of oranges can only be done with a small sharp knife, so don't bother otherwise. I used juicing oranges requiring deft work to remove the pips but the segments are just the right size to mingle with soft, fluffy cooking apple, giving a lovely surprise to most mouthfuls. The flavours, though, are purposely grown-up and depending on your sweetness threshold might require more sugar despite the sweetness of the crumble topping. As always with crumbles, the depth of crumble to ratio of fruit is a matter of taste. I chose a deep gratin-style dish, so ending up with approximately equal depth of fruit to topping, and it was just perfect to my taste. This crumble is lovely with custard but good too with cream or ice cream. When blood oranges are in season, use them for a pretty effect and distinctive flavour.

6 medium oranges

3 cooking apples, approx 750g

3 tbsp demerara sugar

125g cold butter, plus an extra knob

200g plain flour

75g caster sugar

crème fraîche, to serve

Heat the oven to 200°C/gas mark 6. Using a small sharp knife, slice the ends off the oranges and slice away the skin and pith. I find this easiest to do by sitting the orange on one end and slicing down in one curving sweep, continuing thus round the fruit. Carefully slice out the segments, slicing between the skin that covers them, directly into a mixing bowl. Squeeze the juice from what remains of the orange and skin through a sieve over the fruit. Peel and quarter the apples and cut into chunks. Add to the bowl as you go. Mix thoroughly, then spoon the fruit into a 2 litre capacity gratin-style or deeper pudding dish; the shape you choose will dictate the thickness of the crumble. Scatter the demerara sugar over the fruit and cut slivers of butter (the extra knob) over the top.

Sift the flour into a second mixing bowl. Add a pinch of salt and the caster sugar. Cut the 125g of butter into small pieces over the top. Quickly rub the butter into the dry ingredients, lifting and dropping it back as you rub, continuing until evenly crumbed. Spoon the crumble over the apples and oranges, letting it trickle down between the fruit.

Bake in the middle of the oven for 35–45 minutes, until the crumble is golden and fruit juices are bubbling round the edges and making little volcanic eruptions in the middle. Serve hot or cold, with a dollop of crème fraîche.

Thai Sweetcorn Soup with Chicken

SERVES 2–4

A sharp cook's knife held hard to the cob as you slice down in one fell swoop is the way to strip corn from its cob. The corn is perfect for chunky vegetable soups like this but useful too, blanched first then on-hold in the fridge, for all kinds of dishes. Sweetcorn loves roasted red pepper and chilli and here these flavours are enhanced with coconut milk, a handful of chopped coriander and sliced green beans. The soup smells appetizing and looks very pretty but is more satisfying with strips of chicken added at the end, which poach gently in the creamy soup. A big bowlful ticks all the boxes for a comforting, yet exciting, lazy midweek late summer supper. If you are big eaters, it suits being served over tagliatelle-style rice noodles.

1 medium onion	1 chicken stock cube
1 large garlic clove	100g green beans
1 tbsp vegetable oil	2 organic chicken thigh fillets
1 red pepper	165ml tin of coconut cream
1 red bird's-eye chilli	50g fresh coriander
2 corn on the cob	

Halve, trim, peel and finely chop the onion. Crack the garlic with your fist, flake away the skin and chop very finely. Heat the oil in a medium-sized, heavy-bottomed, wide-based, lidded pan – Le Creuset is perfect – and stir in the onion and garlic. Toss thoroughly, then adjust the heat to medium low and cook, stirring occasionally, for 5 minutes or so while you deseed the pepper, slice it into strips and then cut it into small dice. Stir the pepper into the onion and garlic. Trim the chilli, slice into skinny strips, discarding the seeds, and then cut into tiny scraps. Stir the chilli into the vegetables with ½ teaspoon of salt. Reduce the heat slightly, cover the pan and cook for 5–10 minutes, stirring a couple of times, until aromatic and juicy.

Stand the sweetcorn on its flat end and using a sharp cook's knife, slice off the corn in one long sweep. Collect the corn and discard the cob. Boil the kettle and measure off 500ml. Dissolve the stock cube in the boiling water and add to the pan. Return to the boil, add the corn and simmer steadily for 10 minutes while you trim the beans and cut them into 2cm lengths. Slice the chicken into small bite-size pieces. Add the coconut cream to the pan, return to a simmer and add the beans. Simmer for a couple of minutes, then add the chicken. Cook gently for a few minutes, until cooked through. Taste and adjust the seasoning. Chop the coriander and stir in just before serving.

Chili Con Carne y Limón

SERVES 6

I used to make chili con carne once a week when the boys were growing up, always with minced lamb. There was one occasion when I'd added far too much chilli as opposed to mild Mexican chilli powder, and it was so hot no one could eat it. It's a bit of a palaver to make chili properly with diced beef and pork instead of minced beef or lamb, but boy is it worth it. This version is subtly spiced rather than mouth-tinglingly hot and the surprising wow factor ingredient is chopped whole lemon. Serve it with rice, guacamole-style salsa, a bowl of sour cream and tortillas grilled with grated Cheddar.

500g belly pork
700g topside or other lean beef
1 large onion, approx 300g
4 garlic cloves
1 unwaxed lemon
2 tbsp olive oil
75g diced pancetta
3 tbsp Mexican chilli powder or
    mild/dulce pimentón powder

1 tsp ground cumin
1 tbsp flour
2 bay leaves
2 tsp dried oregano
2 tbsp tomato paste
450ml chicken or beef stock
300ml red wine
400g tin of black turtle beans

Run a sharp knife under the fatty pork skin to remove it. Slice the joint into 5mm thick rashers, then into 5mm strips, remove and discard the strip of fat between the layers of meat, then cut into 5mm cubes.

Remove any fat from the topside and dice the meat like the pork. Peel and finely chop the onion and garlic. Quarter the lemon, scrape away the seeds and cut into 1cm chunks.

Heat the oil in a spacious, heavy-bottomed pan, stir in the pancetta and cook until crisp. Stir in the onion and garlic and cook, stirring often, for 10–15 minutes, until slippery soft. Scoop the contents of the pan into a sieve and let it drain back into the pan. Brown the pork in the hot fat, then stir in the beef and brown that too. Add the chilli powder and cumin and, stirring constantly, cook over a low heat for 2 minutes, then add the flour and continue for a further couple of minutes. Add the bay leaves, ½ teaspoon of salt, the lemon, oregano, tomato paste, stock and red wine. Bring to a simmer over a gentle heat and cook uncovered, stirring occasionally to avoid sticking, for 2 hours, until the sauce is thick and the liquid has reduced. Add salt to taste. Cool, then chill, covered, overnight. Reheat with the rinsed and drained beans. Transfer to a large white bowl to serve.

Carpaccio of Pineapple with Mint

SERVES 4

This is a very simple idea that hardly requires a recipe. It is important to choose a pineapple that is very ripe so that it will be sweet and honeyed. Fresh mint complements the juicy fruit wonderfully well but a squeeze of lime points up the flavours. It looks beautiful in a shallow white bowl.

1 very ripe pineapple   1 lime, to serve
about 10 fresh mint leaves

Trim the pineapple and quarter lengthways. Remove the skin, taking care to remove all the hair, eyes and woody core. A thin-bladed filleting knife is best for this. Slice wafer-thin, in whatever shaped and sized pieces you fancy. Pile into a serving bowl, catching any juices. Tear the mint over the top, toss, cover with clingfilm and chill for at least 30 minutes. Serve with lime wedges, if liked, to squeeze over the top.

Leek and Prosciutto Macaroni with Green Beans in Shallot Vinaigrette

SERVES 2

Leeks love ham, particularly the intense flavour of cured ham. There is umami-like alchemy when leeks are cooked with prosciutto and eaten with Parmesan, and you don't need much of any of them. For this quick and easy pasta supper, the leeks are sliced in thick pennies and softened in butter and fat rendered from the ham. They end up impossibly juicy and leeky and the ham will be darker and more like bacon. When this mix is stirred into buttery macaroni with lashings of freshly grated, good quality Parmesan, it is heaven indeed. Quantities are easy to scale up or down, everything is easy to shop for, quick to prepare and the cooking is faster than heating up a ready meal. What's not to like? Don't you just hate that expression?

150g macaroni
5 slices prosciutto or Serrano ham
2 leeks, approx 200g
40g butter
50g lump of Parmesan

For the salad:
350g green beans
a generous pinch of caster sugar
½ tbsp wine vinegar
1 tsp Grey Poupon or Maille Dijon
　　mustard
2–3 tbsp vegetable oil
1 shallot

Cook the macaroni in plenty of salted water according to packet instructions. It is likely to take about 12 minutes, which is more or less the time needed to cook the ham and leeks. Tear or slice the ham across the width into chunky strips. Trim and slice the leeks in thick pennies approximately 1cm wide. Soak in a bowl of cold water to clean, drain and shake dry.

　　Melt 25g of butter in a lidded frying pan or pan that can hold the leeks in a single layer. When it begins to make tiny bubbles, scatter the strips of ham into the butter and leave to shrink, shrivel and darken, turning after a couple of minutes. Add the drained leeks. Stir, season lightly with salt and generously with freshly grated black pepper, cover and cook gently, stirring a few times, for 6–8 minutes, until just al dente, browning on some edges.

When the macaroni is tender, drain and add the remaining butter and half the Parmesan, grated finely. Stir thoroughly, then add the contents of the leek pan. Stir and serve with more grated Parmesan and the bean salad.

To make the salad, boil the kettle or put a large pan of water on to boil. Top and tail the beans. I usually cut them in half to make eating easier. Fill a clean sink with cold water. Boil the beans in 2 or 3 batches for 2 minutes so they stay on the nutty side of crunchy. Scoop into the cold water to chill and arrest cooking. Drain thoroughly.

Dissolve the sugar and a generous pinch of salt in the wine vinegar in a serving bowl. Stir in the mustard and gradually whisk in the oil, continuing until thick and creamy. Peel and finely chop the shallot. Stir into the vinaigrette. When ready to serve, fold the drained beans through the vinaigrette.

Beetroot Gravlax for a Party

SERVES 12–16

This ingenious Scandinavian way of curing salmon with salt, sugar, a little alcohol and humungous amounts of fresh dill is easy to make and impressive to serve. Gravadlax, to spell out its whole name, is actually made up of two words which translate as 'buried salmon': gravad or grave, meaning buried, and lax for salmon. Back in the mists of time, when salmon was ubiquitous in Scandinavian waters, the fish were buried with salt to preserve them and the hidey-hole marked and covered with rocks to keep out the wolves.

It remains an imprecise cure but the pickling mix is approximately one part sea salt to one and half parts white sugar with a little alcohol to bind it. What starts out as a pickling paste melts into syrupy brine and this is what gives the fish its unique flavour. Aficionados adjust their cure according to the fattiness of the salmon and keep additional seasonings a closely guarded secret. Patrick Gwynne-Jones, arguably the first British restaurateur to put gravlax on his menu at Pomegranates way back in 1974, adds a handful of crushed cloves, and saves a smidgen of cure juices to add to the sweet, mayonnaise-style mustard and dill sauce that traditionally goes with gravlax. He is also insistent on white peppercorns rather than black for their pungent flavour. Either will do, but they must be freshly and roughly crushed. Others swear by dried dill instead of fresh, reckoning it gives a better flavour, but the most common deviation is using vodka or cognac instead of aquavit. A Scottish friend uses a really peaty malt whisky.

It takes at least 24 hours to cure the fish and once cured, it has to be rinsed, dried and re-seasoned with fresh dill. The weighting, incidentally, compresses the fish, making it firmer, less flabby and easier to slice. For best results, you will need a very sharp, thin-bladed knife. Gravlax will keep, covered, in the fridge for up to a week. Like smoked salmon, it freezes perfectly but the individual fillets should be snuggly wrapped in clingfilm and then slipped into a sealed plastic bag.

The fish is sliced slightly thicker than smoked salmon and always on the slant so that each slice has a fringe of dill; the depth of angle is a matter of taste and carving skill. The texture is very similar to smoked salmon and this style of preserved salmon is just as versatile. At Baltic, in Southwark, they serve it prettily arranged with a zig-zag of mustard sauce, crisp little potato latkes and a dollop of chrain, the beetroot and horseradish relish. This combination works with blinis (see page 18) or thinly sliced, toasted dark rye bread, but gravlax goes with green salad leaves, particularly rocket and watercress, roast beetroot, avocado, mango or papaya and lime, tzatziki-style cucumber salads and pickled cucumber with plenty of dill.

Gravlax is perfect party food and the beetroot cure, which stains the top of the fish a pretty purple, giving the slices a magenta-coloured frill, has serious wow factor. The recipe can be adapted for a fillet of any size, just be generous with the dill.

For super-easy gravlax without beetroot for 6-8 people, blitz 75g of caster sugar with 75g of sea salt, 2 tablespoons of vodka, 1 teaspoon of ground white pepper and 100g of dill. Spread half the sloppy paste in a dish/plastic box that snugly fits 500g of skinned salmon fillet. Smear the rest on top, cover and chill, turning a couple of times, for 48 hours. Rinse, pat dry, cover both sides with 100g of chopped dill and chill until required. Slice thinly at an angle. For a quickie sauce to go with it, mix together 3 tablespoons of smooth Grey Poupon or Maille Dijon mustard with 2 teaspoons of caster sugar, a squeeze of lemon juice and 3 tablespoons of sunflower oil. Beat in 1 tablespoon of freshly chopped dill, and salt and pepper to taste.

approx 2.25kg Irish or Scottish
   Freedom Food organic farmed
   salmon, filleted and pin-boned
1 raw beetroot
1 lemon
1 tbsp coriander seeds
1 tsp fennel seeds
1 tbsp white or black peppercorns
6 tbsp coarse sea salt
8 tbsp white sugar
4 tbsp aquavit or vodka

200g fresh dill
For the mustard and dill sauce:
1 large egg yolk
2 tbsp Grey Poupon or Maille Dijon
   mustard
1 tbsp runny honey or sugar
150ml groundnut or sunflower oil
2 tbsp white wine vinegar
2 tbsp finely chopped dill
you will also need clingfilm, tinfoil
   and fish tweezers

Lay the fillets, skin side down, on a work surface. Run your index finger up and down the fillet to locate any stray bones and remove with fish tweezers. Trim the sides to neaten up the edges. Lay one fillet, skin side down, on a large sheet of clingfilm placed over a large sheet of foil, large enough to securely wrap the whole fish. Peel and grate the beetroot. Grate the lemon zest. Roughly grind the coriander and fennel seeds and the peppercorns using a pestle and mortar. Mix with the salt, sugar and alcohol to make a gravely paste. Finely chop half the bunch of dill and mix into the paste with the beetroot and lemon zest.

Spread the paste over one fillet of fish, pressing it firmly. Place the second fillet on top, flesh side down, to sandwich the paste. Fold over the clingfilm to snugly encase and then repeat with the foil. Place in a dish or oven tray that holds it snugly and won't spill the juices. Cover with a board and weigh down with weights. Refrigerate for 48 hours, turning a couple of times.

Rinse the fillets under cold water, wiping away the cure and any stray scales. Pat dry with kitchen paper. Finely chop the remaining dill and spread it over both fillets, pressing firmly. Re-sandwich, rewrap as before with new clingfilm and foil, return to the clean container, add board and weights and leave for a minimum of a couple of hours to press the dill into the fish. Keep in the fridge in the foil parcel for up to a week.

To serve, slice thinly on the slant, ensuring that each slice has a dill frill. Lay out on individual plates or a serving platter with a minimal zig-zag of mustard and dill sauce. To make the sauce, place the egg yolk in a mixing bowl and beat in the mustard and the honey or sugar until smooth. Add the oil in a dribble, whisking all the time, alternating with a little vinegar until thick, glossy and smooth. Stir in the dill.

L Lemon Reamer

I have often thought I would like to write a book about lemons, and if I did I'd call it *I'll Be with You in the Squeezing of a Lemon,* the Oliver Goldsmith quote Elizabeth David used for her essay with recipes in *An Omelette and a Glass of Wine.* 'I'll be with you . . .' I say to myself as I squeeze lemon juice over lamb kebabs or grilled fish, into lentil soups and over artichokes or cooking apples to stop them turning brown, while silently running through Mrs David's litany of foods that benefit from a squeeze of lemon. One of the best juicers, she writes, is lump sugar, both for rasping the zest and extracting the juice.

My tool of choice is a traditional wooden lemon reamer. I ram and twist it into lemon halves, collecting the juice through a sieve over a bowl, leaving pith and pips behind. I love its economy of design, a tapered, deeply ridged solid wood dome that acts as a blade, its pointed tip neatly lined up with the centre of the fruit. Its stumpy rounded handle screws into the dome and feels comfortable in the hand. It occasionally needs a friendly twist when it gets loose. I have owned mine for as long as I can remember and the wood is bleached pale and cracked in places. I've seen modern versions with coloured handles, or made entirely of plastic or metal the most dramatic is

Philippe Starck's totally impractical Juicy Salif. It was meant, he says, to start conversations, not squeeze lemons. The whole point of a citrus juicer is to extract maximum juice without pulp, pips and pith, and there are many different designs. I have never been tempted to change. The reamer is small, easy to clean, does the job efficiently and is ageing beautifully.

Here's a little tip for getting maximum juice from a lemon. Warm it first, in the oven, then halve and juice. You will be amazed. And if a recipe calls for zest and juice, zest first and then squeeze.

I leave you with this tip, picked up from *Fruit Recipes* by Riley M. Fletcher-Berry, published in 1907 and which I inherited from Elizabeth David's library.

Baked Lemon for Colds

Bake a lemon whole till thoroughly tender and eat it hot with sugar just before retiring. It is best to do without the evening meal and to fast otherwise as far as possible. Also drink much water. This should be taken three nights in succession.

Home-made Lemonade

MAKES APPROX 750ML

Really delicious and a lovely gift.

8 large unwaxed lemons, preferably Amalfi	250g white sugar
	250ml water

Pare the zest (no white) from the lemons using a potato peeler or zester. Place in a saucepan with the sugar and water. Bring slowly to just below boiling, stirring occasionally until the sugar melts. Simmer gently, covered, for 10 minutes. Cover and leave to go cold.

Place a sieve over the pan, halve the lemons and squeeze the juice through the sieve into the cold liquid. Decant into a bottle or bottles and keep in the fridge for a couple of weeks. Alternatively, freeze in an ice cube tray and make up from frozen. Pour over ice and dilute with soda water, adding sprigs of mint, thin slices of cucumber or fresh lemon or lime, if liked.

Lemon Tart

SERVES 6–8

Every now and again a restaurant dish spreads like wildfire to menus up and down the country, eventually ending up on the supermarket shelf. In the early eighties, at the height of foodieism, when the Roux brothers, Albert and Michel senior, reigned supreme at Le Gavroche and the Waterside Inn, one such dish was their tarte au citron. *This was lemon tart like no other. It was shockingly good, made in a deep tart tin, served at room temperature with a dusting of icing sugar, and the perfect balance of tangy, intensely lemony lemon and sugary cream with a silky, smooth texture that trembled on the tongue. It was a dish to linger over, the pale yellow cream set to just within a wobble of collapse yet firm and beautifully complemented by a thin sweet pastry case.*

It travelled initially with Roux-trained chefs, later available to everyone when a recipe was included in New Classic Cuisine, *published in 1983. Needless to say, some nasty versions were passed off as the real McCoy, and restaurant critics, as I was at the time, pontificated about the best. One of the finest was served at Harvey's, Marco Pierre White's first restaurant, opened in 1987. His recipe, published in 1994 in* Wild Food from Land and Sea, *was virtually interchangeable with the Roux, learnt no doubt during his stint at Le Gavroche. Marco recommends eating the tart when it has cooled to room temperature, while his mentors recommend making it one or two days in advance of eating to allow the flavours to develop.*

Rowley Leigh, one of my favourite chefs cooking today (at Le Café Anglais, Whiteleys, Bayswater), also learnt to make the tart from Albert and he serves it chilled. The really important point, though, is that the middle of the tart remains on the wobbly side of runny when it is taken out of the oven and the tart needs to sit for at least an hour to set, preferably much longer, before slicing. It doesn't really need an accompaniment, although in his days at The Restaurant at the Hyde Park Hotel, Marco served it as part of an assiette citron *with a frozen parfait ice cream and small lemon soufflé. No wonder this short-lived restaurant instantly earned him two Michelin stars.*

For the sweet pastry:
225g plain flour, plus a little extra
a pinch of salt
150g butter, plus an extra knob
75g icing sugar
1 whole egg
1 egg yolk

For the filling:
5 large eggs
4–5 large unwaxed lemons
150g caster sugar
200ml double cream
crème fraîche, to serve
You will need a 22 x 2.5cm deep flan
ring/tin with removable base

To make the pastry, sift the flour into a mixing bowl with the salt. Cut the butter into chunks directly into the bowl and rub it into the flour until it resembles fine breadcrumbs. Sift the icing sugar over the crumbs. Stir. Lightly whisk the whole egg and egg yolk and add to the crumbs. Quickly work everything together and knead a few times. Dust with a little flour if it seems very sticky. Form into a ball, wrap in clingfilm and chill for 1 hour.

Heat the oven to 180°C/gas mark 4. Rub the knob of butter over the inside of the flan ring. Dust with flour, shake out the excess and place on a baking sheet. Dust a work surface with flour and roll out the pastry to make a 28cm circle. If necessary, use a palette knife to ease the pastry off the surface, then roll up on the rolling pin and carefully place over the prepared flan ring, pressing and tucking to neatly line the ring, leaving a 1cm overhang. Drape a sheet of greaseproof paper over the ring and fill with baking beans. Bake for 20 minutes.

Separate one of the eggs required for the filling and lightly whisk the egg white with 1 tablespoon of water. Immediately paint the cooked pastry case with beaten egg white to seal, having plugged any holes with leftover pastry first. Return to the oven, uncovered, for 5 minutes. Lower the oven to 150°C/gas mark 2.

To make the filling, finely zest the lemons to end up with 1 tablespoon of zest. Juice the lemons through a sieve to catch pips and pith. You want to end up with approximately 175ml. Stir in the zest. Whisk the 4 remaining eggs and the reserved egg yolk with the caster sugar, continuing until the sugar disappears. Lightly whip the cream and stir it into the eggs. Add the lemon juice and zest.

Pour the filling into the pastry case and bake for 45–60 minutes, until the tart is just set but still very slightly wobbly in the middle. If the top shows signs of browning, lay a sheet of foil over the top to protect it. Remove from the oven and leave the tart to cool and firm up. Just before you remove the ring, use a serrated knife to carefully shave the pastry overhang. Before serving, dust the tart with icing sugar. If you like, place under a grill or use a cook's blowtorch to caramelize the sugar, repeating a second time for an even crisper finish. Serve with crème fraîche, or not.

Lime-pickled Prawns with Fennel

SERVES 6

And yes, the reamer works with limes too. This quick and easy recipe could be made with raw prawns – ceviche style – but the joy of using cooked is that they are added at the last minute. It makes a great super-quick dinner party starter but is also a clean, vibrantly flavoured light snack to enjoy in the garden on a hot summer day.

2 limes
1 tbsp red wine vinegar
1 tsp fennel seeds
1 tsp crushed dried chilli
3 tbsp olive oil

2 medium-sized red onions, approx
  100g each
60g bunch coriander
400g shelled, cooked prawns,
  preferably North Atlantic
crusty bread, to serve

Halve the limes and squeeze 3 tablespoons of juice into a bowl. Add the vinegar, fennel seeds, chilli, ½ teaspoon of salt and several grinds of pepper. Whisk in the olive oil. Peel and halve the onions and slice wafer-thin. Stir the onions into the dressing and leave, stirring occasionally, for about 30 minutes, until limp and pale yet still crunchy.

Finely chop the coriander. Pat the prawns dry with kitchen paper. Stir the prawns and coriander into the onions and transfer to a serving dish or platter. Serve with crusty bread and butter. If serving as a snack or light meal, pile the prawns over lightly cooked green beans or curls of crisp lettuce.

L Loaf Tin

Over the years I've had phases of keen breadmaking, so keen that I have built up quite a collection of different shaped and sized loaf tins. My favourites, and I have two, are the bog-standard, heavy-duty tins, the sort professional bakers use, that start out silver and end up blackened and scorched, eventually building up a patina that will make them non-stick. If you take a close look at one, you'll see that it is a cunningly clever design made from one sheet of tinned steel, the corners reinforced by their own pleats, and the edges rolled for strength and stability. The base is a ridged double layer to help prevent scorching, also making it easier to extract the loaf. Another identically shaped tin, also solidly made of blackened steel but thinner and lighter with a non-stick coating and red external finish, is a useful tin for beginners.

When my son Henry was twelve, he spent a morning at the Cordon Bleu School with Claire Clark (now with an MBE and regarded as the UK's finest female pâtissière), who was then their pastry chef. All my side of the family is double-jointed in our hands. Henry is double-jointed in all his digits, so much so that we used to tease him about his Ninja fingers, after the dextrous Ninja Turtles in his favourite cartoon. His 'Ninjas', it turned out, make him a natural breadmaker, the perfect kneader, said Claire, who was astounded at his skilled technique. It was wonderful to discover one Sunday morning that Hen had taken himself off to Sainsbury and persuaded the bakers to let him have some fresh yeast; they must have been very surprised that a young lad wanted to make bread. This baking phase eventually petered out but he taught several friends and made weekend rolls many times for breakfast.

When my mother died I inherited all her bakeware and I've kept the large two-pound tin she used for her fruit loaves. Its non-stick surface is scorched and peeling, particularly on the dimpled base, so it has to be lined with baking parchment. I never trust non-stick anyway, and always either oil and flour the inside or line the tin with baking parchment. It's possible to buy loaf tin liners, and they save a lot of fiddling about.

Since a branch of Gail's Bakery opened on my doorstep, I've given up making sourdough bread because I can't compete with their San Francisco loaf. If I want home-made brown bread, I make the super-simple Doris Grant loaf (recipe below) and I return time and time again to the No-fuss White Loaf on page 48. For more bread recipes, check out any book by Dan Lepard. He is the man.

Very Easy Brown Loaf/Doris Grant Loaf

MAKES 1 LOAF

My friend Roger de Freitas introduced me to the Doris Grant loaf, a much-loved recipe first published in Your Daily Bread *in 1944. At the time he was knocking up twenty-odd loaves a week, getting through big sacks of stone-ground flour and slabs of baker's yeast, and selling the loaves for £1 a pop to make money for the school PTA.*

It's a miraculous recipe, producing a densely crumbed proper brown loaf with a challenging crust. A slice of this with marmalade will set you up for the day, but it is particularly recommended with Cheddar and pickles, or to make a fortifying lunchtime ham sandwich. My contribution of adding a little plain white bread flour to the wholemeal lightens the texture.

1 tbsp sunflower oil	450g stone-ground plain wholemeal
1 tsp black treacle, molasses or	flour
golden syrup	50g strong white bread flour
425ml tepid water	1 tsp salt
2 x 7g sachets of dried yeast	You will need a 13 x 20cm loaf tin

Heat the oven to 230°C/gas mark 8. Lavishly smear the loaf tin with sunflower oil. Dissolve the treacle in 150ml of the given water in a small bowl or jug, then stir in the yeast. Leave somewhere warm for a few minutes until frothy and creamy, and smelling yeasty.

Mix the flours and salt in a large mixing bowl. Make a well in the centre, add both lots of water and stir quickly to make a loose dough; it will be too wet to knead. Scrape into the prepared loaf tin. Place somewhere warm, cover with a tea towel and leave for 15–30 minutes, depending on the temperature of the kitchen, until the dough has risen almost to the top of the tin. Bake in the preheated oven for 50–60 minutes, until dark brown and risen to the top of the tin. Tip the loaf out of the tin, tap the base and if it sounds hollow it is done. If not, return to the oven for a few more minutes. Cool on a wire rack before slicing.

Citrus Lokshen Pudding with Crème Fraîche

SERVES 6

Look out for golden sultanas for this variation on an old-fashioned Jewish pudding made with vermicelli. I make it in an elongated 900g, 21 × 10cm silicone loaf mould, but any large loaf tin or a pudding basin would do. I serve it cold, sliced, terrine-style, with crème fraîche but a soft fruit purée or stewed plums are lovely with it too. Greengages are particularly good with the sweet, soft pudding and you will need 500g. Just halve them round their middles, twist out the stones and simmer in a vanilla syrup made with 300ml of water, 2 tablespoons of caster sugar and half a vanilla pod. The plums, laid out in the syrup cut side up, need only a minute or so of direct heat, then leave to finish softening in the hot juices. Serve them cold too.

200g vermicelli
25g butter, plus an extra knob
50g caster sugar
1 juicing orange
1 unwaxed lemon

100g golden sultanas
2 eggs
300ml sour cream
150g cream cheese

Cook the vermicelli in plenty of boiling water, swirling it around to loosen the strands, for 5–10 minutes, until tender. Drain and return to the pan with 25g of butter and the sugar. Stir to melt the sugar and anoint the strands. Zest the orange and lemon and chop the zest finely. Place the sultanas and zest in a small pan and squeeze over the orange and lemon juice. Simmer for about 5 minutes, until the sultanas have absorbed most of the liquid and are plump and juicy.

Whisk the eggs in a mixing bowl. Add the sour cream and cream cheese and whisk until smooth. If using a silicone loaf tin, pour in the mixture. If using a regular 900g loaf tin, butter it first and then line it with baking parchment (buttering makes the parchment stick). Smear with extra butter and then add the pudding mixture. Cut a piece of baking parchment to cover the pudding, smear with butter and loosely cover with the buttered paper. Bake for 45 minutes at 180°C/gas mark 4 until set and firm to a flat hand. Turn out of the loaf tin when cool and serve in thick slices with crème fraîche.

M Mandoline

My mandoline is an old-fashioned Swiss one, worn and weathered after many years of use. Its wooden frame is split and slightly warped but it still works efficiently. It has two blades, one straight, the other corrugated, and both extremely sharp. The angle or depth of slice is adjusted and held firmly with wing nuts on the sides. It has no stand but is held at an angle, keeping it steady with one hand and slicing rhythmically with the other. If I'm slicing potatoes, I do them in the sink, rinsing the blade every now and again with running water. This has its drawback because I don't always want to wash away the copious amounts of starch they produce. This mandoline doesn't have a protective clamp to skewer whatever I'm slicing, so I tend to stop in plenty of time to avoid accidents. After use, it's rinsed and patted dry but I always prop it against the window ledge so the wood dries out before it's bundled away next to my chopping boards. Storing a mandoline requires thought, because if you run a finger across the blade by accident it can be disastrous. Newer models are made entirely of stainless steel and come with stands and covers to clamp over the blades when not in use.

The advantage of a mandoline over a food processor attachment is the control of width of slices. It is particularly good for making potato and other root vegetable crisps. It is also easier to wash up.

Cod, Anchovy and Spinach Boulangère

SERVES 1

Imagine, if you will, a thick fillet of cod topped with succulent silky spinach and salty anchovy, everything hidden under a few layers of thinly sliced potatoes, so thin they cook very quickly. As the sandwich roasts, the anchovies melt against the potato while the top layer turns into a crisp golden crust, the spinach remaining soft and juicy against the firm, yet moist fish.

This impressive dish is just as easy to make for one as it is for two or four, only slightly more demanding to make it for a dinner party. Salting the fish first firms up the flesh and helps stop it producing lots of liquid as it cooks,

but if you are cooking it for four or more, you may need to drain the pan a couple of times. The juices will cause steam and prevent the potatoes crisping.

When making for more than one, scale up all the ingredients in proportion and increase the oven temperature to 230°C/gas mark 8.

1 thick fillet of cod or Cornish pollack	2 anchovy fillets in olive oil
Maldon sea salt	1 potato, approx 100g
50g young leaf spinach	olive oil
	lemon wedge

Place the skinned fish on a plate and dust both sides with salt. Cover with clingfilm and chill for at least 30 minutes – an hour is better. Heat the oven to 220°C/gas mark 7. Boil the kettle. Place the spinach in a bowl and cover with boiling water. Leave for 10 seconds, then drain in a colander and splash with cold water to cool. Drain against the colander. Peel the potato. Use a mandoline or food processor attachment to slice the potato as if making crisps. Do not rinse.

Rinse the fish and pat dry. Line a small roasting tin with foil – shiny side up. Add a splash of olive oil to the middle of the foil and swipe the fish through it on both sides. Place skinned side down on the foil. Squeeze the spinach dry and spread over the fish. Tear the anchovies into a few pieces and place on top. Quickly cover with potatoes, two or three layers deep; the starch will make them stick together. Season lightly with salt and smear with olive oil. Roast for 25 minutes, until the top layer of potato is crusty and the rest is tender to the point of a knife. Serve with a lemon wedge.

Spanish Omelette with Salmorejo Sauce

SERVES 4–8

On the last day of a brief visit to San Sebastián one summer, my friend Tessa and I ducked into a tiny café on the Avenida de la Libertad for a mid-morning coffee. As I sipped my cappuccino and the clock struck noon, out came the tapas. Exquisite sugar-dusted pastries were moved aside for a bowl of silky-grey boquerones *and thickly sliced ham poking out of flat round bread rolls. Huge prawns radiated around a scoop of glossy, wobbly* mayonnaise and saucers were filled with glistening black olives. Last to arrive was the most perfect tortilla patata I've ever seen. Freshly cut wedges were balanced over a diagonal slice of crusty, just-baked baguette, the omelette reassembled like the spokes of a wheel.

It wasn't long after breakfast for me but the sight of such perfection, laid with pride on the bar by the owner, was irresistible. That plump warm omelette packed with firm, creamy potatoes and slippery scraps of onion is now my benchmark for a dish I've been cooking regularly since I wrote my first cookbook, In Praise of the Potato, twenty-odd years ago.

Like housewives all over Spain I usually make Spanish omelette when there are leftover boiled potatoes in need of using up. I dice the potato into dolly-mixture size pieces and mix them with onion softened to melting point in olive oil. I often cheat with Eazy fried onions in a can, the Spanish convenience version of onion confit, available here at selected Sainsbury, Tesco, Morrisons and Asda.

If the tortilla is for a meal rather than a snack with drinks, I ring the changes by adding sliced chorizo with the onion, but the traditional way of making tortilla is simmering thinly sliced potatoes and onions in olive oil. This makes a far richer omelette but if the potatoes are properly drained doesn't, as you'd expect, end up overly oily. Whether you cheat or follow my traditional recipe, it is hard to go wrong with Spanish omelette if you use decent eggs and the right potatoes.

Spanish potatoes are creamy and waxy, so choose one of our salad varieties; larger Jersey Royals or Cornish earlies would be my choice. If cooking potatoes specially, simmered either in olive oil or water, they need to be rinsed thoroughly before cooking. This gets rid of the excess starch that makes the slices stick together.

Salt brings out the flavour of potatoes and eggs, so season generously. The other important point is choosing a frying pan that is reliably non-stick. When it comes to the tricky bit of turning the omelette, a flat pan lid slightly larger than the frying pan is easier to manoeuvre than a plate.

For a lighter omelette, cook the sliced potatoes in water and soften the onion in 4 tablespoons of olive oil. Drain the onion before mixing with the potatoes.

1 medium-large onion, approx 200g
500ml Spanish extra virgin olive oil
4 medium-large waxy potatoes,
  approx 500g
6 organic free-range eggs

For the salmorejo sauce:
25g crustless stale white bread
1 garlic clove
1 shallot
10 cherry tomatoes
½ pointed red pepper
1 tbsp sherry or red wine vinegar
3 tbsp Spanish or other fruity olive oil

Trim, halve and peel the onion and slice wafer-thin. Heat the oil in a non-stick frying pan over a medium heat for 5 minutes. Add the onion. Cook for 5 minutes – you'll see little bubbles – to partially cook. Meanwhile, peel the potatoes and slice on a mandoline as if making thick crisps. Agitate under water, drain in a colander and pat dry. Season with salt and toss to distribute. Submerge the potatoes in the oil. Simmer steadily for 10–15 minutes, until the potatoes are tender but hardly coloured. Remove from the heat and scoop the contents of the pan into a sieve resting over a bowl. Drain the oil from the frying pan (it can be reused repeatedly).

Whisk the eggs in a mixing bowl. Season with salt and pepper. Add the potatoes and onions. Stir thoroughly. Heat a little oil in the frying pan, swirling it round the pan. Add the egg mixture, shaking the pan to settle. Cook over a medium-low heat so the egg quickly turns pale and sets at the edges. Continue cooking, adjusting the heat as necessary, until the omelette looks three-quarters set. Gently shake the pan to ensure it isn't sticking anywhere, cover with a lid slightly larger than the pan and quickly invert. Slide the omelette back into the pan and cook for a few minutes to set what was the top. Take care not to overcook. Slip the omelette on to a plate. Eat immediately, sliced in wedges like a cake.

To make the sauce, tear the bread into the bowl of a blender. Add the peeled, coarsely chopped garlic and shallot, halved tomatoes, chopped pepper, a generous pinch of salt, vinegar and olive oil. Blitz smooth and creamy. The omelette is also good with any tomato sauce.

M Meat Mincer/Grinder

I have clear memories of my mum clamping the mincer, or meat grinder as they are now often called, on to the table ready to mince leftover roast lamb for shepherd's pie. The process seemed to happen quite often, so she must have used it for other things too. As a child I loved cranking the handle and watching the worms, as I pretended they were, curling out of the circle of holes. She wasn't a particularly well-ordered person, my mum, but she did keep all the parts of the mincer in a box and a picture of the order of assembly. I copy her because it's quite a palaver and won't work if it isn't put together properly.

I don't know what happened to Mum's mincer but I bought one specially so I could mince the meat myself for raised pork pies for *The Prawn Cocktail Years*. Mincers have fallen out of fashion now that all our chopping and mincing needs are met by food processors. But if you want to make burgers from scratch, mixing different meats, or wish to control exactly what goes into your minced meat dishes, you need a stand-alone mincer or attachment for your food processor.

If you are buying meat from a butcher or the meat counter of a large supermarket, they consider it part of the service to mince the meat for you. Terrines and sausages, not to mention pork pies, will have a better texture if they are passed through a mincer. Mincers are not expensive, and are extremely satisfying to use.

Meat mincers tend to be made of cast iron or a mixture of stove enamel and plastic – as mine is – with steel cutters and tinned steel discs. All these parts have to be meticulously dried after washing, then lightly oiled, or they will eventually rust and spoil the food. Mine came with a rubber plate that goes between the clamping surface and grinder but my mum had a special piece of wood for the job.

Mincers can deal with fresh and cooked meat, fish or vegetables. They work by dropping the food into a hopper that falls on to a large central screw that runs from the handle to the blades. It's cranked by hand and as the screw winds the food towards the blades or cutting disc, out comes the mince. Mum used to test run and clean the grinder with bread at the beginning and end of the session. I do the same.

Raised Pork Pies

MAKES 1 X 500G PIE AND 4 X 300G PIES

There is something about the combination of textures and flavours of a good pork pie that is hard to beat. The crisp and crumbly yet chewy pastry, with its damp inner lining imbued with meat juices and little pockets of dark, intensely meaty jelly wrapped around a well-seasoned, terrine-like porky filling, is particularly good when daubed with a smear of bright yellow English mustard. For me, pork pie is picnic food, or the centrepiece of a leisurely lunch in the garden on one of those perfect summer days when a gentle breeze stirs the blossom and cools the brow as the sun beats down, ripening growing strawberries in front of your very eyes.

Melton Mowbray is the home of the raised pork pie. It started over 200 years ago as a by-product of Stilton, when the dairy pigs flourishing on the unwanted whey led to an excess of pork. The grocer and the butcher got together and came up with a pie of uncured pork in a pastry coffin made from rendered lard, flour and boiling water. It proved popular with labourers out in the field, and later in the season, when they swapped labouring for grooming at the many local hunts, the pies caught on with the hunting set.

The pastry, now known as hot water paste, ends up like warm plasticine and is surprisingly easy to mould or 'raise'. Traditionally, butchers formed their pies around a wooden pie mould called a dolly, worn smooth with use. I've tried using a jam jar instead of a dolly but had far greater success, more fun and wonderful results from moulding or raising small pies with my hands. The final shaping is done around the filling and the pastry is then nipped and tucked to make a narrow aperture before the lid is pressed into position. I always tie a double thickness of baking parchment around the pie to give extra support and protect the lid from cooking too fast. I have also experimented with a tall pork pie tin with a removable base. The result was a huge success too but the straight sides of the pie looked wrong. Another route – shock horreur – is to roll the pastry and make a large pie in a prettily decorated, lozenge-shaped, hinged pie mould. In Melton Mowbray that would never do. Their pies are traditionally raised by hand and cooked without support, giving them a distinctive bow-shape. The gap between pastry and meat is generously filled with melted jellied stock, contributing the final part of the trinity that sets a good pie apart from an ordinary one.

For the jellied stock:
bones from the meat used to make
the filling or 1 chicken carcass
1 pig's trotter
1 large carrot
1 unpeeled onion, quartered and
stuck with 3 cloves
herb bundle: fresh thyme, sage,
rosemary and a bay leaf
6 peppercorns
2 litres water

For the pork pie filling:
250g rindless smoked back bacon
800g boned shoulder of pork or
spare ribs, with approx ¼ fat to
¾ lean meat
1 tbsp anchovy sauce/paste
1 tbsp finely chopped sage
½ tsp each ground cinnamon,
nutmeg and allspice
For the hot-water crust:
500g plain flour
½ tsp salt
250ml water
175g lard
1 egg
You will also need baking parchment

Begin this recipe 48 hours before you plan to eat the pies. Start with the stock. Put all the ingredients into a pan and simmer steadily for 3–4 hours. Strain the stock into a clean pan, cool, then chill overnight and remove the thick layer of white fat.

Simmer the stock until you have about 600ml. Cool, then refrigerate until required. This liquid will set to a firm jelly, and is much better than the stock plus gelatine recommended in some pie recipes.

To make the pie filling, finely dice 4 bacon rashers and some of the best bits of pork; you will always get a better texture if some meat is finely chopped rather than minced. Mince the rest of the pork and bacon together (or ask the butcher to do it for you). The bacon, incidentally, improves the colour of the pie on account of the saltpetre: without it the filling would look rather grey when the pie is cut.

Add the anchovy, sage and spices – the anchovy gives a savoury saltiness without a hint of fishiness – and the diced meat, and mix thoroughly. Fry a small amount and taste to see if adjustments are needed. Chill, covered, until required.

To make the pastry, sift the flour and salt into a mixing bowl. Bring the water and lard to the boil. This happens very quickly with a lot of spluttering, so watch out. Stir, then tip it into the flour, mixing deftly with a wooden spoon. Quickly form into a smooth dough with your hands. Leave to cool slightly.

You can make a pork pie any size you like, just allow an equal weight of meat to pastry. For a 500g pie, take 250g of pastry, setting aside 50g for the lid. Put the ball of pastry into a 500g pork pie or cake tin with a removable base. Quickly and lightly push the pastry up the sides of the tin, being careful to leave no cracks. If the pastry collapses into a dismal heap, it is a little too hot, so wait and try again.

Having raised the crust, loosely pack with 250g of meat slackened with 2 tablespoons of warm jellied stock. Roll the pastry lid, lay inside the raised walls and pinch and trim together, leaving a 1cm collar-cum-seal. Use a small sharp knife to cut out a central hole the size of a shirt button.

For small free-form pies, you will need 125g of pastry, 25g of which is for the lid. Put the pastry in your left hand (if right-handed) and use the thumb and fingers of the right hand to raise a wall, turning constantly with your left hand, pressing, pushing and raising a 'cup'. The walls will gape out, so use your right-hand thumb and fingers to pinch the top together in little pleats and use this new thickness to continue raising; you need the wall to go 1cm higher than the filling.

Fill with 125g of meat slackened with 1 tablespoon of warm stock. Roll the pastry lid, lay inside the wall and pinch together to seal, leaving a 1cm collar. Tie a 5cm fold of baking parchment around the pies, rising slightly taller than the lid.

Place the pies on a baking sheet. Heat the oven to 200°C/gas mark 6. Bake for 30 minutes, then lower the heat to 170°C/gas mark 3 and leave for a further hour for the large pie, 30 minutes for small pies.

Remove the pies from the oven. Stand the tin on a jam jar to remove the casing (or untie the baking parchment) and peel off the base. Brush the sides with beaten egg and return to the oven for 10 minutes or so to give a glossy sheen.

Rest the pies on a cake rack to cool. Pour warm jellied stock through the central hole, using a tiny kitchen funnel or a cone of cardboard. Top up several times as it disappears into the pie.

Leave the pies for 24 hours before eating; they keep, covered, in the fridge for a week. Serve with English mustard and pickles.

M Metal Mixing Bowls

When I had my kitchen extension done and moved around the house setting up a temporary culinary oasis, my equipment was minimal. A plug-in double hotplate, kettle, whisk and wooden spoon, favourite knives, a knife sharpener and chopping board, a few pots and pans, and a couple of metal chef's mixing bowls.

Metal mixing bowls are endlessly useful. They are inexpensive, light and unbreakable, hygienic, heatproof and stackable. I have various sizes for different jobs, but the most useful are larger than the average colander, with wide, rounded, sloping sides and a narrow lip. Apart for the endless mixing and whisking, separating, cooling and temporary storing, I use them to make pastry and prove bread dough, for lentil and vegetable salads, hydrating couscous and bulgar, soaking beans, mixing meatballs, marinating meat, for acidulated water when I'm preparing apples and artichokes, and for moving food around the kitchen. Smaller bowls are useful for quick little jobs like collecting chopped onion and other vegetables ready for the wok or stew pot. If I ever run out of big white bowls to serve food in – unlikely, but it happens when there is a big party – I use my metal mixing bowls.

Perhaps it is because it looks so sleek and shiny, but the most expensive large bowl, made of stainless steel, so heavier and more stable than the others, is always my last choice. It has straight sloping sides, a deep lip and wide flat base. It lives at the bottom of the pile. The others get slammed around the place while this one is too posh for such goings-on. Curious, isn't it, how even metal bowls have characters?

Stuffed Vine Leaves with Tzatziki

SERVES 4–8

Mine is a typical postage stamp London garden with lousy soil depleted by ivy grown to hide the fence and block out the neighbours. Three things flourish: jasmine, honeysuckle and a vine. The vine, now twenty years old, produces small sweet green grapes and in late May, June or July, depending on the weather, prodigious amounts of leaves. It gives me huge satisfaction to cook with them, wrapping them round quail and red mullet to roast in the oven, but mostly I make dolmades. *I love those plump, dark green bundles and make them all year round with preserved vine leaves (widely available preserved in brine or dried, in cans), but I particularly like making them with my own vine leaves. I serve them at the drop of a hat, with drinks or as a starter with home-made tzatziki, take them on picnics and make them to assuage hunger when the barbecue isn't ready. I love them hot from the oven with a chunky tomato sauce, cool Greek yoghurt and new potatoes fried in olive oil with lemon juice.*

Everyone is always hugely impressed by home-made stuffed vine leaves, but they require no cooking skills whatsoever and anyone who has ever rolled a cigarette with a modicum of success can make them. Once you get the hang of it, and it's quite addictive, you'll be begging leaves from friends with vines. Stuffed vine leaves feature in most cuisines where vines flourish but are particularly familiar in Greece. I learnt to make them from Claudia Roden's seminal A Book of Middle Eastern Food *but soon went off piste, as it were, using minced chicken instead of lamb and coriander instead of flat-leaf parsley, making do with dried mint instead of fresh, and I've never had a failure. It really doesn't matter which soft herbs you use, or in what ratio, because home-made stuffed vine leaves are always going to taste far superior to anything you can buy. I usually go to town with the herbs if I am making them without meat, and like the texture and extra interest of toasted pine kernels and raisins.*

Mint, flat-leaf parsley, dill and marjoram or oregano, and basil are all suitable, and spices such as saffron and cinnamon, for a Middle Eastern note, and marjoram or oregano with mint for Greek, are equally delicious. You can use any rice you like (despite what anyone might tell you) but it is usually used raw, soaked first in boiling water to soften, swelling in the water or stock poured over the closely packed bundles before they are covered and baked in the oven. Many recipes tell you to weight them down to stop them unfurling but I find a snugly tucked sheet of foil punched with a few air-holes works perfectly. The most important point is to pack them with the leaf end underneath. I sometimes get fancy and post slivers of garlic between the dolmades and lay them over sliced tomato, but it's simpler to inject extra flavour with stock rather than the more usual water.

This mix is based on a Bulgarian recipe and is quite meaty – pork and beef with paprika, onion and carrot, quickly stir-fried with the rice so everything is lightly cooked before the rolling begins. To be authentic, sarma is flavoured with chubritza, *the Bulgarian herb that gives a distinctive flavour to many*

local dishes. I made do with herbes de Provence *(it includes summer savory, the closest* chubritza *equivalent), plus plenty of fresh parsley and mint.*

So, prepare to be impressed: the essential long, slow cooking results in tender, moist morsels that leave you wanting more. Serve hot, warm or at room temperature; chilled from the fridge is not recommended.

40 fresh vine leaves or 250g
   brine-preserved leaves
6 spring onions
1 medium carrot
50g fresh flat-leaf parsley
2 tbsp olive oil
300g minced pork
300g minced beef or veal
1 dsp *herbes de Provence* or
   chubritza
1½ tsp paprika

200g basmati rice
1 chicken stock cube
about 20 flourishing mint leaves
For the tzatziki:
1 garlic clove, preferably new season
300g sheep's yoghurt
1 tbsp lemon juice
1 tbsp olive oil
2 Lebanese/small cucumbers
2 tbsp chopped fresh dill

Soak fresh vine leaves in boiling water for 5 minutes, or follow packet instructions for preserved leaves. Drain. Trim and finely slice the spring onions, scrape and grate the carrot. Finely chop the parsley stalks.

Heat the oil in a spacious frying pan and stir-fry the spring onions, carrot and parsley stalks for a couple of minutes before adding the meat. Brown thoroughly, then add the *herbes de Provence* and paprika. Stir-fry briefly, then add the washed rice. Season generously with salt and pepper. Dissolve the stock cube in 600ml of boiling water. Add 250ml of stock and simmer briskly, stirring occasionally, for 5–10 minutes, until moist rather than wet. Chop the parsley and mint leaves and stir into the mix. Tip into a mixing bowl and spread out to cool.

There is plenty of stuffing for at least 32 sarmi, but work in batches, laying out a few leaves, smooth side down, on a work surface. Place a scoop of filling – how much depends on leaf size – at the base. Fold the base 'wings' up over the filling, then the side 'wings' to the middle and carry on rolling upwards, tucking in the sides of the leaf as you go, ensuring the package is secure. Make two layers, the join underneath, packing snugly in a lidded sauté pan. Add the remaining hot stock. Cover with excess/damaged leaves, make airtight with foil, then add the lid. Simmer gently for 30 minutes. Serve hot from the pan or allow to cool before arranging attractively on a platter.

To make the tzatziki, peel and crush the garlic with a pinch of salt. Beat into the yoghurt with the lemon juice and olive oil. Peel the cucumbers, halve lengthways and use a teaspoon to scrape out the seeds. Slice into chunky half-moons and stir into the yoghurt with the dill.

Ⓜ Mezzaluna

It was very clever of my sons to work out that one bit of kitchen kit I didn't own was a mezzaluna. It was even cleverer to buy a decent one, get in touch with Henry's old art master who has etching materials, drive to his studio and etch a birthday message on the blade. I keep it, message facing out, on a specially made little wooden arch above one of my knife racks, close to the kettle. My eyes slide over their handwriting every day as I choose a knife or wait for the kettle to boil. Without being cheesy, but I know I am, I think of them as I rock the blade from side to side, annihilating a bunch of parsley or whatever it is I'm chopping.

Mezzaluna in Italian means half-moon and, in the culinary sense, is a half-moon-shaped, deep blade with sturdy vertical extensions at either end that are capped by plump, smooth wooden handles which fit comfortably into the palm of each hand. They are sometimes sold with a wooden bowl or thick board for chopping.

The mezzaluna works by holding the handles in both hands and rocking the blade from side to side. It feels odd to begin with, but with experience you will soon find that food can be quickly chopped to various degrees of delicacy. Double-bladed mezzalunas supposedly chop twice as much, twice as fast.

Pork and Lettuce Parcels with Nuoc Nam

SERVES 2, OR 4 AS A SNACK/STARTER

Curls of little gem lettuce heart lined with sprigs of coriander are the perfect two-bite size for a crumbly mound of soy-seasoned minced pork cooked with spring onions and beansprouts. The tastebuds are jerked into life with a garnish of crushed toasted nuts and a spoonful of Thai-style sweet-sour sauce.

Everything is laid out in bowls and it's a hands-on, do-it-yourself kind of supper, so the hot pork filling doesn't get a chance to wilt the crisp lettuce.

If this sounds rather complicated to make, or eat, you must trust me that it isn't. Far from it. Everything can be prepared in advance with minimal effort and the actual cooking takes minutes. In a restaurant, this style of dish is usually part of a spread to share but it's a popular main course in my house and a great way to diet.

If you are very big eaters, boiled rice is a good chaser-cum-accompaniment. The parcels are also good cold. Arrange as described on a platter and eat with fingers or knife and fork.

4 spring onions	1 tbsp dark soy sauce
100g beansprouts	2 tbsp Thai sweet chilli sauce
2 little gem lettuce hearts	*For the sauce:*
25g fresh coriander	2 garlic cloves
50g peanuts, cashews or hazelnuts	2 tbsp Thai fish sauce (nam pla)
2 tbsp groundnut oil	1 tbsp fresh lime juice
300g minced pork	1 tbsp Thai sweet chilli sauce

Trim and finely slice the spring onions. Use a mezzaluna to chop the beansprouts into short lengths. Unfurl, wash and shake dry the lettuce leaves. Arrange on a platter and drape each one with a sprig of coriander.

Peel, chop and crush the garlic to a paste with a generous pinch of salt. Place half the garlic in a ramekin or similar small dish. Add the fish sauce, lime juice and 1 tablespoon of chilli sauce. Mix thoroughly to make the sauce. Use a pestle and mortar to crush the nuts or place in a plastic bag and smash into pieces with something heavy like a rolling pin. Heat ½ tablespoon of groundnut oil in a spacious frying pan and stir-fry the nuts for a couple of minutes, until golden. Tip on to kitchen paper to drain. Place in a suitable dish.

Wipe out the pan and add the remaining oil, placing over a high heat. When very hot, crumble the pork into the pan, stirring to separate the grains. Add the soy sauce and stir-fry for 2–3 minutes, until amalgamated. Add the reserved garlic, spring onions, beansprouts and 2 tablespoons of chilli sauce. Stir-fry over a medium heat for 3–4 minutes.

Use the mezzaluna to chop the coriander and stir it into the mix just before tipping into a bowl for serving. To eat, spoon the pork into a curl of lettuce, adding a sprinkling of nuts and a spoonful of sauce.

M Mouli-Légumes Food Mill

A Mouli-Légumes food mill is a curious-looking contraption but a really useful and inexpensive gadget for puréeing and soup-making. It is a sophisticated sieve-cum-masher with three metal discs with different sized holes for puréeing. It clicks apart as easily as it clicks together and is invaluable for making mashed potato. The sturdiest, least likely to force out the centrifugal bolt that holds it together, is made of steel. Other, cheaper but less durable presses are made of plastic. Mine has legs that fold out and clamp on top of the pan or bowl. I've owned several over the years and would never be without one. I always use it for mashed potato and super-soft pommes purée.

Pommes Purée with Smoked Haddock and Dijon Mustard Sauce

SERVES 2

Pommes purée is silkier, richer and more liquid and sauce-like than mashed potato and is always made with waxy-type La Ratte-style or Belles de Fontenay French potatoes. It is vital that the potatoes are mashed smooth and the Mouli-Légumes is the tool of choice, although others swear by a ricer. The potato purée acts as a sauce-cum-mash and is the perfect rich and creamy foil for robustly flavoured smoked haddock.

It is sure to be a French idea to serve this lovely fish with a Dijon mustard sauce and it really is a match made in heaven. This is one of my favourite combinations of food and looks very pretty with the mustard and chive sauce. The chives add quite a strong onion flavour. A good addition, if you really want to be greedy, is a soft-poached egg. The yolk will give a second, even richer sauce.

2 fillets of naturally cured smoked haddock
1 bay leaf
4 black peppercorns
300g large Charlotte potatoes
50g unsalted butter
75ml hot full-fat milk
1 dsp Grey Poupon or Maille Dijon mustard
2 tbsp crème fraîche
1 tbsp finely snipped fresh chives

Place the fish, skin side down, in a pan that can hold it in a single layer. Add the bay leaf and peppercorns and just cover with water.

Now make the pommes purée. Put the potatoes into a pan, cover with water, add salt, semi-cover the pan and cook for 20–30 minutes, until tender. Drain. Spear with a fork and use a small, sharp knife to whip off the skin. Return the potatoes to the pan, cover and leave for 5 minutes.

Pass the potatoes through a Mouli-Légumes (or a ricer; *do not* use a food processor) back into the pan. Shave the butter over the top and use a wooden spoon to beat thoroughly until smooth and glossy.

Have ready the hot milk and add gradually, beating constantly with the wooden spoon until pale, fluffy and runnier than British mash. Taste and season with salt. Cover with a tea towel to keep warm or place, covered, in a low oven.

Cook the fish for 3–4 minutes a side, ending skin side up, until just cooked through. Ease off the fish skin.

Spoon the pommes purée into the middle of two warmed plates. Arrange a fillet of fish on top and spoon over the sauce, made by quickly warming 4 tablespoons of fish cooking liquid with the mustard, crème fraîche and chives. *Bon appétit.*

N Nutcracker

When I was growing up, we had a lovely nutcracker shaped like a Dandy Dinmont terrier, with jaws that cracked the nut. I suspect it made us children eat more nuts, particularly at Christmas when the bowl was piled with walnuts, Brazils, almonds and cobnuts, all in their shells. I looked in vain for something similar when my sons were young but ended up with a sleekly elegant modern take on the classic nutcracker design (see page 275). It's made of heavy, satin finish stainless steel, the handles subtly shaped to be extremely pleasing to hold, and seamlessly hinged. The serrated crackers are strong enough to deal with the most resistant Brazil or awkwardly shaped walnut. It offers control, too, so just the right amount of pressure is applied to each type of nut, so the kernel isn't shattered to smithereens. Being Italian, it is called Schiaccianoci. You don't need me to translate.

Nuts, like apples and oranges, were always there for the taking when I was growing up. We never thought about how old the nuts were but the thin skin that clings glove-like to nuts is what makes the kernel bitter. It dries and turns flaky with age. These days, it's only at Christmas that we think of buying nuts in their shells, although walnuts are always available. Cobnuts, actually large hazelnuts – which I used to pick in my school holidays – and almonds are sometimes on sale as they come into season in the spring and early summer, and both are so much more interesting to eat then. We are used to buying nuts without their shell, with or without their inner skin rubbed away.

Every so often someone comes up with a new nutcracker design. They are usually variations on the classic design like mine, or the screw-in-the-bowl-shaped cracker, winding slowly until the nut cracks, or a ratchet job that reminds me of the tool box. One such is a German-designed stainless-steel Mono Pico walnut *opener*, stylish enough to wear as a piece of jewellery. It is strung on a short leather thong and works like a key, splitting the shell (see page 275).

I suspect, though, that the nutcracker trade is a dying one. Conversely, old nutcrackers like the one from my childhood are highly collectable. The local antique shop is the place to look.

Pasta with Walnuts and Dill

SERVES 2

The paucity of ingredients in this simple pasta dish belies its deliciousness. It makes a lovely quick supper but works well as an accompaniment to lemon-and-olive-oil-splashed grilled white fish.

8 walnuts	4 tbsp Greek or other fruity olive oil
2 garlic cloves	about 8 mint or basil leaves
10g bunch dill	100g Greek feta
200g pappardelle	rocket or lettuce salad, to serve

Use the nutcracker to carefully crack the nuts so the halves aren't broken. Roast the pieces in a heavy frying pan, tossing them around for a couple of minutes until aromatic and slightly darkened in colour. This intensifies their flavour. Cool slightly and break into chunky pieces. Crack the garlic, flake away the skin, chop finely, then crush to a paste with the flat of a knife. Tear the leaves off the dill stalks and chop.

Cook the pasta according to packet instructions in plenty of salted water. Drain and add 2 tablespoons of oil and the garlic to the pan. Cook, stirring constantly for a couple of minutes until aromatic. Return the pasta and stir to mix. Shred the mint or basil. Add the walnuts, dill and mint or basil. Crumble the feta over the top and mix. Serve with a generous splash of olive oil and a simple rocket or lettuce salad.

N Nutmeg Grater

If you've ever been lucky enough to lay your hands on fresh nutmegs, brought back perchance by a friend visiting the Moluccas, Sri Lanka or Indonesia, they are likely to be covered in bright red lace. This pretty camisole is mace. It is a quite different hauntingly aromatic spice with a perfumed, sweet scent and clean bitter flavour. The nutmeg itself is inside a thin, almost ceramic dark brown shell that needs to be cracked and discarded. Nutmeg is not a nut but the kernel of a seed. It is roughly egg-shaped and about the size of an acorn, the colour pale brown with a grey hue. It is solid and hard, almost woody, but once you start grating or slicing, it is deceptively crumbly. Inside it has a delicate veined surface reminiscent of a white truffle. It is exceedingly aromatic with an instantly recognizable flavour that complements all sorts of things, from rum punch and milky foods like rice pudding and cheese sauces, to spicy food, potatoes and some surprises like Brussels sprouts (see page 262).

All box graters feature a small grater punched with tiny holes for grating nutmeg because it has always been a popular spice in dried fruit cakes and puddings. Separate nutmeg graters come in various shapes and sizes. I own several but all have been usurped by my Peugeot nutmeg grater. Whole nutmegs sit awaiting their destiny around a central chamber inside an acrylic dome that twists on to a pale, natural wood base with chrome trimmings. A small handle on the side grinds effortlessly – Peugeot have been making grinders (as well as cars) since 1840. When the nutmeg is finished, it can be quickly replaced by one of the decorative spares.

Nutmegs retain their qualities almost indefinitely but are best stored out of direct light and away from heat or damp.

Spinach Malfatti with Gorgonzola Sauce

SERVES 4–6

In early 2000, the Guardian *newspaper ran a series of interviews with well-known people about their perfect meal. John Mortimer – or was it Rumpole of the Bailey? – chose a starter of spinach malfatti. The description was short yet so enticing that I tore out the article and filed it. A few years later, I had a go at the recipe (adapted by Jeremy Lee, now at Quo Vadis) and as nutmeg is such a crucial ingredient, it was an obvious choice for inclusion here. Try as I might, I couldn't find my carefully saved tear-out anywhere so in the end I made up my own recipe.*

Malfatti are a very delicate gnocchi made with ricotta, eggs, Parmesan, a little flour and lots of nutmeg. Malfatti means 'badly made' and the mixture is so soft, it is hard to shape. I picked up a clever solution using a wine glass from Rose Gray and Ruth Rogers of the River Café. It sounds odd, but all is revealed in the recipe.

Like all gnocchi, malfatti need only a few minutes cooking in boiling water before they're ready to eat. At the River Café they serve chard malfatti with sage butter, made by melting about 25g of butter with two or three sage leaves per serving. It is a slightly lighter alternative to this rich creamy sauce, but either goes very well with spinach malfatti. Tomato sauce would be another good alternative. Semolina flour, incidentally, can be made by grinding semolina or polenta in a food processor.

500g young spinach leaves
250g ricotta
2 large eggs
2 tbsp '00' or potato flour
½ whole nutmeg
100g finely grated Parmesan

approx 6 tbsp semolina flour
For the sauce:
125g Gorgonzola dolce or dolcelatte cheese
100ml whipping cream
6 tbsp milk

Rinse the spinach carefully and pile into a colander. Put a large pan over a high heat and add the spinach with only the water clinging to its leaves. Add a pinch of salt, cover and cook, turning over the leaves a couple of times, for 3–4 minutes, until soft and wilted. Spread out on a tray to cool. When cool enough to handle, squeeze out as much liquid as possible. Finely chop the mound of spinach. Place the ricotta, eggs, flour, freshly grated nutmeg and 50g of finely grated Parmesan in a mixing bowl and use a fork to mix thoroughly, adding a pinch of Maldon sea salt and a few grinds of pepper. Stir in the spinach thoroughly. Scatter half the semolina flour over a small tray. Place about 1 tsp semolina flour in a wine glass. Gently drop a scoop of mixture, about a dessertspoonful, into the bottom of the glass, gently swirl it round in the flour to make a shape and gently drop it on to the floury tray. Repeat until all the mixture is used.

Next make the sauce. Break the cheese into a pan, add the cream and place over a medium heat. Stir as the cheese melts, stirring in sufficient milk to give a glossy, thick finish.

To finish the dish, place a big pan of water over a high heat, bring to a boil, and drop in as many malfatti as will sit comfortably at once. When the malfatti rise to the surface – a couple of minutes – they are done. Have ready a hot platter or serving plates. Add a little hot sauce (or melted butter; see above) and the malfatti, lifted one at a time with a slotted spoon. Spoon over some of the sauce and finish with freshly grated Parmesan, this time grated on a larger hole so the pieces are spiky.

Caramelized Rice Pudding with Vodka Plum Purée

Every time I grate nutmeg I'm back in Pringle Cottage watching my mum pouring a huge amount of milk into an absurdly small amount of rice and sugar, cutting off chunks of butter, then wiping her hands on her apron before grating the nutmeg. It was my favourite pudding, but my brother Jonathan used to hide in the downstairs loo when it was served (the same place he lurked when it was time for his washing-up shift). When my sons were growing up, I always seemed to be looking around for last-minute pudding ideas and one was to stir yoghurt and caster sugar, with a few toasted almonds, into leftover rice and serve it with soft fruit purée.

If I wanted to make a proper rice pudding I had to plan ahead. This one, an all-time favourite, takes ages. To end up with the desired creamy texture and thin skin that billows like a tarpaulin as it cooks but settles and softens again once the pudding is out of the oven, it needs long slow cooking. The skin on my mum's version, which she regularly burnt, stayed like tarpaulin and became a vital component of rice pudding. She served it with the top of the milk – in those days gold-top milk was like pouring cream – and home-made strawberry jam (see page 99). Other good accompaniments include cooked strawberry or raspberry sauce (see page 167) and puréed plums. Both are served lukewarm or cold, so a great make-ahead pud.

50g butter	*For the plum purée:*
75g caster sugar	2 bay leaves
100g pudding or other round-grain rice	½ split vanilla pod
	300ml water
1 litre full-fat milk	3 strips of orange zest
1 vanilla pod, split lengthways	3 tbsp vodka
150ml double cream	3 tbsp demerara sugar
nutmeg	6 large, ripe plums

Heat the oven to 140°C/gas mark 1. Begin the cooking in a sauté pan and have ready a deep gratin dish of 1.5 litre capacity to transfer the pudding into. Melt the butter in the sauté pan. Add the sugar, stirring gently over a medium-low heat until straw-coloured and gooey. Add the rice and continue stirring, until the rice looks puffy, pale golden and syrup-sticky. Add the milk, stirring as the liquid heats to disperse any clumps of rice. Add the vanilla pod, squashing it around a bit so it releases its seeds. Add the cream and salt and bring to the boil. Season generously with freshly grated nutmeg, stir, then place in the oven for 2½–3 hours, until just starting to set but still slightly liquid-looking in the centre. Leave to cool. As it cools, it will firm slightly more. Serve lukewarm or cold, as milk puddings have very little flavour eaten piping hot.

For the plum purée, place the bay leaves, half vanilla pod, water, zest and vodka in a pan that can accommodate the chopped plums in a single layer (but don't add them yet). Simmer, uncovered, for 10 minutes. Stir in the sugar to dissolve. Remove the bay leaves and vanilla. Slice the plums off their stones in big chunks into the pan. Simmer, covered, for 5 minutes.

Liquidize the plums with sufficient liquid to make a thick purée. Pour into a bowl or jug and leave to go cold.

O Oven Grill

I grew up thinking the oven grill was for cooking toast. And cheese on toast, or grilling tomatoes and bacon. Sometimes we would have grilled pork chops with charred crackling running down the side and kippers grilled for breakfast on high days and holidays. The grill wasn't even used to toast crumpets and teacakes – that was done in front of the fire.

I use my grill – in fact I have two as mine is a double oven – for cooking a wide range of things. It is useful for fish fillets, whole mackerel and slip soles, for charring aubergines to make moutabal, and scorching the skin off red peppers so they peel easily. I like slowly grilled sausages and quickly grilled lamb chops that make sparks as the fat melts and spurts up to the grill. I always use the grill to cook bacon.

In fact, I use my oven grill a lot. Mine is at eye level, so it's easy to see what's going on. It is even more efficient if whatever is being grilled is laid on shiny-side-up aluminium foil.

Harry's Grilled Aubergine with Feta and Parsley

SERVES 4

At lunchtime Harry, the chef patron of the favourite beachside taverna at Thanos on Lemnos (see page 89), is usually cooking or toiling in the adjacent fields that supply the kitchen. One day he joined friends for lunch. From my table I couldn't make out what they were eating but on the way out we stopped to chat. What intrigued me most was the big, stunningly pale aubergine in the middle of the table. It was peeled and slashed lengthways so the buttery-soft flesh almost oozed under its cloak of crumbled feta, surrounded by Harry's signature chopped parsley and swirl of fruity olive oil. It tasted garlicky and lemony, creamy and unimaginably delicious. It took days to wheedle the recipe out of Harry but it is ludicrously simple and I've cooked it many times and published the recipe in my Times *column. Harry served his with lamb shanks braised in the oven with potatoes, but it adapts to virtually any size and shape of aubergine and is interesting enough to serve on its own. It's become a favourite home alone supper but makes a great starter. Both my sons make it regularly and so will you.*

4 medium or 2 large aubergines, approx 800g
1 large garlic clove
1 lemon
5–6 tbsp fruity olive oil
1 tbsp very finely chopped flat-leaf parsley leaves
100g Greek feta cheese

Heat the grill. Run a small, sharp knife round the base of each aubergine stalk, just cutting through the skin. Make 4 evenly spaced shallow cuts down the length of the aubergine. Cook under the grill, turning every 10 minutes two or three times to cook evenly, until the aubergine feels soft but before the skin hardens over sagging flesh. Transfer to warm plates or a platter and use a fork and knife to quickly lift and remove the skin. Slash the aubergine from stalk to end without cutting it in half.

During a lull in proceedings, peel and finely chop the garlic. Scatter chopped garlic over the aubergine and add a generous squeeze of lemon juice, a splash of olive oil and most of the parsley. Crumble feta over the top. Garnish over and around with a little more parsley and finish with a swirl of olive oil.

P Paella Pan

My brother Jonathan was the person with Spanish links in my family and he gave me my first paella pan. It was not much larger than a frying pan and made of carbon steel, with a dimpled base and red handles. Despite the fact that it instantly rusted and I didn't know it had to be oiled between uses, it followed me around various flats and has ended up with one of my sons. In the part of Spain where my brother lived, paella reigns and there are many restaurants that specialize. Everyone owns a complete paella kit stand, burner, gas fittings, a special long-handled ladle and various pans. I have one too and there is another at Zach's house and one in Cornwall. Discovering the Paella Company (see page 275), who sell various kits and numerous pans of different sizes and finishes, has had a huge effect on my family. We have pans that will feed 10–12 and another that caters for 25. With a Calor gas cylinder for fuel, it means paella challenges the barbecue for a way of feeding a gang of people with minimal trouble. It is similar to the barbecue in that all the preparation can be done in advance and stashed in the fridge in plastic boxes.

Paella is more of a muck-in meal than a barbecue and it's fun extending the Spanish mood with wines and impromptu tapas, gathering round the pan, savouring the anticipation as supper gently simmers unaided.

Anyone who is into paella will tell you that it is all about cooking the rice and giving it as much flavour as possible. The look of the dish is immaterial. I have made paella very successfully with basmati rice but to be authentic you need round-grain Bomba or Calasparra rice, or failing that, Arborio, the risotto rice. Like risotto, which paella resembles, the rice swells as it cooks, but unlike risotto, once the initial *sofrito* has been made, and the rice and the main ingredients added, all the stock goes into the pan in one go. It is stirred only once, apart from the occasional prod to ensure even cooking, and left to do its thing. If some of the rice sticks and ends up slightly burnt, that is regarded as the choice mouthful and even has its own name; the *socarret*.

Alberto Herraiz has written a masterful book called *Paella* (Phaidon, 2011) which charts everything there is to know about Spain's national dish, its history, the various pan types, the range of paella possibilities, the constituent ingredients from the rice to the pimentón and saffron. He discusses cooking paella outside, inside, in the oven, on hob and grill.

Monkfish, Squid and Chorizo Paella with Prawns

SERVES 6

Pretty much anything goes in the name of paella, but the favourite combination in my household is spicy chorizo with mildly flavoured, creamy and meaty monkfish or tender (and blessedly inexpensive) squid, with a few prawns to finish. A good tip from food photographer Jason Lowe – who cooked three paellas, each for fifty, for his wedding feast – is to cover the paella with spinach for its 10-minute (covered) rest before serving, then stir it into the paella with a pesto-style paste made with flat-leaf parsley, garlic, saffron and a slick of olive oil. This optional extra gives the paella a burst of vitality, livening up the look as well as the flavour of the dish.

1 large Spanish onion or 400g tin of Eazy onions

4 large garlic cloves, preferably new season

150g Iberico chorizo

2 pointed red peppers

4 tbsp olive oil

1 large beef tomato or 5 plum tomatoes

2 very generous pinches of saffron threads, softened in 1 tbsp hot water

1kg monkfish tail fillet or 500g monkfish tail and 500g small prepared squid

350g Bomba, Calasparra or Arborio rice

1 litre fish stock, light chicken stock or water

8 large shell-on raw prawns or 12 medium-sized ones

350g young spinach

2 large lemons

For the parsley paste:

60g bunch flat-leaf parsley

4 garlic cloves

2 generous pinches of saffron threads, softened in 4 tbsp hot water

3 tbsp olive oil

Heat the oven to 200°C/gas mark 6. Keeping separate piles, peel, halve and finely chop the onion and garlic. Sprinkle the garlic with ½ teaspoon of salt and use the flat of a small knife to crush it to a paste. Run a knife down the chorizo and peel away the skin. Slice chunkily. Arrange the peppers on a roasting tin and bake for 10 minutes, then turn and repeat. Remove to a plate, cover with clingfilm, leave for 10 minutes, then remove the skin. Halve lengthways, scrape away the seeds and chop.

Heat the oil in a 35cm diameter paella pan or in two large frying pans placed over a medium heat. Stir in the onion and garlic and cook for 3–4 minutes before adding the chorizo. Cook for a further couple of minutes to release some of the fat and flavour from the chorizo. Pour boiling water over the tomato. Count to 20, drain and remove the skin. Chop the tomato. Add the peppers to the onion. Stir well, then add the tomato and saffron. Leave to cook while you remove any trace of the slimy membrane covering the monkfish and chop it into kebab-size pieces. If using squid, remove the tentacles from inside the sac and quarter the sac lengthways.

Stir the seafood into the onion mixture. Increase the heat slightly and cook for 5 minutes to seal the fish. Season with salt and pepper. Stir in the unwashed rice and cook for a couple of minutes while you heat up the stock. Stir the stock into the pan, return to boiling then reduce the heat to a steady simmer. Cook for 20 minutes or until all the liquid has been absorbed into the rice and the grains are swollen and tender. If necessary, fold the food together rather than stir it, encouraging the paella to cook evenly. Push the prawns into the rice, and when they turn pink, cover the entire paella with the spinach leaves. Cover with foil and punch a few steam holes. Weight the foil with folded newspapers and leave for at least 10 minutes.

To make the parsley paste, blitz the parsley leaves, peeled garlic, saffron liquid and olive oil, adding extra water if too stiff. To serve, fold the wilted spinach and parsley paste into the rice. Serve the paella from the pan, with lemon wedges.

Zarzuela Fish Stew with Garlic Parsley Crumbs

SERVES 6

Zarzuela is the Spanish equivalent of the merging of two legendary French fish soups, bouillabaisse *and* soupe aux poissons. *What these refined fishermen's soups-cum-stews have in common, apart from a mix of seasonal, local fish, is a rich, thick broth based on* sofrito, *a mound of sloppy, soft onion cooked in olive oil. It could be made with water, or fish stock from the bones and shells, maybe with a splash of wine, but for maximum flavour*

*I use light chicken and fish stock, with a goodly squeeze of tomato purée.
The soup is thickened with a rich and robustly flavoured paste called a
picada, made with creamy Spanish Marcona almonds and rustic bread,
both fried in olive oil with flat-leaf parsley, saffron and mild, so-called 'soft'
or 'sweet', paprika. I find that the smoked version, widely available in small
red tins under the La Chinata label, gives a haunting extra dimension to the
flavours, but not everyone likes it.*

*As with all fish soups and stews, a mixture of seafood is the most
interesting to eat, but stick with firm fish that won't fall apart in the pot.
Monkfish, cod and sea bass, all tagged and seasonally sustainable from
Cornwall, are perfect, and so are Pacific cod, Cornish pollack, gurnard and
hake, if you can get it, and farmed tilapia (for more about eco-friendly fish,
see page 276). I particularly rate squid in dishes like this. I buy it frozen, in
500g or 1kg bags, the tentacles tucked back inside the cleaned sac, from my
fishmonger, Waitrose and Sainsbury. Shellfish, particularly prawns, mussels
and clams, when available, look dramatic and give a paella-style finale to
this substantial dish. Add them at the last minute; in the case of mussels,
cover the dish to encourage speedy cooking.*

*Zarzuela is a wonderful sharing dish. I love the fact that all the
preparation, including cooking the onions to melting, can be done in
advance. The actual cooking is fast, furious and fun; a great dish to cook in
a large paella pan over the barbecue. It's eaten with thick slices of bruschetta
and the fiery snap of raw garlic contributes to the overall flavours. It's a rich
and satisfying one-dish meal, so you really won't want much else, maybe
some fruit, a salad, or a snicket of cheese.*

2 pinches of saffron threads
1 sourdough-style loaf
8 tbsp olive oil
30g Spanish Marcona almonds
80g bunch flat-leaf parsley
2 heaped tsp smoked sweet/soft/
  doux paprika
2 large Spanish onions
500g large vine tomatoes
2 tbsp tomato purée
300ml dry white wine
300ml fish or light chicken stock, or
  a mixture

500g prepared fresh or frozen small
  squid, defrosted
6 fillets of hake, cod, pollack, sea
  bass or other firm, white non-oily
  fish
400g monkfish fillet
2 large garlic cloves
280g organic raw prawns
6 large tiger prawns
4 lemons
a bottle of Spanish olive oil

Soften the saffron in 4 tablespoons of warm water. Cut a thick slice from the loaf (approximately 50g) and tear it into pieces. Heat 2 tablespoons of olive oil in a spacious, lidded frying pan and stir-fry the almonds, tossing until light golden. Scoop out of the pan. Fry the bread in the oil until golden. Tip both into the bowl of a food processor. Add three-quarters of the parsley leaves, the paprika, saffron and its water, and 2 tablespoons of olive oil. Blitz to make a grainy, loose paste. Scrape into a bowl.

Peel and finely chop the onions. Add 2 tablespoons of olive oil to the frying pan. Stir in the onions. Cover and gently soften, stirring occasionally. Allow 20–30 minutes for this; you want them melting soft. Meanwhile, prepare everything else. Immerse the tomatoes in boiling water. Stab with a sharp knife and when the skin splits, after about 30 seconds, drain. Cut out the core and remove the skin. Chop. Stir the tomato purée into the white wine and stock. Keeping separate piles (in bowls or plastic bags), prepare the remaining ingredients. Remove the tentacles from inside the squid sacs. Trim the top of the tentacles to quickly remove the hard beak. Slice the sac in half lengthways. Following the grain of the hake fillets, slice into 2 or 3 pieces. Cut the monkfish into kebab-size chunks. Peel the garlic and leave whole.

Tip the cooked onion into a paella pan, spacious *cazuela* or roasting tin with 2 tablespoons of olive oil. Reheat, then add the squid and monkfish, stir-frying for 5 minutes until all the pieces have stiffened and changed colour. Add the chopped tomatoes and 1 teaspoon of salt. Let the stew bubble away for 5 minutes or so, then add the tomato purée, wine and stock. Bring the liquid to a simmer, then scoop a ladle of the hot stock into the almond paste and stir it back into the dish. Simmer for about 10 minutes, giving the odd stir, before you check the seasoning, adding extra salt if needed. Stir in the organic raw prawns. Tuck the hake into the liquid evenly across the dish, followed by the large tiger prawns. As the prawns change colour, from grey to pink, and the white fish is just cooked through, scatter over the remaining chopped parsley. Serve in shallow soup bowls with forks and spoons, with lemon wedges to squeeze into the terracotta juices.

While the stew finishes cooking, toast thick slices of bread. Serve them in a pile with the peeled garlic and a bottle of olive oil for people to do their own rubbing and anointing (see page 158).

P Pastry Brushes

At the latest count there are eight wooden pastry brushes tucked in with my wooden spoons. Often I use several of them for one batch of pastry. One will be dipped in oil to grease a pie tin, another will flick surplus flour from the rolled-out pastry, a third will be charged with milk or beaten egg to glaze the pie and I might need the fourth to apply melted jam to fruit tartlets.

Each brush has a specific job; the oldest and most whiskery is useful for fine work whereas the wide, flat brush is perfect for spreading jam on rolled marzipan for a cake. The best pastry brushes are either round-headed or flat, with natural bristle firmly glued in a plain wooden handle. Flat brushes look exactly like a small decorator's paintbrush with the bristles glued and held in place with a steel band. Avoid pastry brushes with plastic bristles. The hard, square-ended filaments can mark soft pastry and can't 'hold' water or egg as efficiently. Pastry brushes are a bit like wooden spoons; they develop their own character as they age. Watch out, though, for moulting.

Walnut and Pistachio Baklava with Rose Water and Cardamom

SERVES 12

Home-made baklava is surprisingly easy to master and tastes out of this world. When I produced one for a dinner party, it received such fulsome praise that I'm thinking of going into business, using metal baking trays the same size as the filo pastry sheets, as I did the other night, so it looks professional. Baklava is made by sandwiching two layers of coarsely ground nuts in sheets of butter-painted filo. The surprisingly sturdy 'pie' is then etched into portions – traditionally lozenge, square or oblong – and baked for an hour. Once out of the oven it is immediately drenched in sweet syrup made with sugar or honey or a combination of the two. The stunning tray of baklava is then left to cool and soak up all the liquid. It will keep, covered, in a cool place, not the fridge, for several days.

Sticking with one type of nut, particularly hazelnuts or walnuts, is delicious, but mixing different nuts in whatever combination and proportion takes your fancy (or you find at the back of the store cupboard) is part of the fun of making baklava.

Roasting enriches the flavour of most nuts and many seeds and it's a quick and easy job that fills the house with delicious smells. Sesame seeds, in particular, are transformed by roasting. Apart from turning a pale caramel colour, they glisten when their natural oils are released and turn deliciously nutty. It is possible to buy most nuts ready roasted, but with the exception of the superb roasted cashews I bought at Dammas Gate in Shepherd's Bush, you get better results doing it yourself.

Serve baklava with coffee or mint tea, or as a stupendous dinner finale with fresh fruit – strawberries, slices of mango and pineapple – laid out on an accompanying platter decorated with sprigs of mint. It is also the perfect feed-the-five-thousand picnic or barbecue dessert.

For the syrup:
350g sugar
450ml water
juice of 1 lemon
1 tbsp rose water

For the filling:
100g pistachio kernels
20 green cardamom pods
300g walnut kernels
2 tbsp palm sugar
200g lightly salted butter
400g filo pastry, at room temperature

First make the syrup. Dissolve the sugar in the water, stirring regularly. Add the lemon juice and simmer gently for 30 minutes, until slightly reduced and syrupy. Stir in the rose water, cool, cover and chill.

Heat the oven to 180°C/gas mark 4. Set aside 12 of the greenest pistachios. Remove the seeds from the cardamoms and crush them lightly. Place in the bowl of the food processor with the walnuts and the rest of the pistachios. Pulse until coarsely chopped. Tip into a bowl and stir in the palm sugar. Melt the butter.

Unfurl the filo and keep covered with a damp tea towel. Lay one sheet of filo in a baking tin approximately 20 × 30 × 3cm deep. Use a pastry brush to carefully paint the filo with butter. Repeat 10 times. Scatter half the nuts over the buttered filo. Top with another sheet of filo, paint with butter and cover with the remaining nuts. Continue with 10 more sheets, finishing with butter. Use a sharp knife to divide into portions, cutting right through to the tin; I cut four straight lines and seven at an angle to make modest lozenge-shaped portions. Bake for 30 minutes, then reduce the temperature to 150°C/gas mark 2 and cook for a further 30 minutes until golden.

Reinforce the portions by cutting down the lines, then pour the chilled syrup over the top, working from the outside in so everything is drenched. Place the reserved pistachios in a plastic bag and crush to dust with something heavy. Sprinkle little mounds of ground pistachio in the centre of each portion. Leave to completely cool before serving.

P Pie Dishes

The everyday pies of my childhood, and they were everyday, tended to be made on a thick enamel plate with a wide rim and slightly curved base, rather like a shallow, old-fashioned soup bowl. They were always double-crust pies, by which I mean pastry top and bottom, usually filled with fruit, often apples, but rhubarb, gooseberries, blackberries and plums came and went with the seasons. Fruit pies came with custard or white sauce and meat pies with gravy, lots of it.

Big meaty pies like steak and kidney – one of Mum's specialities – were made in a pie dish. These can be any shape but tend to be oval, made of stoneware, earthenware or, in our case, Pyrex. A flat rim runs round the top of the dish for the pastry to sit on over the filling, and the dish slopes gently to a far smaller base. The filling, often uncooked, goes almost to the top of the dish, and a thicker than usual pastry lid rests on the rim.

Pies like this need a pie funnel. This is a small ceramic funnel, about 8cm high, and always hollow. It is placed in the middle of the pie and pokes through the pastry. Its function is twofold. It supports the pastry and allows steam to escape from the filling.

Very plain funnels started to appear in kitchens by the late 1880s, and you may happen upon one stamped with Nutbrown, a name synonymous with the earliest funnels. In the mid-thirties, ceramicist Clarice Cliff was inspired by the English nursery rhyme of the King's blackbird pie to add a blackbird funnel to her catalogue and it became the most popular and much copied design. Hers are now extremely collectable (see page 275).

An elephant, with its trunk swinging up to expel steam, a cook baker, his hat the funnel and coloured blackbirds (made by Le Creuset) are also collectable but the most interesting and prolific potter specializing in pie funnels is Stuart Bass. He's been making them at his Exmoor pottery since the mid-seventies (see page 275). Collector June Tyler has produced a book – *Collecting Stuart Bass Pie Funnels* – based on her extensive collection, with a website (see page 275) showing new designs since the book was published in 2010. The funnels are highly decorative, amusing and very beautiful. A fox, snowman, great tit, various ladies, including Flo and Dot, are just the tip of the iceberg.

Chicken (or Rabbit), Bacon and Mushroom Pie

SERVES 4

We ate a lot of pies when I was growing up and pastry-making was a loathed kitchen task. Cold hands, cold ingredients and minimal handling were my mum's tips for successful pastry. She used lard, which produced light, flaky pastry with a rich flavour, but when I started pastry-making for myself I switched to butter, thinking it would be better. These days I tend to use a mixture, either half-and-half or erring one way or the other depending on the filling.

Despite the fact that one of my dad's sisters reared rare breed chickens, first in Surrey and later in Cornwall, chicken was a treat. My mother always made stock from the bones, having already made the bird last two meals for a family of six. I love the sense of occasion that comes with sharing a pie, the anticipation of what's inside – in this instance, big chunks of tender chicken, although it could be rabbit, and mushrooms in a rich, tangy white wine sauce.

300g plain flour, plus a little extra
a pinch of salt
100g butter, plus an extra knob
50g lard
5–6 tbsp cold water
4 rashers of smoked streaky bacon,
   approx 70g
1 tbsp vegetable oil
1 onion
1 tsp chopped thyme leaves

6 medium chestnut mushrooms,
   approx 200g
350–500g diced chicken thigh fillet
   or rabbit
1 tbsp seasoned flour
1 dsp Grey Poupon or Maille Dijon
   mustard
100ml dry white wine
50ml water
1 egg, whisked

Sift the flour into a mixing bowl with the salt. Cut the butter and lard in small chunks into the flour. Quickly rub the fat into the flour until it resembles breadcrumbs. Add the water, 1 tablespoon at a time, mixing with a knife until it clumps together. Quickly form into a ball. Pop into a plastic bag and chill for 30 minutes.

To make the filling, chop the bacon and fry gently in the oil in a spacious frying or sauté pan over a medium-low heat, tossing as the fat begins to run, until crisp. Add the peeled and finely chopped onion and the thyme, tossing together for 10 minutes or so until the onion begins to soften and turn glassy. Wipe and quarter the mushrooms and stir into the onion, tossing often until they start to sweat. Toss the meat in seasoned flour and add to the pan. Brown thoroughly, then stir in the mustard, wine and water. Simmer briskly, scraping up the brown goo as you stir with a wooden spoon. Taste and adjust the seasoning with salt and pepper. Leave to cool.

Butter a 1 litre capacity enamel pie dish or similar. Dust a work surface with flour and roll two-thirds of the pastry to fit the dish. Trim the excess. Roll the remaining pastry to make a lid. Tip the cooled filling into the pastry case, smear the border with water and fit the lid. Crimp with a fork to seal. Paint the pie with egg and make a few steam holes with a fork. Heat the oven to 200°C/gas mark 6. Bake the pie for 15 minutes, then reduce the heat to 180°C/gas mark 5 and cook for a further 20–30 minutes, until the pastry is puffed and golden.

Quince and Apple Batter Pudding

SERVES 4–6

This recipe is embedded in my memory as I used to make it as a child with my grandmother, who lived next door. The heady scent of quince wafted round the kitchen as I peeled its downy skin, slicing the tough, grainy flesh directly into acidulated water to stop it turning brown. The quince is stewed with cooking apples and a little sugar, then piled into a pie dish and covered with the sponge mixture. It's really Eve's Pudding with quince. After thirty minutes in a hot oven the topping puffs into soft golden sponge and the smell of the fruit will be driving you crazy with anticipation. Serve it warm, with a sprinkling of caster sugar and home-made custard or a bowl of whipped cream.

a squeeze of lemon
400g quince
400g cooking apples
2 tbsp white sugar
a knob of butter

For the sponge:
50g butter
50g caster sugar, plus 1 tbsp
1 egg
75g self-raising flour
1–2 tbsp milk

Heat the oven to 200°C/gas mark 6. Put the squeeze of lemon and 3 tablespoons of water into a medium-sized lidded pan. Peel the quince and then, using a small, sharp knife, slice small, thin chunks off the core directly into the pan. Stir to coat with the acidulated water. Quarter, peel, core and chop the apples and add to the pan. Add the sugar.

Cover the pan and cook over a low heat, giving the occasional stir until the sugar melts, for 10–15 minutes, until the quince is soft and the apple fluffy.

Butter a 23cm pie dish and add the fruit. To make the sponge, cream the butter until soft, add 50g of sugar and continue beating until pale and fluffy. Whisk the egg lightly with a fork and add gradually, beating until smooth, adding a little sifted flour if it shows signs of curdling.

Fold the remaining flour into the mixture, adding sufficient milk to give a dropping consistency. Spoon the mixture over the fruit. Bake for 25–35 minutes, until the sponge topping is firm and golden. Dust with 1 tablespoon of caster sugar and serve warm; leftovers are delicious cold.

P Piping Bag

This is what you need if you want to make rosettes or pyramids with icing on a cake, or control the shape and size of meringues or pavlova, or fill profiteroles, pipe cream or chocolate, or make neat little French-style macaroons.

The proper name for a piping bag is a forcing bag, because that is what happens: the wizard's-hat-shaped bag is fitted with the appropriate nozzle in the slit at the point of the bag, then filled with whatever is to be piped, and the filling forced out, rather like pumping the bagpipes.

There is a skill to filling the bag. Once the nozzle is fitted and pulled firmly into position, it is held thus with one hand while the sides of the bag are folded back as the filling begins. Once filled, the soft goo is held firm by gathering in and twisting the empty remains of the bag. The filling is forced out by squeezing and tightening the emptying bag with one hand, while directing the nozzle with the other one.

The bag works in conjunction with a set of nozzles, with different sized and shaped holes to give different effects. My set is made of metal, although they are also made of plastic or nylon. I keep them in their own bag so none go missing.

I have various forcing bags. One is made of plastic, another rubbery one is made of thin silicone, but the best is a medium-sized professional standard bag – they come in three sizes – made of waterproof nylon with a loop for hanging it up to dry. I often slob-out, using a strong plastic bag instead, cutting off the corner to hold the nozzle. It gets thrown away after use and there is no messy clearing up.

I also quite like the novel design of the Lékué Decomax (see page 275). It's shaped like a bowl with a spout and made of coloured silicon with a twist-off, see-through lid. A set of six hard, durable plastic nozzles clips on to the spout. It's simple to fill and use and goes in the dishwasher. It's neat.

D-I-Y Eton Mess with Strawberry Sauce

SERVES 8

Eton Mess, an old-Etonian friend once told me, means taking tea in your room with 'a mess' of one or two other boys. He remembered banana mess with mashed banana, two scoops of ice cream and 'lots of cream' but there are countless stories about the origin of the strawberry version, most of which revolve around 'accidents' at the 4th of June College picnic, held every year to celebrate the birthday of King George III.

The College librarian dug out the Eton College recipe for me, dated 1936, and mentioned Pellaprat, a famous French chef regarded with the same reverence as Escoffier. He disguised over-ripe strawberries with a fluff of whipped cream and the fool was served with sponge fingers. Somewhere along the line someone else had the idea of stirring chunks of sweet, chewy meringue into the fool at the last moment.

I like deconstructing Eton Mess, providing all the ingredients for people to make their own mess. It's fascinating: some people go the classic route, others sandwich meringues with whipped cream, others put some of everything on their plate and begin to create. It's certainly a conversation starter.

½ lemon	1.5kg British strawberries
3 egg whites, at room temperature	400g very ripe strawberries
150g white caster sugar, plus 2	1 juicing orange
tablespoons	500ml whipping cream
a knife point of vanilla seeds	caster sugar, to serve

Heat the oven to 150°C/gas mark 2. Smear the scrupulously clean bowl of an electric mixer with lemon juice. Add the egg whites and fit the whisk. Start the machine slowly at first, then, as the whites begin to froth, increase the speed, continuing at top speed until they hold firm peaks. With the machine still running, add the 150g of sugar, one tablespoon at a time, and the vanilla, until the mixture is glossy and stiff.

Line a baking sheet with baking parchment, using a spoonful of meringue to stick the parchment securely. Wet your hands and wipe them across the baking parchment to dampen. Fill a piping bag fitted with a large nozzle and gently squeeze egg-sized swirls-cum-stunted-witch's-hat shapes on to the parchment, leaving space between for expansion. Place the tray in the oven and immediately reduce the heat to

100°C/just below gas mark ¼. Bake for 1½ hours and leave in the oven with the door open to cool.

Rinse then hull the 1.5kg of strawberries and pile them into a large bowl. Hull the very ripe strawberries directly into a saucepan and add the 2 tablespoons of sugar and the juice of the orange. Place the pan over a low heat and stir as the sugar melts. Simmer for 5 minutes, then tip into a sieve over a jug or bowl, forcing as much through as possible with the back of a wooden spoon, scraping underneath so nothing is wasted. Cool. Serve the meringues in a large bowl, with whipped cream in another, the strawberries and jug of strawberry purée and sugar separately, passing everything for people to help themselves.

Profiteroles

SERVES 6, VERY GENEROUSLY

When my sister and her boyfriend arrived from Sydney via India en route for Europe, I made profiteroles for her birthday. We had a big family supper and everyone loved these hollow choux pastry balls stuffed with whipped vanilla cream, dripping with chocolate sauce. Making the pastry is a bit alarming. It requires melting butter with double its weight of water then stirring in about a third of their combined weight of flour. This has to be done in one hit before stirring the ungainly mixture like a whirling dervish until it turns into a stiff yet malleable paste. If this isn't tricky enough, the next bit is even trickier. Whole eggs then have to be quickly beaten into the mixture, beating like mad with a wooden spoon until the slippery paste is once again smooth and taking on a glossy, slightly oily sheen. I don't want to put you off having a go because it is actually very simple once you understand that it is essential to really go for it, beating the paste with a quick blast of energy, working the mixture into submission but without letting any escape from the pan. Fortunately, all this is done off the heat. To begin with, when the eggs are added, the mixture resists them, not allowing the egg to amalgamate, but you just have to keep going and it suddenly all comes together.

The thick, sticky pastry-cum-dough is then spooned into a piping bag and that's good fun too; mucky fun. I like piping food, and choux pastry behaves surprisingly well. Don't worry if your piping technique gives less than perfect results because you can quickly and easily round the walnut-

sized balls of floppy pastry when the top is painted with beaten egg. Alchemy takes place in the oven and the little balls rise and swell, becoming crisp and hollow. Once punctured to allow the hot air to escape, they go back into the oven until golden brown. They are left to cool before filling. It is best to do this at the last moment so the filling doesn't have a chance to make the pastry soggy, although yesterday's profiteroles have a chewy appeal of their own.

It's fun to pile the surprisingly sturdy little puffs into a pyramid, using a smear of the accompanying chocolate sauce to glue them together. You are then heading towards making croquembouche. This showy centrepiece encased in a spun-sugar cage is traditional at French weddings, christenings and first communions.

Whichever presentation you settle on, profiteroles are usually served with lashings of chocolate sauce. Any leftovers of that – some hope – will be delicious poured over vanilla ice cream with a lavish garnish of sugary, toasted almonds. Ice cream, incidentally, or lemon-flavoured crème Chantilly, are good alternative fillings for the profiteroles.

125g plain flour
a pinch of salt
75g butter, plus an extra knob
150ml water
3 medium eggs
1 whisked egg
For the chocolate sauce:
200g dark chocolate (minimum 70% cocoa solids)

300ml water
100g caster sugar
For the filling:
300ml Jersey double cream
½ tsp vanilla extract (optional extra)
You will also need greaseproof paper and a piping bag

Sift the flour and salt together into a bowl. Put 75g butter and 150ml water into a medium-sized saucepan (that can hold all the ingredients) over a low heat. Once the water has boiled and the butter melted, turn off the heat. Add the flour in one hit and immediately start stirring with a wooden spoon, beating vigorously until the mixture forms a stiff dough and comes away from the sides of the pan. This happens very quickly, within a minute. Leave the dough to cool for a few minutes to avoid the possibility of the eggs cooking when added. Crack one egg into a bowl or cup and add to the pan. Beat briskly and thoroughly until the egg is incorporated; unlikely though it seems at first, all will be well. Repeat with a second and third egg.

Heat the oven to 200°C/gas mark 6. Spoon the choux dough into a piping bag fitted with a plain nozzle. To prevent the balls from sliding and the greaseproof paper from slipping, butter a baking sheet and line with lightly buttered greaseproof paper. Pipe balls about the size of a walnut about 2cm apart, not worrying if you can't form a perfect ball. Paint the tops with the whisked egg, using the brush to smooth the top. Cook in the oven for 15 minutes, then reduce the heat to 190°C/gas mark 5 and cook for a further 10 minutes. Remove from the oven and pierce the side of each ball with a sharp knife. Return to the oven for a further 5 minutes, until crisp and golden. Transfer to a wire rack to cool.

To make the chocolate sauce, break the chocolate into a pan with the water and melt over a low heat, stirring until smooth. Add the sugar and continue stirring until dissolved. Bring the sauce to the boil, then reduce the heat and simmer for 10–15 minutes, until the sauce is thick and syrupy with a good coating consistency.

Lightly whisk the cream (with the vanilla extract if using) until it holds soft peaks. Thirty minutes before serving, slit one side of each profiterole and fill with a spoonful of whipped cream. Arrange 3 or 4 profiteroles on each serving plate and pour the hot chocolate sauce (reheated just before you are ready to serve) into a jug for people to serve themselves and be as greedy or abstemious (ha!) as they wish. There is plenty.

P Platters

I love serving food on platters, the bigger the better, with plenty of room for building a feast. The faux dresser by the French windows that give on to my back yard is where I keep most of my collection. Centre stage, as it were, on the top shelf, is my beloved Chinaman, with long sleeves that cover his hands like my old Joseph jersey. He holds a flower in one drooping arm and around him are smaller replicas, all slightly different and framed in almost heart-shaped bubbles. He holds his head despondently and probably laments lost love; he certainly has a tale to tell. He used to live on the top shelf of the oak dresser in the dining room of my childhood home and was a gift to my mother from an aunt married to one of her brothers. After he died, when she was still young, she lived and worked in Hong Kong and shipments of goodies arrived all through my childhood. My mother built up a huge collection of blue and white Chinese porcelain and this platter was always my favourite, eventually becoming mine. It is oblong with a wide lip, curving down to make a large shallow platter-cum-bowl, so good for sauced food or perilous piles. I use it for special occasions because it is too precious to risk mishap.

Other favourites include two large creamy white hexagonal platters, also with a deep curved base, with a blue-painted etched fringe trim. They are surprisingly light and fragile and stamped on the back with '15' in a French typeface but no other markings. These platters were a gift from my friend Christian when he was clearing his capacious armoires prior to moving to the Dordogne after closing his restaurant for the last time. Circular and oblong white platters line up next to a square tray-cum-platter advertising Finest Mince in huge black letters on one side, and stamped in the middle with Smith and Stevenson, Butchers' Complete Outfitters, 207 Gallowgate, Glasgow. It was a gift from my friend Tessa before she left for Sydney, but probably belonged to David, her collector-holic Scottish boyfriend.

I love serving complete meals on platters. It might be meatballs, pasta and sauce, couscous salad, lentil salad, roasted and griddled Mediterranean vegetable salad, leeks vinaigrette, Lebanese tabbouleh resting in curls of lettuce, falafel with sesame sauce, freshly picked crab, fried fish with lemon halves, pea salad with feta and mint, tomato salad, mounds of asparagus, not forgetting fruit salad, the fruit prepared and arranged by type, say strawberries, raspberries, melon and white peach, with sprigs of mint and a bowl of cream. That is my favourite way of serving food, so everyone just tucks in to whatever they fancy, whenever they want it.

Chorizo and Chickpea Salad

SERVES 6

A colourful platter of food to eat on its own or as part of a buffet.

4 large fresh eggs	1 lemon
½ red onion, approx 100g	1 sprig of rosemary, approx 8cm long
2 tbsp red wine vinegar	5 tbsp olive oil
2 new season garlic cloves	2 x 400g tins of chickpeas *(cont.)*

150g Iberico chorizo sausage
4 vine tomatoes or 2 roasted red
  peppers (from a jar)

about 20 mint leaves
a small bunch of chives

Boil the eggs for 5 minutes. Drain, crack all over under cold running water and flake away the shell. Halve lengthways. Very finely slice the onion. Place in a bowl and soak in boiling water for 10 minutes. Toss with the vinegar. Peel and chop the garlic, then crush with a pinch of salt to make a paste. Remove the zest from half the lemon in paper-thin scraps. Strip the rosemary off the stalk and chop to dust with the lemon zest. Squeeze the lemon juice into a mixing bowl. Stir in the garlic paste and rosemary dust, then whisk in the olive oil.

Rinse the chickpeas under cold running water in a sieve. Shake dry and stir into the dressing. Run a sharp knife down the side of the chorizo and peel away the skin. Slice thinly. Core then chop the tomatoes. If using peppers, slice in strips. Squeeze the vinegar out of the limp onions and stir them into the salad. Shred the mint and finely snip 2 tablespoons of chives. Stir the tomatoes or peppers, mint and chives into the salad. Season with salt and lavishly with freshly ground black pepper. Stir again and serve, or chill, covered, until later. To serve, tip on to a platter and edge with hard-boiled egg halves decorated with snipped chives.

P Potato Masher

I have always loved my mum's potato masher. It was probably very ordinary in its heyday but its neat, efficient design went out of fashion years ago. By the time it came back into my life after my mother died, it presented me with a serious conundrum. I had become used to making mashed potato with a Mouli-Légumes (see page 145). The latter gives almost identically good results, is far quicker for mashing a lot of potatoes but far more of a pain to wash up.

I had searched in vain over many years to find a masher like Mum's and here it was, the Real Thing, in my clutches. The downside, I discovered, is that it now rusts. It's made by Tala – who these days specialize in retro bakeware (see page 275) – from hard carbon steel now with the last knockings of what was once a shiny coating. The round disc that does the mashing is covered with cleanly punched holes of two different sizes. This disc is wielded by a sturdy and strong central spine-cum-handle that feeds into a deep wooden handle bleached by constant washing and smooth from years of hot handling.

For a long time, I ignored my Mouli and used Mum's masher, scrubbing it after use with a scourer. Very recently, I discovered a masher (see page 275) that gives it a run for its money. It is German-made from high-quality stainless steel, so it will never rust, and it comes with a lifetime guarantee. The actual mashing disc is almost twice as large as Mum's, and oval rather than round. It too has holes right up to the edge, so it can be worked round a pan to get the last lump of potato. The handle is welded into the sides at the deepest point and rises up flat, so it's perfect for whacking the rim of the pan to shift all the potato lodged in the holes. The actual handle is plump and comfortable, allowing hand and arm to engage in a steady rhythm, making mashing a joy. It looks stumpy and businesslike, which it is.

I love using both Mouli and masher but tend to use the latter for small quantities of mash, and for crushing potatoes, peas or beans. Mum's masher has pride of place on the tool rail behind my hob. Its presence in a kitchen enabled by an inheritance after she died makes me feel grounded. It instantly whisks me back to my childhood and the memory of how we children detested being asked to mash the potatoes for supper. It has the power to make me smile and cry.

Roast Lemon Hake with Crushed Potatoes and Watercress

SERVES 4

Boiled potatoes crushed with watercress and garlic softened in olive oil go with everything, from simply cooked fish like this to roast chicken, pork chops and steak. It's an idea to play around with: instead of the watercress, try adding halved, pitted black olives with chopped flat-leaf parsley and a crumble of feta cheese, or lemon juice and very finely grated zest with extra olive oil, with or without grated courgettes.

Look out for hake, a member of the whiting/cod family we should embrace more. It is much prized by the Spanish, who buy the majority of the hake caught in the British Isles. I've seen fillet upon fillet of merluza, as it's called in Spain, laid out on the wet fish counter at Mercadona, my brother's local supermarket in Moraira, but it can be hard to find here. It's softer than cod, with a milder flavour, but has similarly large bones that are easy to detect. It roasts perfectly.

1kg King Edward potatoes	4 fillets of hake, pollack, cod
2 garlic cloves	or sea bass
4 tbsp olive oil	½ lemon
100g watercress	lemon wedges, to serve
1 small lemon	a splash of your best olive oil

Peel the potatoes, cut into even-sized chunks, rinse and boil in plenty of salted water. Drain. Peel the garlic, chop finely, sprinkle with a little salt and work to a paste. Put 2 tablespoons of olive oil and the garlic in the potato cooking pan and stir-fry briefly over a medium heat. Return the hot potatoes and coarsely chopped watercress. Give a couple of stirs with a wooden spoon to mix, then mash a few times to crush. To cook the fish, heat the oven to 200°C/gas mark 6. Line a small roasting tin with foil, shiny side up, and add a splash of the remaining olive oil. Arrange the fish fillets over the oil then splash with a little more. Squeeze the lemon over the top and season with salt and pepper. Roast for 8–12 minutes, depending on thickness, until just cooked through. Carefully drain the juices from the cooked fish into the potatoes and give a final stir. Serve the fish with the mash and a lemon wedge, adding a splash of your best olive oil.

P Potato Peeler

There are half a dozen potato peelers in my kitchen drawer and a pecking order for using them. One is particularly good at removing paper-thin citrus zest, another is perfect at making optimum-thickness Parmesan curls and another has a light glide which is superb for peeling peppers, tomatoes, celery and other dainty jobs.

It's difficult to recommend a particular potato peeler because they all vary slightly and what is good for me might not suit you. I peel away from my body (except when making Parmesan curls) and I'm right-handed. I like to work quickly with a regular rhythm and my favourite peeler for potatoes for years had a carbon steel blade, recently replaced by an almost identical thin, vertical steel peeler, bought for a pittance from Ikea.

The good news is that potato peelers are incredibly cheap and widely available, so it makes sense to have several and to use them for different jobs. A decent potato peeler makes light work of spud-bashing but is also good for all root vegetables, celery, capsicums, apples and pears, lemons and other citrus fruit.

There are countless potato peeler designs but they tend to be variations on three themes: the horizontal swivel-head, Y-shaped peeler; the vertical swivel peeler; and the old-fashioned rigid metal peeler with a string-bound handle. The latter two types are the most useful for jobs other than peeling. The pointed 'blade' can dig out blemishes and makes neat working of coring apples. Having said that, I have just put in an order for a Fissler potato peeler made of heavy-gauge stainless steel with a rigid blade, suitable for left- and right-handed users. It's dishwasher proof and comes with a lifetime guarantee (see page 275).

Parsnips Molly Parkin

SERVES 4 (6 WITH ROAST LAMB)

Molly Parkin has been described as the Queen of the Sixties because of her pivotal role at the time as fashion editor of the Sunday Times. *Denis Curtis, a food writer friend of Molly's, knew she hated parsnips and invented Parsnips Molly Parkin to persuade her that parsnips could be okay.*

Combining their sweetness with acidic tomatoes and plenty of butter and cream changed her mind. It's what we used to call a layer-bake, in this case thinly sliced, lightly fried parsnips, peeled and seeded tomatoes, grated Gruyère and cream, with a breadcrumb crust.

I was introduced to it at a dinner party given by Dudley Winterbottom, another friend of Molly's, who's been making the dish for years. He likes a rustic, juicy version with thick slices of parsnip and tomato, which he doesn't bother to peel or seed. The next day, after dinner at Dudley's, I looked up the recipe in the Reader's Digest Cook Book *(page 294, published by* The Reader's Digest Association, 1973*) and followed it almost exactly, slicing the parsnips thinly, frying them in oil, peeling and seeding the tomatoes, adding brown sugar and lashings of butter. Later, after a long conversation with Molly's daughter Sophie, I picked up a tip for slicing the parsnips super-thin with a potato peeler and doing away with frying them. I peeled but didn't seed the tomatoes, ditched the sugar and cut down the amount of butter. It's a dish that is best cooked long and slow so it remains moist and creamy with a thick gratinéed crust. Try it next time you plan a roast or serve it alone with a garlicky escarole salad.*

6 medium parsnips, approx 1 kg	50g butter
6 plum tomatoes, approx 600g	300ml single or double cream
150g Gruyère cheese	50g crust-free white bread

Heat the oven to 170°C/gas mark 3 and boil the kettle. Trim the parsnips, then peel and use a potato peeler to slice them; size and shape is immaterial. Work quickly, slicing away from you, until you hit the woody core. Discard this. Cover the tomatoes with boiling water. Count to 30, drain, then cut out the core in a cone shape and swipe away the skin. Slice the tomatoes. Grate the cheese.

Smear a 1.5 litre capacity casserole dish (deep is best) with some of the butter. Reckon on four layers. Start with parsnip, salt, pepper and a little cream. Cover with a layer of tomatoes. Spread with more cream and some of the cheese. Continue thus, finishing with cream and cheese. Tear the bread into pieces, blitz to make crumbs and sprinkle over the top. Dot lavishly with butter. Bake for 1 hour.

Limoncello

MAKES APPROX 2 LITRES

All through art school, my eldest son Zach worked a shift a week and holidays at the River Café. His best friend from school, Alan Simeoni, is half Italian and together they hatched a plot to make limoncello. Alan got the recipe from an old couple that lived up the hill from the family house near Rome, who had a vineyard and make their own wine. Zach collected hock-style bottles from the River Café bottle bank and bought yellow-ended cork stoppers for the bottles. He hand-painted and scripted elongated lemon-shaped labels. Alan brought grain alcohol back from Rome (it's on sale in Italy but not here) and Zach a tray of Amalfi lemons from the restaurant. I remember coming home to a sticky floor, a freezer full of bottles and a lot of giggling. It's thanks to Alan's dad, Manfredo, that the recipe was tracked down for me to include here.

There is a website devoted to making limoncello (see page 276), with more tips than it's possible to imagine. If you go to Naples, check out Limone on via del Tribunali, and buy the real thing dispensed into slim bottles from what looks like a giant tea urn.

8–10 lemons, preferably unwaxed ones from Amalfi or Sorrento	1 litre water
1 litre pure alcohol (or vodka)	600g sugar

If the lemons are not organic and unwaxed, wash them in warm water before you start. Use your favourite potato peeler to peel them, sweeping down the length of the lemon. Remove only the zest; you do not want any white pith. Place the zest in one or two large jars with lids and add the alcohol to cover. Fit the lid and leave for at least 15 days and up to 40, swirling the jar most days.

When the time is up, place the water and sugar in a pan and boil for 7 minutes, stirring initially until the sugar has melted. Strain the alcohol to collect the lemon zest, then strain again through muslin or a very fine sieve into the jars. Add the cooled sugar water to the alcohol, mix well, and leave in a cool dark place for at least 1 month. Use kitchen paper to blot any residual particles accumulated in the neck of the jar. Strain into bottles, add labels and hey presto, it's done. Store in the freezer.

P Pudding Basins

My mother kept her collection of cream-coloured china pudding basins stacked inside an extra large mixing bowl, hidden away in the cupboard under the stairs. They came out at Christmas for the inevitable puddings, but one or two were used regularly during the colder months for steamed sponge and suet puddings. The bowls were all identical, deep with sloping sides and a ridge on the outside rim for securing the square of torn sheet she used, tied on with string, then knotted over the top to make a handle to lift the basin in and out of the pan. I own some of her basins, mine by default, never returned after we'd eaten the Christmas pudding she made every year, long after I'd left home and started my own family. Sometimes, of course, she was with us but I'm glad I have those original Mason Cash basins, now deemed vintage (see page 275) and selling for three or four times the price of new basins.

Mason Cash is one of only a few companies making traditional ceramic kitchen equipment from traditional materials in the traditional way. The origins of the company go back to the early 1800s, and a pottery in Church Gresley, Derbyshire, run by a succession of master potters. In 1901, when Tom Cash acquired the pottery, it was run by 'Bossy' Mason, and it became Mason Cash and Co. The design of the basins, and their much-copied tawny-glazed stoneware mixing bowl, remains virtually unchanged. Although they don't have a royal warrant, the basins are chosen by the Royal Household for the plum puddings traditionally given out to staff at Christmas.

The basins come in a range of sizes: my favourites are no. 42, the diddy 7.5cm high by 13.5cm diameter, which holds 400ml, and no. 30, which holds just over a litre and is the perfect size for a family pudding.

They are widely available, even in sets of six (see page 275).

Steak and Kidney Pudding

SERVES 8, MAKES 2 PUDDINGS

Of all the dishes that epitomize British comfort food, something we crave on chilly, dark winter nights, it has to be steak and kidney pudding. I've got a couple steaming away right now in my kitchen. The aroma is almost palpable, truly rich and intense as the suet pastry swells and burnishes against the pudding bowl while it soaks up the thick, meaty juices from slowly cooked steak and kidney. When I mentioned to friends, particularly male ones, that I planned to make steak and kidney pudding, everyone went into rhapsodies. If my straw poll is anything to go by, the king of steamed puddings is without doubt one of our culinary national treasures.

For my mother, and her mother before her, making suet pudding was only possible if the butcher had kidney fat to spare. This would be grated or finely chopped and used instead of lard to make the pastry. These days most people, including me, rely on Atora. The contents of the packet look like little white worms and it takes a bit of kneading to work it into what becomes an incredibly soft and malleable pastry that will swell like bread dough if left for too long. When cooked it has a soft, slightly spongy texture that is all at once creamy and cakey but undeniably pastry-like. As an experiment, I made one of my puddings with marginally less calorific vegetarian 'light suet'. It looks, responds and tastes pretty much like the real McCoy, which is surprising because it's made from palm oil and rice flour. The other surprise is that steak and kidney pudding is incredibly simple to make and economical too, requiring an inexpensive cut of stewing beef like chuck or skirt, or a mixture of the two, and calf or ox kidney. Traditionally all the ingredients go into the pastry-lined pudding bowl raw, although the cooking time can be halved – from 4 to 2 hours – if they are cooked first. I prefer the taste and texture of the former and like to savour the build-up of appetizing smells that go with it, although the steam fug created isn't so great.

Mashed potato or mash with celeriac is what you want with steak and kidney pudding. I ran out of milk when I made mine and substituted mascarpone, resulting in very superior mash. Leftovers were whizzed with chicken stock and a little milk to make a sublime cream of potato and celeriac soup garnished with chives and freshly grated nutmeg. Carrots and sprouts complete this truly comforting meal.

I used two medium-sized traditional pudding basins, Mason Cash's no. 30, which each hold just over a litre of liquid. You could use smaller or larger basins or make one pudding instead of two – just adjust the ingredients accordingly. Leftover pastry, incidentally, should you have any, is superb for Cornish pasties and you'll find recipes in Pasties, *published by Mabecron Books (2008).*

For the pastry:
500g self-raising flour, plus 1 tbsp
250g Atora shredded suet or
   vegetarian 'light' alternative
approx 8 tbsp cold water
For the filling:
1 large onion
1½ tbsp vegetable oil
250g calf or ox kidneys
approx 2 tbsp flour

1 tsp finely chopped thyme, optional
approx 25g butter
750ml beef stock (cubes are fine)
English mustard and redcurrant
   jelly, to serve
For extra gravy:
1 tbsp soft butter
1 tbsp flour
1 tsp redcurrant jelly

Sift the flour into a mixing bowl, then mix in the suet and ½ teaspoon of salt. Add the water, a little at a time, to bind into a light, spongy pastry. Rest for 30 minutes while you prepare everything else.

Halve, peel and finely chop the onion. Soften in the oil in a frying pan. Tip on to a plate to cool. Trim away the fat and sinew from the steak and cut into kebab-size chunks or 1 × 1 × 3cm strips. Cut the kidneys into slightly smaller pieces, discarding the white core. Mix the meat and kidneys and dust lavishly with flour. Mix with the onion. Season with salt and pepper, adding chopped thyme if liked.

Halve the pastry and flour a work surface. Lavishly butter 2 × 1.1 litre capacity pudding basins. Working on one pudding at a time, set aside just over a quarter of the pastry for a lid. Roll the pastry into a circle to fit the basin with a 2cm overhang. Repeat with the second pudding. Add the filling and sufficient stock to moisten but not drench or cover the filling. Roll each lid to fit. Moisten the overhang, fit the lid and pinch and roll the two together to seal securely. Pleat a large piece of tinfoil and place loosely over the top. Tie it securely, going round twice, with string under the rim of the basin, then loop a handle across the top of the pudding, allowing plenty of room for the pudding to expand. As it will. Roll the excess foil up and over the string and lift the puddings into two large saucepans with well-fitting lids. Add sufficient boiling water to come two-thirds the way up the basin, fit the lid and boil for 4 hours. Check every hour or so and top up with more boiling water.

To make the gravy, mash the butter and flour together. Bring the leftover beef stock to the boil. Add the redcurrant jelly and scraps of butter and flour, whisking to incorporate. Taste and adjust the seasoning with salt and pepper. Pour into a jug to serve.

To serve, lift the pudding out of the bowl on to a plate. Remove the foil. Wrap a napkin around the basin with the top crust showing and serve from the basin with extra gravy, vegetables, English mustard and redcurrant jelly.

Marmalade Sponge Pudding

SERVES 6–8

When I was a child growing up in the fifties and sixties, family meals always included pudding. Pies, crumbles, steamed sponge and suet puddings, rice pudding and semolina, puddings designed to fill you up, and usually far more desirable than the main course. I loved them all, particularly jam roly-poly and syrup sponge pudding, but my all-time favourite was steamed sponge pudding with marmalade. My mother was a great one for cooking just about everything in a pressure cooker, but I associate steamed pudding with the kitchen and hall windows fugging up and a constant rattling of china (this was from the upturned saucer at the bottom of the pan which avoided direct heat to the pudding) as the pudding steamed away.

It was years before I made one myself, but with the help of a food processor, they are as quick and easy to make as a sponge cake. The ingredients and method might be similar, but the results are quite different. Long, slow steaming in water (rather than above it) gives the texture a swollen, almost crumbly, damp finish. It's light but somehow very rich and dense. The colour of the crumb ends up different too. While a sponge cake is pale, a sponge pudding made with caster sugar turns golden and surprisingly dark when made with soft, pale brown sugar.

I made this one after a bout of marmalade-making. That's what my mother and her mother before her used to do, using up what was left in the pan, not quite sufficient to fill a jar. Also waiting to be tidied away was the remains of a jar of stem ginger, and I decided to marry the two. The result, even if I say it myself, is fantastic. Be sure to serve it with custard.

125g soft butter

100g caster sugar

2 large eggs (at room temperature)

100g self-raising flour

1 tsp baking powder

2 tbsp milk

4 tbsp Seville orange marmalade (see recipe opposite if you want to make your own)

50g stem ginger in syrup

Boil the kettle. Dice 100g of butter into a mixing bowl. Add the sugar and beat until light and fluffy. Whisk 1 egg at a time, beating into the mixture. Sift the flour, baking powder and a pinch of salt together. Add to the bowl gradually, beating until smooth. Slacken the mixture slightly by beating in the milk. Chop the ginger into dolly-mixture size pieces. Fold 1 tablespoon of chopped marmalade into the mixture, followed by the ginger.

Cut out a disc of baking paper to fit the top of a 1.1 litre capacity pudding basin. Lavishly butter the basin and use the rest to smear one side of the baking paper. Spoon the remaining marmalade into the basin. Add the pudding mixture, swirling from the outside in to avoid dislodging the marmalade. Rest the buttered side of the baking paper on top and cover with a sheet of tinfoil pleated in the centre to allow room for the pud to expand. Tie with string to secure, looping the end over the top to make a handle. If you have a plastic basin that comes with a lid, don't bother with the foil. Place an upturned saucer in a lidded pan that can hold the pudding comfortably. Sit the pudding on the saucer and fill with boiling water from the kettle, to come about two-thirds of the way up. Cover with the lid. Place on a medium-low heat and simmer for 2 hours. Check occasionally to see if the water needs topping up; it shouldn't, but check just in case.

When the pudding is ready, carefully remove from the pan and even more carefully – watch out for the steam – remove the foil or lid. Quickly run a palette knife round the inside edge of the basin. Place an upturned deep plate or dish over the pudding and quickly invert. Serve with custard.

Seville Orange Marmalade

FILLS 6-8 X 340G JARS

10 Seville oranges
2 lemons
2 litres water

2kg sugar, 500g of which should be
preserving sugar

Place the oranges and lemons in the given water in a large lidded pan placed over a very low heat. Cover and simmer until soft. Use a saucepan lid to keep them immersed, piercing the fruit after about 20 minutes to encourage immersion. The time for this varies depending on the quality of the fruit, but allow at least 45 minutes. Lift the fruit into a colander over a bowl and leave to cool. Dissolve the sugar in the orange water.

Halve the softened fruit, scrape out the seeds and place in a jelly bag or fold of muslin. Tie with string and hang over the side of the pan. Slice or chop the peel thinly; I do all of it because I like chunky marmalade, but how much peel is a matter of taste. Stir the peel into the liquid. Bring to a simmer, stirring to ensure the sugar is dissolved, then boil hard, stirring occasionally, until setting point is reached. This varies and may be as little as 5 minutes but is more likely to be 15. Once it begins to look syrupy, test by placing a teaspoonful on a saucer. Cool, then push with your finger. If it wrinkles it's done. Pour into hot sterilized jam jars, cover and cool before storing. Ready to eat immediately.

Q Quarter Pounder Burger Press

Even if you aren't a McDonald's habitué, you are sure to be aware of the Quarter Pounder. It was created by Al Bernardin, a McDonald's franchisee, in 1971 after spotting a niche for an adult burger with a higher ratio of meat to bun. A year later it was on McDonald's national American menu, soon spreading to branches all over the world. Thanks to *Pulp Fiction*, the movie, we all became familiar with the Quarter Pounder's other names, Hamburger Royale or McRoyal, but most particularly the cheese version, Royale with Cheese.

It's easy enough to make burgers without any special equipment but I've fallen for a modest little gadget called the Quarter Pounder Burger Press, from Lakeland (see page 274). It comprises three pieces of white plastic. They fit together to mould and press whatever you want to turn into a burger. It could be minced steak or lamb shoulder, duck, chicken, pork, even venison, or finely chopped fish. The result is a neat burger approximately 10cm in diameter.

The kit comes with 100 'easy-release' waxed paper circles, so burgers can be stacked and frozen, just like they are at the supermarket.

Vietnamese Chicken Patties with Mint Salad and Roasted Peanuts

SERVES 4

Minced chicken or pork is what you need for these light and bright pattie-cum-burgers. Flavoured with kaffir lime leaves, lemongrass, ginger, chilli and fresh coriander, they are fried, chunkily sliced, and piled over a noodle salad laced with thinly sliced cucumber and fennel, mint and more coriander. A nuoc nam-style dressing with garlic, nam pla, lime juice and sweet chilli sauce sets the flavours singing. The finale is crushed roasted and salted peanuts and a zig-zag of sweet chilli sauce. Bean thread noodles, incidentally, end up transparent. If peanuts are off radar, use cashews instead.

25g finely chopped shallots
1 tbsp fresh lime juice
1 lemongrass stalk
4 kaffir lime leaves
25g fresh ginger
15g bunch coriander
1 red bird's-eye chilli
500g organic minced chicken or
    pork
1 tbsp vegetable oil
For the salad:
100g vermicelli bean thread or rice
    noodles
125g cucumber

1 small fennel, approx 125g
10g bunch coriander
5g small mint leaves
For the dressing:
1 garlic clove
1 tbsp Thai fish sauce (nam pla)
2 tbsp fresh lime juice
1 tbsp Thai sweet chilli sauce
For the garnish:
2 tbsp roasted salted peanuts
1 tbsp Thai sweet chilli sauce

Put the shallots and lime juice into a mixing bowl. Extract the inner lemongrass shoot and finely chop. Cut out the lime leaf spines, make a pile of the leaves, slice into thin strips, then into tiny dice. Peel the ginger and grate very finely. Finely chop the coriander. Split the chilli, scrape away the seeds, slice into thin batons and then into tiny dice.

Crumble the meat over the shallots and scatter with the prepared seasonings. Season lightly with salt. Use your hands to mix and mulch. Divide into four. If using a quarter pounder burger maker, line with a wax disc, add a quarter of the mix, press evenly with your fingers, cover with a second waxed disc, then press to form a neat burger shape. Continue with the remaining mixture. To make the patties by hand, form each quarter of the mix into a disc approximately 10cm diameter × 2cm deep. Keep chilled (up to 24 hours or freeze) until required.

To make the salad, soak the noodles in cold water for 10 minutes until soft enough to cut into manageable lengths (approximately 8cm). Drain, cover with boiling water and leave for 15 minutes to soften. Peel the cucumber, use a teaspoon to scrape out the seeds, then slice into thin half-moons. Trim the fennel and halve lengthways. Slice thinly across the halves. Chop the coriander. Drain the soft noodles.

Peel and chop the garlic and crush to a paste. Mix with the remaining dressing ingredients. Add the noodles, mix thoroughly, then add the rest of the salad ingredients. Mix. Place the peanuts in a plastic bag and bash to crumbs with something heavy.

To complete the dish, heat the oil in a non-stick frying pan and fry the patties for 3–4 minutes a side, until golden and just cooked through. Slice on the slant into 4 roughly equal pieces. Give the salad a final toss, pile into the middle of four plates or bowls and top with the pattie slices. Scatter with peanuts and a swirl of chilli sauce.

R Ramekins

Ramekins look like dolls' tea party soufflé dishes. They are identical to their big brothers, just scaled down, a miniature version of a white porcelain, straight-sided soufflé dish. While they can be used for individual soufflés and gratins, they are great for any portion-control baked or chilled dish – pies, baked custards, sweet and savoury mousses, jellies and sponge cakes. They are perfect for potted shrimps, for crème brûlée and crème caramel, and any little creamy pudding. They're handy too for nuts and olives, dips and sauces, cheese and egg dishes like coddled eggs, *oeufs en gelée* and *oeufs en cocotte*. Dishes that need high temperatures, or to go under the grill, or be fired by a blowtorch, or to go in the fridge or freezer, these cute little dishes can cope with everything. They are made in various sizes: I have diddy ones that hold 50ml, but most are 150–250ml capacity. Look out for them in charity shops and jumble sales. You will notice that they vary very slightly but quite noticeably from manufacturer to manfacturer – the thickness, size and depth of the rim, weight, etc. – my favourites are French Pullivuyt.

Lemon Posset with Roast Rhubarb

SERVES 6–8

Lemon posset is the cooked equivalent of syllabub and similarly quick and simple to prepare. Both are made by souring and thickening cream with lemon juice and sweetening it with sugar. For posset, the sugar is dissolved in the cream and boiled briefly in a large pan so it can rise and expand before the lemon juice is added. As the cream cools in individual little pots it sets firm, like home-made lemon curd, but melts on the tongue in exquisite mouthfuls of creamy, lemony angel food. It is the perfect make-ahead dessert and was on the menu for the twenty-first birthday celebrations at the Blueprint Café overlooking Tower Bridge. It was also Jeremy Lee's swansong before he left for Quo Vadis. He served the creamy little puds topped with similarly soft, impossibly slender slices of pale rhubarb. Such a clever idea; here's how to do it.

600ml double cream	2 large lemons
150g caster sugar	200g rhubarb

Heat the oven to 180°C/gas mark 4. Pour the cream into a medium-large pan. Add 125g of sugar and the zest from 1 lemon. Squeeze the lemons into a measuring jug – you want 100ml of juice. Bring the cream slowly to the boil, stirring with a wooden spoon as the sugar melts. Increase the heat and boil for 2 minutes.

Take off the heat and whisk in the lemon juice. Cover the pan with a stretch of clingfilm to avoid a skin forming and leave for 15 minutes to infuse. Strain into a jug and pour into 6 or 8 ramekins, stumpy glasses or similar, leaving room for the rhubarb. Drape a sheet of clingfilm over the top, cool, then chill for at least 60 minutes and preferably several hours.

Trim, rinse and cut the rhubarb into slices approximately 5mm thick. Arrange, snuggled up closely, on a shallow roasting tin. Lightly dredge with the remaining 25g of sugar. Cover tightly with foil. Roast for 8 minutes.

Remove from the oven and leave, still covered, to cool. Keep thus in the fridge until you are ready to scoop with a metal spatula on top of the little puddings.

R Roasting Rack

A roasting rack is designed to fit inside a roasting pan and hold the joint above the fat and juices released as it cooks. Some are simple trays that sit inside the base of the pan, others are adjustable in a V-shape to hold different sized joints or birds.

Many, like mine, which also has handles in the middle to enable easy lifting, are sold with the roasting pan. In my case, I made the mistake of assuming the professional quality roasting pan with big easy-to-grip welded handles would fit into my oven. It didn't. So I kept the rack and gave the pan to one of my sons. There is a moral there.

Gressingham Duck with French Peas and Potatoes

SERVES 4

A Gressingham duck is a cross-breed of wild mallard and Pekin. One duck tends to weigh two kilos, providing plenty of meat for four hungry people, with sufficient leftovers to fill Peking pancakes for two with spring onions and plum sauce, a noodle soup supper with rice noodles, peas and coriander or duck Parmentier with gratinéed mash. It is meaty and gamey and has a high proportion of breast meat. I like it roasted so the skin is very crisp and dark and the meat cooked brown rather than rosy.

For this delicious roast, some of the fat is used to roast diced, blanched potatoes, and peas with scraps of bacon and shallots are cooked in stock made from the giblets. I like to carve the duck and pile the meat over the peas on one big platter but you may prefer to carve it at the table. Full details of how to carve a duck can be found on the Gressingham Foods website (see page 276), but basically, remove the legs, then the breasts in whole fillets, then get slicing.

Usefully, duck preparation, stock, the first stage of potato cooking and preparing and cooking the onions with the bacon, can all be done 24 hours in advance. Remove the duck from the fridge an hour before you start cooking it.

2kg Gressingham duck

2 onions

1 carrot

1 bay leaf

a bunch of thyme

20 shallots

5 rashers of rindless streaky bacon

15g butter

900g potatoes

500g frozen petits pois

1 tsp flour

2 tbsp chopped flat-leaf parsley

redcurrant jelly, to serve

Boil the kettle. Remove the giblets from the duck. Set aside the liver for another meal. Place the rest in a pan with 600ml of water, 1 chopped but unpeeled onion, the carrot, bay leaf and half the thyme. Simmer for about 45 minutes. Strain; you want 400ml, so simmer to reduce if necessary.

Heat the oven to 220°C/gas mark 7. Pierce the duck all over with a fork. Rinse with boiling water from the kettle to make the holes open. Drain and pat dry. Trim, peel and quarter the second onion. Rinse out the cavity, season with salt and pepper and fill with the onion and the remaining thyme. Place on a roasting rack inside a roasting pan. Roast for 20 minutes, then reduce the heat to 180°C/gas mark 5 and cook for a further 1 hour 40 minutes, or until the skin is crisp and dark golden, and the juices run clear when it is pierced with a skewer. During the cooking, drain (and save) the fat a couple of times.

Re-boil the kettle. Place the unpeeled shallots in a bowl and cover with boiling water. Leave to soak for 10 minutes. Make a bacon pile and slice across the rashers into lardons. Separate the pieces. Melt the butter in a medium-small, heavy-based, lidded pan, add the bacon and cook for a few minutes until the fat begins to melt. Drain the shallots, trim the ends, remove the skin and separate any 'double' shallots. Stir into the bacon, cover and cook gently, stirring every so often, for at least 30 minutes, until the shallots are cooked through and the bacon is crisp.

Boil or steam the potatoes until tender. Drain, leave until cool enough to handle, then peel and cut into dice about the size of a large sugar lump. Twenty minutes before the duck is ready to come out of the oven, pour 4 tablespoons of duck fat into a shallow roasting pan. Add the potatoes, turning them through the fat. Place on the top shelf of the oven.

When the duck's time is up, transfer it to a warmed platter and cover loosely with foil. Rest for at least 15 minutes before carving. Keep an eye on the potatoes, turning if necessary; you want them golden and crusty. Cook the peas in salted boiling water. Drain.

Drain the fat from the roasting pan, leaving behind about 1 tablespoon of fat and any meaty juices. Stir the flour into the pan, then add the stock and stir briskly to make a thin, smooth gravy. Stir in the hot shallots, bacon and drained peas. Simmer together for a few minutes to consolidate and reduce the liquid slightly. Stir in the parsley and any duck juices. Transfer to a hot serving dish. Place the potatoes in a second dish. Carve the duck at the table or before you plate up the peas and potatoes, and serve with redcurrant jelly.

R Roasting Tins

I keep my roasting tins lined up on their sides in a deep, wide cupboard under my oven, which was built at eye level into the old kitchen chimneybreast. They are arranged by size next to the baking sheets, pizza pans and pans that came with the oven. My favourites look bright and new but aren't. They are made of heavy-duty, hard-anodized aluminium by Alan Silverwood (see page 275). They won't warp in very hot ovens, or over direct heat (when making gravy) and are magic to clean, only needing a soak and scrub with a mild scourer to bring them back to rights. Vim and Viakal are my solutions for burnt-on food.

The pans divide into two types: the shallow tins, in two sizes (21 x 30cm and 37 x 27cm) and two depths (1.5 and 2.5cm), and large deep ones. Two of the smaller size fit side by side on my oven shelves and are the perfect size for roast potatoes for two. These pans are deceptively Tardis-like, and will hold up to a dozen round or pointed red peppers, four mackerel, a brace of game birds or a spatchcocked chicken. I have two favourite large pans, both 24 x 36cm and 7cm deep. The oldest cost a fortune and is made of heavy stainless steel with a reinforced base and a slightly raised central panel that means the joint is raised above the fat or juices that swim around it. It has slightly curved sides and a deep lip at each end for lifting the pan in and out of the oven. It's been in constant use for twenty-odd years but still scrubs up like new. The other, newer pan, from Lakeland (see page 275), is made of heavy steel with a rolled rim and all-over non-stick surface. It has no lip or handles, so is a bit tricky to manoeuvre with a big joint of meat, but I love it for party-size dishes like moussaka, pastitsio and stuffed peppers. It is useful too for marinating kebabs and large pieces of meat for the barbecue, for baked apples for a blow-out and stuffed marrow from the allotment.

My advice would be to buy the sturdiest pans you can afford. Treat them well and they will last a lifetime.

Char Siu and Rice

SERVES 2

The supermarkets have caught up with our predilection for belly pork, selling large pieces as joints and packs of neatly trimmed slices. Either is perfect for this approximation of char siu, the dark, glossy roast pork that hangs glistening in many Chinatown restaurant windows. With boiled rice and a few sprigs of coriander it makes a delicious prepare-ahead, greedy hands-on supper.

500g pork belly slices
150g basmati rice
about 8 sprigs of coriander
For the marinade:
2 tbsp runny honey
1 tsp rice wine

1 tbsp soy sauce
1 tbsp tomato ketchup
1 tsp water
3 tbsp hoisin sauce

Make 2 or 3 diagonal cuts in the belly slices in opposite directions, cutting halfway through the width; when cooked the meat will fan in traditional char siu style. Mix together 1 tablespoon of honey with all the other marinade ingredients. Return the pork to its container or place in a shallow dish and pour over the marinade. Cover with clingfilm and chill for at least an hour and up to 24 hours.

Heat the oven to 200°C/gas mark 6. Place a cake rack over an oven tray half-filled with water (to catch drips) and line up the belly slices. Roast for 30 minutes. Turn, smear with marinade and roast for a further 30 minutes.

To cook the rice, rinse until the water runs clean, place in a pan and cover with boiling water. Stand for 5 minutes, swirl to remove the starch, then drain and place in a pan with 225ml of water. Bring to the boil, turn the heat very low, cover the pan and cook for 10 minutes. Turn off the heat, do not remove the lid and leave for 10 minutes. Fork up the rice before serving. Glaze the pork with honey and serve over the rice with a few sprigs of coriander.

Turbot in a Salt Crust with Aioli

SERVES 6

Cooking a large fish to share with family and friends is always a bit daunting, with the fear of over- or undercooking the beast. For a special fish like a large turbot or sea bass, encasing the fish in gravelly sea salt is a stunning solution. The salt sets hard and the fish steams evenly and very quickly, ending up perfectly seasoned. The pearly white flesh with its dense yet delicate texture slides off the bone in pleasingly silky flakes and is delicious with mild aioli, just garlicky enough to be noticeable but not enough to swamp the delicate fish. All you need with this is new potatoes. Steam or boil them before you toss them with butter and chopped chives or a little parsley. A good alternative, though, if you are off carbs, is lightly cooked green beans topped with a generous mound of finely diced tomato, the merest hint of red wine vinegar and a splash of your best olive oil.

approx 2kg turbot or sea bass,
   gutted but not scaled
fennel stalks (optional)
1kg rock salt (unrefined coarse
   Atlantic sea salt)
2 large lemons

For the aioli:
2 new season garlic cloves
2 fresh egg yolks
2 tsp Grey Poupon or Maille Dijon
   mustard
200ml olive oil
½ lemon

Heat the oven to 220°C/gas mark 7. For the turbot, spread half the salt in a parchment-lined roasting tin that can hold the fish snugly. Top with the fish, black skin uppermost, and cover with the remaining salt, not worrying if head and tail aren't submerged. To cook a sea bass, rinse inside and out and pat dry with kitchen paper. Stuff the cavity with fennel stalks, if you have them. Spread half the salt in a foil-lined roasting tin that can hold the fish comfortably. Lay the fish in the middle. Pull up the sides of the foil so the salt rests against the fish, crushing the foil so it makes a salt-lined boat-cum-coffin for the fish. Cover with the remaining salt, not worrying if head and tail aren't submerged. In both instances, sprinkle with about 6 tablespoons of cold water to moisten the salt and encourage it to harden. Slacken the foil around the sea bass so it isn't tight.

Bake the fish on a middle shelf for 20 minutes. Take it out of the oven and leave for 5 minutes. Carefully lift the fish on to a serving platter. Crack the salt shell and use a metal spatula to carefully lift it off in pieces. Slice down the backbone to halve the skin and peel it away to reveal the pearly flesh. Slide the spatula under the flesh from centre to side and remove the fillets. Remove the backbone before tackling the rest of the fish. Serve with a lemon wedge for each person.

I usually make aioli in my large, granite mortar. Chop the garlic and crush to a paste with a pinch of salt. Mix the egg yolks and mustard into the garlic with the pestle or a wooden spoon. Add the olive oil in a dribble whilst beating constantly with a wooden spoon, adding a squeeze of lemon juice every so often. Continue until thick and wobbly.

R Rolling Pin

One of my regular Sunday morning 'pocket money' jobs from quite a young age was to make the pastry and then the custard – Bird's – for lunch. The flour was measured out in tablespoons into a big china mixing bowl with a pinch of salt added. I was given a chunk of lard, sometimes margarine or butter too, which had to be cut into small pieces into the flour. The trick, I was told, was to work quickly, rubbing the sticky lard into the flour with my fingertips. I couldn't bear the feeling of the soft, slippery fat stuck under my fingernails, and hurried to finish so I could rush upstairs to the bathroom and scrub my nails back to normal.

I was never allowed to roll the pastry. That was a job for Mum. She had a slim, long wooden rolling pin, probably made of beechwood, with fixed handles, that she floured deftly, sliding the pin up and down her floury hands until dusty white. She cut the pastry into two pieces, rolling one to cover the pie plate, then the other for the lid. Her rolling technique was very particular: always away from her body, quickly moving the pastry with her hands so it could be rolled evenly, gauging with her eye the size she wanted. When she was done, she loosely rolled the pastry round the pin, then lifted and gently unrolled it under or over the filling, pinching and tucking, smoothing and positioning. I loved watching her work so quickly and neatly, trimming the edges and using the trimmings to cut out leaf shapes to decorate the top. Afterwards, clearing the floury surface and scraping up the little bits of pastry that stuck to the surface was my job.

I felt a similar awe years later when I watched Valeria and Margherita Simili, better known as the Simili sisters, thinly roll pasta dough for tortellini at their house in Bologna. They used long wooden rolling pins that tapered very gradually to the ends, giving greater control for very thin pastry or paste, and small shapes. A much smaller version of a *matarello* is used for chapattis. It comes with a special round chapatti board with three little feet that make it easier to turn the board to achieve a perfect circle. One day I am going to treat myself to one.

When I first moved to London the only pies my flatmates and I ate were Fray Bentos. When I went home for a visit, I would beg my mother to make a real steak and kidney pie or a gooseberry or rhubarb pie with thick Bird's custard and me having all the skin. I didn't attempt pastry-making myself for years and years. When I did, all those memories came flooding back. The flat where I lived wasn't strong on kitchen equipment, so instead of a rolling pin I used a milk bottle. Any smooth bottle will do the job perfectly but given the choice I'd choose a hock bottle because it's longer and thinner than most other bottles. Professional chefs use rolling pins without handles and I own one myself, made (though sadly no longer) by Eddingtons. It's long and slim and made of red silicone-wrapped metal, so it's always cool, but if I remember, I pop it into the fridge just before baking. I use Mum's old beech rolling pin for the many other jobs a rolling pin can help with. Crushing nuts (in a sealed plastic bag), rolling dried bread into toasted crumbs, bashing digestive biscuits for cheesecake base, and curling *tuiles* (thin almond biscuits) around. It is perfect, too, for pounding meat for escalopes.

There is a boggling choice of rolling pins available in various materials apart from wood. I've seen bamboo and basketweave pins, although stainless steel, marble and glass are thought to be particularly good because they are so cold. When I bought my house it coincided with Richard Shepherd clearing out the huge basement below Langan's Brasserie. My builder and I went along for a recce and came away with enough marble for all my kitchen work surfaces. So, when I slap my pastry around, I sometimes think of the chefs who toiled at this incredibly thick, icy cold marble, way back when Langan's was Le Coq d'Or.

Chicken Escalopes, Tomato Sauce and Linguine

SERVES 2

Fresh tomato sauce, particularly one made with butter and very little else, is always a revelation. For an intense tomato taste, it's vital, of course, to use so-called vine tomatoes, preferably grown in soil and natural conditions. I used a huge, ridged tomato weighing half a kilo that had been sitting on my windowsill for a week, too beautiful to cook immediately. It's a coeur de boeuf (bull's heart), grown in the south of France and many areas of Italy, available from discerning greengrocers such as Andreas (see page 276), who supply the River Café. With a hint of garlic and a few leaves of basil, the sauce has a clean flavour worthy of the extra effort involved in skinning and seeding the fruit. Here it's spooned over linguine, making the perfect accompaniment to crunchy little chicken escalopes, the whole lot served with a generous grating of Parmesan. A lovely plate of food.

500g large vine tomatoes	50g fresh breadcrumbs
1 garlic clove	150g linguine
40g butter, plus an extra knob	1 tbsp groundnut oil
3 chicken thigh fillets	15 fresh basil leaves
2 tbsp flour	freshly grated Parmesan
1 egg, beaten	

Pour boiling water over the tomatoes. Count to 30, then drain, core, peel and quarter. Place a sieve over a bowl. Scrape the seeds into the sieve (the surrounding jelly is richly flavoured). Dice the flesh. Crack the garlic, skin, chop and crush to a paste with a pinch of salt. Melt 25g of butter in a frying pan over a medium-low heat. Stir in the garlic and cook, stirring constantly, for a couple of minutes before adding the tomatoes. Stir. Press the seed juices through the sieve with the back of a wooden spoon and add that too. Simmer, stirring occasionally, for about 10 minutes, until thick and smooth. Season to taste with salt and pepper, then beat in scraps of the remaining butter to thicken further.

Slice each chicken fillet on the diagonal into four similar-sized pieces. Arrange on a sheet of clingfilm, cover with a second sheet and bash a few times with a rolling pin. Place the flour in one shallow bowl, the egg in a second and the crumbs in a third. Dip the chicken into the flour, shaking off excess, then into the egg, then press into the crumbs, transferring to a plate as you go. Cook the linguine according to packet instructions. Toss with a splash of cooking water and the knob of butter. Heat the oil in the wiped-clean frying pan and fry the escalopes in two batches for a couple of minutes a side, until golden and cooked through. Shred the basil, stir it through the sauce and serve the pasta topped with sauce and with the escalopes on the side. Hand round the Parmesan.

Apple Strudel with Golden Sultanas

SERVES 8

My sister has an annoying habit of saying she can't cook. What she actually means is that she prefers someone else to take on the day-to-day cooking. Despite this feigned disinterest, she is always on the lookout for recipes with wow factor to impress her friends, so when it comes to entertaining, which she does often, she always has something special up her sleeve. Most of the time, though, she relies on a tried and tested repertoire she's been cooking for years. One such favourite is apple strudel with almond ice cream. She likes the fact that both recipes can be made up to 48 hours in advance. The strudel, she reckons, actually improves after a day or so in the fridge. At the cookery course she attended before she got married – see what I mean? – everything was made from scratch, including rolling a large sheet of tissue-thin strudel pastry. Cheating with filo, which is what a lot of cooks do, is not an option. The pastry is undeniably the tricky bit of making this roly-poly apple pie but it's a revelation how a small lump of pastry can be cajoled beyond the size of a tea towel. The occasional tear doesn't matter a jot because it's likely to be hidden in the roll.

Any apple, eater or cooker, is suitable for apple strudel but green-skinned, crisp and dry, slightly tart eaters like Granny Smith or Golden Delicious are particularly well suited. The peeled and sliced apples are strewn over the sheet of pastry with buttery, fried breadcrumbs and golden sultanas to soak up the apple juices. Lemon zest and finely chopped toasted almonds, cinnamon and demerara sugar add extra interest and depth of flavour and they all sing out with the apples and pastry as the strudel bakes in the oven. The pastry will have been carefully rolled into a plump, ungainly sausage, the ends sealed and the surface glazed with butter. It is usually curled into a horseshoe shape to fit neatly on to a baking sheet and will be baked until crisp and golden. The strudel can be served immediately or left, as my sister advises, for up to 48 hours before it's brought up to room temperature and then given a 15-minute blast in a hot oven to warm it through and re-crisp the outer pastry. While it cooks, the apple and pastry merge against each other and end up deliciously light and gooey with an almondy apple flavour, but it's the sultanas and background hint of cinnamon that make the dish. Some recipes advise soaking the sultanas first in alcohol – rum or Calvados – but it really isn't necessary.

Like all apple pies, apple strudel goes with cream, ice cream and custard. The cream could be whipped with icing sugar to make crème Chantilly, or with a little rum or Calvados. Decent shop-bought vanilla ice cream is a good easy option, but why not have a go at almond ice cream? Based on meringue rather than custard, with home-made praline stirred into the mixture, it's not the simplest of ice cream recipes but at least you won't need an ice cream maker.

For the pastry:
250g strong white flour, plus a little
  extra
½ tsp salt
1 egg, beaten
1 tbsp vegetable oil
75ml tepid water
For the filling:
75g butter
50g blanched almonds, preferably
  Marcona
75g white breadcrumbs
1 lemon
1kg green eating apples
100g sultanas
2 tsp ground cinnamon
75g demerara sugar
1 egg, beaten
25g icing sugar

Sift the flour and salt into a mixing bowl. Whisk the egg in a small bowl, add the oil and water and mix thoroughly. Make a well in the middle of the flour and pour the liquid into the middle gradually, beating flour and liquid together with a wooden spoon, continuing until it clumps together and is neither wet nor dry. This is a dodgy moment because adding the liquid too quickly makes it lumpy. Work the dough, kneading and slapping it on to a work surface for about 10 minutes until smooth and shiny and obviously elastic. Cover the bowl with a tea towel and leave in a warm spot for at least 30 minutes to relax the pastry.

Now prepare the filling. Melt 15g of butter in a spacious frying pan and when bubbling, stir in the almonds. Stir-fry until golden, then tip on to a fold of kitchen paper to drain and cool. Wipe out the pan and add 35g of butter. When melted, add the breadcrumbs and stir constantly until crusty and golden. Tip on to a fold of kitchen paper to cool and crisp. Place the cooled almonds in a plastic bag and crush with something heavy until chopped into crumbs. Remove the zest from the lemon and chop finely. Squeeze the lemon juice into a mixing bowl. Quarter, core and peel the apples, then slice thinly down the quarters directly into the lemon juice. Toss occasionally to prevent excessive browning.

Give the pastry another quick kneading. Choose a clean tea towel with a strong pattern – I chose one covered with strawberries – and spread it out on a work surface. Dust the tea towel lavishly with flour and rub it into the fabric. Plonk the pastry in the middle. To begin with, as you roll and pull the pastry, your task, to roll it so thin you can clearly see the tea towel pattern and big enough to overhang the edges, will seem impossible. The pastry will resist and want to spring back on itself, but just keep on rolling, stretching it gently with your hands. As it gets larger, slip your hands under the pastry, carefully easing it off the tea towel, to gently stretch and pull the dough, using your forearms and later the backs of your hands to support it. It helps if you can roll the pastry on a work surface or table that enables you to get at the pastry from different angles, although you could just move the tea towel. Keep on keeping on until the pastry is tissue-thin and large enough to just overhang the tea towel. Don't worry about the odd tear but choose the end with the least damage to finish on. Trim the edges. If you haven't already, ease your hand under the pastry to ensure that none of it is stuck to the tea towel. Have ready a buttered baking sheet lined with buttered baking parchment.

Melt the remaining 25g of butter and paint it over the pastry. Leaving a 2cm border, scatter the pastry with the chopped almonds, sultanas and breadcrumbs. Drain the apples and mix with the cinnamon, sugar and lemon zest. Spread evenly over the crumbs. Bearing in mind which end you wish to end on, roll the pastry with the aid of the tea towel. Use beaten egg to glue and seal the end of the roll and the side ends, tucking the seal under the roll. Carefully manoeuvre the roll on to the prepared baking sheet and ease it into a horseshoe shape. If you wish, you could keep the strudel on hold at this point. To cook, heat the oven to 180°C/ gas mark 4 and bake it for 20 minutes. Increase the oven to 200°C/gas mark 6 and cook for a further 30 minutes, until the surface is crisp and golden and your kitchen smells like Christmas. Dust with icing sugar and ease on to a serving platter. Serve warm rather than piping hot, cut in slices.

S Salad Bowl

I've just broken my favourite salad bowl, a huge, crystal-clear, thick Perspex hemisphere that has lived for years upside down balanced over several Le Creuset dishes. It was the perfect family salad bowl, capacious but light, with matching fork and spoon and dishwasher safe. I bought two, one for me and one for the house in Cornwall. They are made by Guzzini, an Italian company who make smart, modern kitchenware in brightly coloured plastics and glass. This one had been showing signs of a potential fissure for some time, but cracked apart spectacularly into two almost identical curls as it hit the kitchen floor. It made a shocking noise, going off like an amplified shotgun, making me jump right out of my skin.

I don't relish the thought of choosing another. If it had a downside, it was to do with the washing up. All salad bowls are unpleasant to wash up. There is always something left in the bowl. It might be just sufficient for another meal but usually not, more likely to be a few stray bits and pieces and an unpleasant slimy smear of dressing that clings to the bowl, never satisfactorily dealt with in the dishwasher. Salad bowls really need to be washed and dried by hand. Perhaps I don't mind this extra chore because I've been liberated from Wooden Salad Bowl Syndrome. Strange though it seems now, in the seventies a wooden salad bowl was as familiar on the wedding list as a set of Egyptian cotton sheets. It was only supposed to be used for green salads and was always wiped and never washed. Ours developed an unpleasant stickiness and eventually turned rancid and had to go, despite having cost an arm and a leg. It was usurped first by a glass salad bowl and then the more practicable Perspex one.

The point about a salad bowl as opposed to a bowl for a dressed salad is that it must be large enough to toss the salad thoroughly. I always make the dressing in the bowl or pour it into the bowl. If it is a lettuce salad or one with soft leaves, I make a cross with my salad servers then pile the salad over the top. It can sit happily for ages, to be tossed at the table just before serving.

There is a huge choice of salad bowls available in every imaginable material including wood, but I have failed to find an alternative to my ricocheting salad bowl and have temporarily retrieved its identical sibling. I am tempted by a similar sized Guzzini bowl, 14.5 x 30cm, called Mirage (see page 275), made in a pretty pale yellow plastic with white interior, but I really want another see-through bowl. If Zuperzozial's coconut white salad bowl (see page 275), made of biodegradable bamboo and corn powder, came in a larger size (it's 11 x 24cm), I'd probably go for that. It feels like stone, doesn't stain, is dishwasher safe and you get change from £12.

Chicory, Walnut and Parsley Salad

SERVES 6–8

A crunchy, zingy salad to get the tastebuds buzzing.

6 cornichons or 1 pickled cucumber	4 tbsp light olive oil
4 Belgian chicory	1 tbsp water
50g bunch flat-leaf parsley	50g walnut pieces
1 tbsp smooth Dijon mustard	1 small baguette or ciabatta
½ tbsp red wine vinegar	Gentleman's Relish or tapenade

Chop the cornichons into small pieces. Trim the chicory, halve lengthways and slice down the halves into 5mm strips. Pick the leaves off the parsley stalks. Put the mustard into a salad bowl. Mix in the vinegar, pinch salt, pepper and sugar, then whisk in the olive oil gradually to make a thick vinaigrette, slackening with 1 tablespoon of water. Toss the chicory, parsley leaves, walnuts and cornichons in the dressing. Thinly slice the bread, toast and spread sparingly with Gentleman's Relish or tapenade. Pile the toast on to a plate and serve with the salad.

S Saucepans

When I got married I was already living with my husband-to-be in a well-stocked home. Our wedding was low-key so there were hardly any guests, let alone a wedding list. Top of my list would have been a set of Le Pentole pans. These sleekly elegant, satin-glazed stainless steel Italian pans are beautiful. Every detail, from their distinctive hoop-handle lids (which are bought separately and are interchangeable) to their sturdy, heavy base made of three layers – steel, copper, steel – is function as well as form. Craftsmanship shines through the timeless designs, so it's no surprise to learn that they are the most consistently popular range of pans stocked by classy cook shop David Mellor (see page 275). One of these days, I am going to clear out my motley collection of pans and replace them with Le Pentole. They do, of course, cost two arms and two legs (the lids start at £30) but they occasionally come up on eBay, and 'bargain' sets can also be bought (see page 275).

I am very happy with a Le Pentole-style, Italian-made (Irradial Plus by Lagastina) milk pan I bought many years ago at Habitat. Its glossy finish and loop handle are in complete contrast to my little aluminium egg pan with a stumpy red handle that found its way into my kitchen from my dad's family home via an aunt. I am also very happy with a stainless steel set of various sized pans, plus sauté pan and very large pan, bought for a song many years ago at Ikea. All have a heavy base, good-fitting lids, and the three larger pans have side handles rather than the long handle of the sauté and smallest (1.5 litre capacity) pan. I do think Ikea is excellent for kitchen basics.

My latest pans, a Stellar Eazi store pan set (cook's shops or Lakeland, see page 275), are the Russian dolls of the cooking world. The pans (16, 18 and 20cm) and their riveted handles stack neatly with their vented glass lids on top. They are brilliant if space is an issue. And I am becoming addicted to pans with glass lids.

Pheasant and Lemon Broth with Egg and Parmesan

SERVES 2

Whenever I roast a bird, I always save the bones for stock. Pheasant produces remarkable stock, clear like consommé, virtually fat-free, golden and richly flavoured. It gives zuppa alla Pavese, *an exquisite but simple soup from Pavia, a new lease of life. Apart from good stock, it requires very few ingredients – an egg and a slice of dense-textured sourdough-style bread per person, olive oil and freshly grated Parmesan. In the original, the bread sits at the bottom of the bowl, the hot broth is added and the egg cooks in the soup, the yolk enriching the broth and the bread thickening it. My version is made with fried toast and the egg is poached separately. I add lemon to the stock and finish the soup with freshly grated Parmesan. Your butcher may be able to supply pheasant carcasses.*

For the pheasant stock:
1 pheasant carcass (2 is better)
1 onion
2 stalks of celery
1 garlic clove
1 carrot
1 bay leaf
a few sprigs of thyme
1 lemon

For the soup:
1 tbsp wine vinegar
2 eggs
2 slices sourdough or similar
  dense-crumbed bread
25g butter or 3–4 tbsp olive oil
freshly grated Parmesan
500ml pheasant stock (see above)

To make the stock, break up the raw carcass and roast for 15 minutes at 200°C/gas mark 6. Transfer to a pan with the chopped, unpeeled, onion, chopped celery and carrot, the garlic, cracked with your fist and peeled, the bay and thyme. Add a pinch of salt and 1.5 litres of water. Simmer, uncovered, for an hour, then strain. If necessary, simmer to reduce and concentrate the flavour; you want 500ml. Taste and adjust the seasoning with salt and lemon juice.

Half-fill a small pan with water, bring to a simmer and add the vinegar. Crack one egg at a time into a tea-cup, then slip the egg into the vortex of briskly stirred, simmering water. Cook for a couple of minutes, until just set. Use a slotted spoon to lift the eggs out of the pan and rest on a fold of kitchen paper to drain. When you begin preparations for the eggs, place a griddle or heavy frying pan over a high heat. When very hot, smear both sides of the bread with olive oil or spread with butter, then toast both sides on the griddle. Place in shallow bowls. Add an egg to each bowl, dust with Parmesan and pour over the hot stock. Serve with extra Parmesan and black pepper.

Lemonade Pork with Soy, Greens and Rice Noodles

SERVES 4

I have a huge collection of cookery books and am always running out of shelf space. In an attempt to solve my storage problems, an architect friend designed a new shelving system. One day, when a layer of sawdust covered everything in the house, Roger the builder told me about a 'brown pork stew' cooked by a Chinese Australian staying in a flat he once worked on. The list of ingredients sounded intriguing but his description of the taste had me scribbling a shopping list. Belly pork and lemonade, soy and Thai fish sauce, and onions. It might sound odd, but trust me, this recipe really is a gem.

One tip: if you are concerned about the vast amount of fat in belly pork, make the dish 24 hours in advance and leave to chill overnight. Remove the disc of white fat, reheat and add the beans.

2 large onions, 225g each	400ml cold water
3 tbsp vegetable oil	freshly grated black pepper
approx 750g meaty belly pork joint	500g green beans
2 tbsp Kikkoman soy sauce	400g tagliatelle-style rice noodles
3 tbsp Thai fish sauce (nam pla)	(rice sticks)
200ml lemonade	25g bunch coriander

Trim, halve, peel and chop the onions. Heat the oil in a spacious sauté pan and brown the onions. Allow at least 25 minutes, stirring often. Use a slotted spoon to scoop them into a spacious heavy-bottomed, lidded saucepan. Run a sharp cook's knife under the pork skin to remove it. Cut the meat into kebab-size chunks. Brown the meat in batches in the sauté pan, using the remaining oil. Transfer to the other pan as you go. Add the soy to the sauté pan and swirl around to lift any residue. Add to the other pan with the fish sauce, lemonade and water. Season generously with black pepper. Bring to the boil, then establish a steady, gentle simmer. Cover and cook for 90 minutes.

Remove the lid and simmer for a further 15–30 minutes, until the meat is meltingly tender and the sauce slightly reduced. Top, tail and halve the beans and cook in boiling water for 2 minutes. Drain and stir into the stew. Soak the noodles in warm water for 10–15 minutes, until soft. Drain, then cover with boiling water for 2–3 minutes to heat through. If adding coriander, stir it through the drained noodles. Serve the noodles in bowls topped with the pork 'n' beans and the amazing juices. Serve with a fork and spoon.

⬛ Sauté Pan

A sauté pan, or sauteuse, is a frying pan with deep, straight sides and a long handle. Mine is made of stainless steel and has a heavy base and a lid. In the States it's called a chicken fryer. Its point is to fry larger pieces of food, like chicken, that can't be safely cooked in a frying pan, but I use mine for all sorts of things. The high sides limit fat splattering when frying but the pan is just the right size for risotto for four, and is perfect for simmering fruit such as plums, apples and pears which need to be immersed in liquid in a single layer.

Afghani Turkey Korma with Cardamom and Orange

SERVES 4–6

This is a dish to remember when you are facing leftover Christmas turkey. Having said that, I make it for a picnic with the remains of any roast bird, including chicken, but gamey birds like pheasant are best. If there is one of those handy packs of Merchant Gourmet ready-cooked Puy lentils stashed away in the food cupboard, this is the time to whip it out. The aromatic, fruity seasonings with the turkey and lentils are at their best warm rather than chilled, but it could be a hot dish with rice, naan and mango chutney.

2 large onions	250g cooked Puy lentils
2 tbsp vegetable oil	2 large navel oranges
9 cardamom pods	1 lemon
400–600g leftover dark turkey meat	100g pomegranate seeds

Halve, peel and finely chop the onions. Heat the oil in a spacious sauté pan, stir in the onions and cook steadily, stirring often, until soft and golden, allowing at least 20 minutes. While the onions cook, crack the cardamom pods, extract the seeds and pound them to powder. Tear the turkey into large bite-size pieces.

Stir the cardamom into the softened onion and stir-fry for a couple of minutes before adding the turkey. Stir-fry for a few minutes, then fold in the lentils. Squeeze the juice from the oranges and lemon over the top and stir-fry to heat through and send the juices through the food. Fold in the pomegranate, and either serve immediately or reheat later.

Roast Tomato Risotto with Saffron

SERVES 4

There is something extraordinarily uplifting about the smell of slowly roasting tomatoes and for this lovely risotto, it will mingle with the smell of buttery shallots gently softening in the pan. These are the prelims of a simplified risotto, a cheat's version made by adding the saffron and honey-flavoured stock in two batches rather than the usual ladle after ladle. Within thirty minutes you will be enjoying this luscious risotto finished with a lump of pale Italian butter and those gooey, intensely flavoured roasted tomatoes.

500g ripe tomatoes, plus 6 more

1 tbsp olive oil

2 shallots

75g unsalted butter, preferably Italian or French

2 chicken stock cubes

1 tsp honey

a generous pinch of saffron threads

350g risotto rice

Parmesan, to serve

Heat the oven to 200°C/gas mark 6. Halve the 6 tomatoes round their middles, or lengthways if using plum tomatoes. Arrange cut side up on a foil-lined baking sheet and smear the cut surface with olive oil. Place in the oven without waiting for it to come up to temperature. Peel and finely chop the shallots. Melt half the butter in a large sauté or similarly wide-based pan and gently soften the shallots. Cover the 500g of tomatoes with boiling water and count to 20. Measure 1 litre of the water into a jug. Remove each tomato core in a pointed plug shape and discard the skin. Chop into small pieces.

Dissolve the stock cubes in the tomato water and stir in the honey and saffron. Stir the rice into the shallots until glistening all over, then add the chopped tomatoes. Cook until hot, then add half the stock. Simmer, stirring occasionally, until the liquid begins to dry out. Stir in the remaining stock and continue cooking for a further 15 minutes or so, until the liquid is absorbed and the rice is tender with a slight bite in the centre. Stir in the remaining butter, cover and leave for 5 minutes. Slide the roast tomatoes off their skins. Stir the tomatoes and their juices into the risotto and serve with plenty of finely grated Parmesan.

S Scallop Shells

I've had a soft spot for these pretty shells for as long as I can remember, way before I knew they contained something delicious to eat. When I was very little, my art mistress aunt gave me a book of famous paintings and my favourite, where I lingered longest, was Botticelli's impossibly beautiful Venus, her long blonde hair swirling behind her as she perched on a giant scallop shell. At school scallop shells decorated the shields of Crusaders in my first history book and later I discovered that these distinctive shells were worn by early pilgrims to signify a pilgrimage to the shrine of St James (St Jacques in French, hence *coquilles St Jacques*) at Santiago de Compostela in Galicia, the region of Spain famous for scallops. The pilgrim route to the cathedral is marked out with a scallop shell symbol and when you get to the city, the pavement leading to its doors is marked out with golden scallops embedded in the pavements.

The scallop shell remains a popular image but these days it filters into our awareness at the Shell petrol pump. The distinctive fluted-edged, tapered and curved shape of the shell, with two little wings at its base, that enters our subliminal consciousness still isn't associated with food. Aficionados might relish the moist, sweet meat, but most people regard scallops as an expensive choice at the fish counter and worrisome to prepare. That's a pity, because scallops are quick and easy to cook well and the sweet, tender meat is a versatile ingredient as popular in Chinese and Asian cuisines as it is in French *haute cuisine*. Happily, scallops are abundant and sustainable in British waters, especially prolific in Cornwall, Scotland, Ireland, Wales, the Isle of Man and on the south coast, particularly in and around the Cinque Port of Rye. In fact the town holds an annual scallop week at the end of February (see page 276), when local chefs celebrate with sample menus showcasing scallop dishes from around the world.

There is always a stack of scrubbed scallop shells teetering on the middle shelf of my kitchen dresser. They remind me of my beloved Cornwall with every glance, and although they get used as ashtrays and soap dishes, the bigger ones for nuts and dinner party pats of butter, I really keep them to make *coquilles St Jacques*, or other scallop dishes that need a shell. It's the curved half shell, the part that holds the

scallop, not the flat lid, that's required for such dishes. It's illegal to land scallops below 11cm across their width, but what you really need for stuffed dishes is 12–14cm wide shells.

What you want is diver, hand-caught king scallops which are lifted without disrupting the ocean bed and to strict quota controls. This laborious but ocean-friendly, sustainable way of catching scallops makes them the expensive option, particularly as they're in limited seasonal supply and in great demand from restaurants, but they are worth it on many counts. Divers can pinpoint and measure as they catch, whereas scallop dredgers scoop up anything and everything on the ocean floor and that includes immature and damaged shells that go to waste, not to mention spoilage caused by compacted sand in the shells.

The shells clean up beautifully, keep indefinitely and are dishwasher, freezer and microwave safe. It's not always easy to buy scallops on the half shell unless you buy them in season and at a decent fishmonger, or in a seaside town like Newlyn, in Cornwall, where there is a thriving scallop fishing industry. They tend to be sold neatly cleaned up and out of their shell, often without their coral. There are hundreds of different scallops but the choice boils down to king and queen scallops. King scallops, which have a creamy white shell, are the bigger of the two and most highly prized. Queen scallops, known as queenies, are much smaller, with an average shell size of 4–6cm, but it's rare to see them on their distinctive browny-red shells. Particularly fine Isle of Man queenies can be bought vacuum-packed online (see page 276). They keep for four days in the fridge and up to six months in the freezer.

If asked, any fishmonger will get scallops on the half shell for you or they can be ordered, diver-caught in Cornwall or Scotland, for overnight delivery (see page 276). They also sell sterilized shells. For greater quantities and different sized shells, see page 276. At a pinch, saucers or small, shallow bowls would suffice but most cook shops sell fine porcelain scallop shells made by French manufacturer Apilco, which come in four sizes: 8, 11, 13 and 14cm.

Although I feel strongly about buying British diver-caught scallops and eating them in season, I sometimes weaken and buy the widely available Canadian Atlantic or Patagonian scallops. These sustainable Marine Stewardship Council (MSC) certified scallops are cleaned up and frozen at sea, sea freighted to the UK and sold frozen or defrosted, sometimes singly. Be warned, though: frozen scallops give off a lot of liquid as they defrost, so give them a gentle squeeze and then pat dry with kitchen paper before cooking.

The scallops inside their pretty shell need minimal cooking, just enough to 'set' the dense disc of white meat and creamy orange coral. I love them quickly fried to burnish the surface and served au naturel with a squeeze of lemon, but Rowley Leigh's accompaniment of pea purée and mint vinaigrette is a pretty close second. Scallops can also be steamed, grilled or roasted. They can even be eaten raw, ceviche-style, 'cooked' with lime or lemon juice. Their sweet, creamy taste complements a wide range of seasonings, including soy, ginger and spring onion, chilli and garlic, or bacon and mushrooms. The best scallops are fresh from the sea, their salty-sweet flavour needing nothing more than a flash in the pan with a splash of olive oil and a squeeze of lemon, and maybe a hint of garlic and a pinch of salt.

To prepare live scallops, rinse unopened shells in plenty of cold water to remove sand inside. Hold the scallop with the flat shell uppermost. Working from the base of the shell, slide a sharp, strong knife between the shells, pressing the blade flat against the top shell whilst feeling for the ligament that joins the shell to the white muscle meat. Cut through with one sweep. Lift off the flat shell and pull out the black stomach sac and frilly 'skirt' surrounding the white meat and orange coral. Rinse away sand and debris and drain before cooking. To remove the scallop from the rounded shell, run a knife under the white meat where it is attached to the shell. If necessary, trim the hard edge.

Chinese Steamed Scallops with Ginger

SERVES 4

Variations on this recipe, grilling rather than steaming the scallops, adding garlic or crushed black beans, more of this and less of that, are on most Cantonese dim sum menus. It should be made with scallops still attached to the shell, but it's also pretty good with loose scallops in cleaned shells.

12 king scallops on the half shell	2 tbsp soy sauce
1 tbsp toasted sesame oil	1 tbsp groundnut oil
25g fresh ginger	1 tbsp finely chopped coriander
2 spring onions	leaves

Half-fill the base of a steamer with water and bring to the boil. Using a pastry brush, lightly smear the scallops with the toasted sesame oil. Peel the ginger and slice into very thin matchsticks. Sprinkle the ginger over the scallops. Place in the steamer tray – you may need two layers or to cook in two batches – balancing them against each other so the ginger doesn't fall off. Cover and steam for 3–4 minutes, until just set.

While they cook, trim and very finely slice the spring onions. Arrange the scallops on four plates, add the soy sauce and sprinkle with the spring onions. Place the oils in a small pan and bring quickly to the boil. Pour the hot oil over the scallops. Scatter with coriander and eat immediately. Use a chopstick or fork to loosen the scallop from the shell, and eat in one or two bites with a slurp of juices.

Scallops Mornay

It isn't necessary to buy scallops on the half shell for this dish but you will need four decent-sized curved shells. The idea is to edge the shell with stiff mashed potato, fill the middle with diced scallops in a thick, creamy white wine-flavoured sauce and pipe more mash in thick wavy coils over the top. The shells are finished with a sprinkling of butter-fried fresh breadcrumbs and are ready to eat after 15 minutes in a hot oven. Two make a lovely supper treat with salad to follow, but one would be adequate as a starter.

For the mash:
600g potatoes
25g butter
1 beaten egg
For the filling:
1 small lemon
1 sprig of fresh thyme
150ml white wine
150ml fish or light chicken stock

300g king scallops or queenie scallops
1 shallot
25g butter
25g flour
1 tbsp crème fraîche
For the gratin:
25g slice of bread
25g butter

Peel, chunk, rinse and boil the potatoes until tender in salted water. Drain and mash with the butter. Cool slightly, then beat in the beaten egg. Spoon into a piping bag with a jagged nozzle. Pipe a generous border of potato round each shell. Simmer a strip of lemon zest with the thyme, wine and stock for 5 minutes while you separate the corals from the scallops, trim away the hard bit at one side, rinse and pat dry. Halve large scallops horizontally. Simmer the scallops and corals for 2 minutes in the stock. Scoop out of the pan, cool then cut into big dolly-mixture-size dice. Boil the stock to reduce to 200ml. Discard the zest and thyme.

Heat the oven to 200°C/gas mark 6. Peel and finely chop the shallot. Soften in 25g of butter, stir in the flour, then add the reduced stock, beating to make a smooth sauce. Simmer for 3 minutes. Stir in the crème fraîche, season to taste, then add the scallops and a squeeze of lemon. Spoon into the shells and pipe the remaining mash over the top. Blitz the bread to make crumbs and fry briefly in the remaining butter to saturate. Sprinkle over the mash. Arrange the shells on a baking sheet, balanced against each other, and bake for 15 minutes, until crusty and golden.

S Sieve

When I went on maternity leave at the end of my first pregnancy, I astounded my doctor by losing weight. At the time I was fascinated by a chef called Michel Guérard, who runs a three Michelin star restaurant within a Spa hotel at Eugénie-les-Bains, in south-west France. His intelligent gourmet diet food was captured in a book called *Cuisine Minceur*, and I decided to cook the book. Many of the dishes required small amounts of quite complicated vegetable purées, and a vital bit of kit to achieve perfection was a conical sieve. Mine cost an arm and a leg. The sieve was strong and fine, a double sheet of tinned wire held within a steel frame that echoed its shape with a hook to hang over the side of a pan or bowl. It was a devil to use, acting as a chinois rather than a sieve, requiring much pushing and shoving to get any results. It remains indestructible.

For some years that sieve has remained at the back of the cupboard. I prefer a bowl-shaped, round sieve made of shiny wire mesh and a similar but stronger conical sieve. I use both most days, for straining anything and everything that is too fine or such a small amount that a colander isn't appropriate. Both are useful too for sifting flour, which I always do for pastry and cakes, and for washing rice, lentils and bulgar cracked wheat. If I am deseeding several tomatoes, I always scrape the seeds into a sieve placed over a bowl then crush them with the back of a wooden spoon to catch the juice. This is full of flavour and should be saved for sauces, vinaigrette and Bloody Mary. It can be kept in a jam jar in the fridge for several days.

Tunisian Salade Mechouia with Tomato Bread

SERVES 4

When I was twenty-five, I worked for several weeks on an international arts festival at Tabarka on the north-west coast of Tunisia. My job was to produce a daily Gestetnered paper of what was going on. Part of the brief was sussing out the restaurants, of which there were many. I became an aficionado of Tunisian food. The salads were stupendous but mechouia, *sometimes served on a slab of bread soaked in olive oil and tomato juice, was particularly good. It is clearly related to* salade Niçoise, *but the red peppers and tomatoes are grilled (*mechouia *means 'grilled' and often refers to a kebab cooked with peppers and tomatoes). This salad is often served with chunks of canned tuna and scraps of Moroccan-style salt-preserved lemon peel, which gives the dish an unexpected twist.*

For the salad:
3 red peppers
3 garlic cloves
6 vine tomatoes, approx 600g
4 tbsp olive oil
a pinch of sugar
3 eggs
8 pitted black olives
4 anchovy fillets
2 salt-preserved lemons (optional)
1 tbsp capers

1 tbsp chopped flat-leaf parsley
 leaves
juice of 1 small lemon
For the tomato bread:
6 over-ripe tomatoes
1 tbsp red wine vinegar
a pinch of sugar
4–5 tbsp olive oil
1 garlic clove, cut in half
4 slices of sourdough bread

Heat the grill. Arrange the peppers on a foil-lined grill pan. Cook under a high heat, turning them as the skins blacken. Transfer to a plate, cover with a stretch of clingfilm and leave for 20 minutes before removing the skin. Slice into chunky ribbons, discarding seeds and white filaments. Halve the vine tomatoes, lengthways if plum, through their middles if round, and lay out on the grill pan. Paint the cut surfaces with a smear of olive oil. Season with salt and pepper and a little sugar. Grill at a medium heat until soft and the surfaces blistered and scorched. Leave to cool. Boil the eggs for 6 minutes. Drain, then crack the shells and remove. Cut lengthways into quarters. Cut the olives in half through their middles. Halve the anchovies lengthways. If using preserved lemons, quarter then scrape away the seeds and pith and slice into skinny strips.

To make the tomato bread, place the over-ripe tomatoes in the bowl of a food processor. Blitz to a purée with the vinegar and sugar. Pass through a sieve placed over a bowl to catch pips, etc. and whisk in 1 tablespoon of olive oil. Season with salt and pepper. Toast the bread, rub with garlic and smear one side with olive oil. Place in shallow soup bowls or on large plates, drench with the puréed tomato and arrange the salad on top. Decorate with the olives, anchovy, capers, parsley and preserved lemon, if using. Whisk the lemon juice with the remaining olive oil and spoon over the top.

S Soufflé Dishes

The perfect soufflé emerges from the oven puffed and golden, rising out of its dish with the merest hint of a wobble. Inside will be creamy and soft and just set as the spoon dives in. The timing of a soufflé is critical. It is not an occasion for late arrivals; everyone must be at the table before the oven door is opened and the hope is that the soufflé will stay inflated long enough for the inevitable oohs and aahs. At Langan's Brasserie in Mayfair, they only serve their famous spinach soufflé with anchovy sauce in the downstairs dining room, never upstairs in the Venetian Room.

A soufflé could be made in any round, deep-sided ovenproof dish, but the dish for the job is modelled on a timbale, a high-sided container whose name derives from *at-tabl*, the Arabic for drum. Soufflé dishes are made in porcelain, fireproof glass, occasionally stoneware. The shape is round so the heat can penetrate evenly to the centre and the mixture can rise smoothly to its maximum height. The traditional fluted surface resembles a chef's toque but the design is based on the pleated paper cases used to hold ramekins, once a soufflé-like cheese dish, now the name of an individual soufflé dish (see page 187). The base of some soufflé dishes is unglazed so that as it stands on a baking tray in the oven the heat can quickly penetrate. Likewise the rim at the top of the dish helps the heat to penetrate but is also useful for tying string around if the soufflé needs a collar. That is necessary if there is too much mixture and the soufflé is filled almost to the top, the collar giving the dish extra depth. A chef friend who used to specialize in function catering told me about an occasion when he was cooking soufflés in an unfamiliar travelling oven and all the collars caught fire.

There are lots of stories about soufflé dramas but making a soufflé is kitchen alchemy, faster and more dramatic than baking a cake and even more intriguing. The mix is based on eggs and is made in two parts. The yolks slacken a thick, creamy sweet or savoury sauce and stiffly beaten whites are folded into the mixture just before it goes into the oven. All the components, egg yolk and white and sauce ingredients, affect how the soufflé behaves. An extra egg white or two makes the soufflé lighter but the flavour blander. As a rule of thumb, use three yolks to five whites, or four yolks to six whites. Flour helps stabilize the mixture but too much makes it heavy and hinders the rise. Soufflés can be flavoured with almost anything, but strong flavours, particularly smoked fish, cheese, mushrooms and spinach, that stand up to the bland eggs, work best.

The soufflé mix can be made, even poured into the dish, as they do at Langan's, hours before it needs to go in the oven. When my sons worked, first as dishwashers then as waiters, at Christian's restaurant in Chiswick, one of the specialities was mature Cheddar cheese soufflé. Christian Gustin-Andrews would season the milk (cooked with onion, bay and black pepper) for the Dijon mustard-flavoured béchamel in the morning and make the sauce just before the restaurant opened, so the mix was at room temperature, ready for adding the whisked egg whites to order. He kept twice-buttered, large ramekins in the fridge and baked his soufflés at 180°C/gas mark 4.

Soufflé dishes are available in various sizes. Mine are glazed porcelain by Pillivuyt; one is 1.5 litres capacity and 9cm tall, the other 2 litres capacity and 9.5cm tall. My ramekins (also Pillivuyt) are unglazed on the base and round the rim.

Smoked Haddock Soufflé

SERVES 4

The creamy mild flavour of Dijon mustard goes deliciously well with smoked haddock and gives a mild background tang to this lovely soufflé. Dusting the inside of the deep, straight-sided dish with finely grated Parmesan creates a thin, golden cheesy shell for the soufflé and this crusty carapace is always the favourite mouthful. It is not a good idea to open the oven wide during the cooking time but it is very important not to overcook the soufflé. It should rise spectacularly over the top of the dish, and running your thumb or a knife around the inside edge before it goes into the oven will create an impressive cap. The middle should still be just set but a tad wobbly.

300g naturally smoked haddock	1 tbsp Maille Dijon mustard
350ml milk	4 whole eggs
75g butter	2 egg whites
2 tbsp flour	3 tbsp freshly grated Parmesan

Heat the oven to 180°C/gas mark 4. Place a baking sheet on the shelf where the soufflé dish will end up, ensuring there is plenty of space for rising. Lavishly smear a 2 litre capacity soufflé dish with 25g of butter.

Dust with most of the Parmesan, turning the dish in your hands so that base and sides are evenly coated. Chill for at least 30 minutes. Simmer the haddock in milk for 4–6 minutes, until just cooked. Flake the fish on to a plate and strain the milk, including any left on the plate, into a jug.

Melt 50g of butter in a medium pan and stir in the flour to make a stiff roux. Stir in the mustard, then add the reserved milk gradually, first stirring then whisking until smooth. Simmer gently, giving the odd stir, for a few minutes to cook the flour. Season lightly with salt and generously with black pepper. Remove from the heat.

Separate the eggs. Beat the yolks, one at a time, into the hot sauce. Whisk the egg whites, including the extra ones, to soft peaks. Using a metal spoon, fold 2 tablespoons of egg white into the sauce to slacken it. Stir in the fish. Gently fold the remaining egg white into the mixture and pour into the prepared dish. Lightly dust the top with the rest of the Parmesan. Make a deep groove with your thumb round the inside edge of the soufflé. Bake for 30–40 minutes, until the soufflé has risen above the top of the dish and the top is crusty and golden. Serve immediately.

S Steamer

One of my childhood Christmas memories is driving with my dad to his family home and borrowing the steamer. It was a huge, multi-layered pan, large enough to cook several Christmas puddings. My mother made loads, enough for us and various relations, and I remember the steaming going on all day, the kitchen and hall windows fugging up. Every now and again the timer would go off, reminding her to top up the pan so it wouldn't boil dry.

My first attempts at steaming food were made using a curious expanding basket I found in the cupboard of a rented flat. It folded in on itself but was a series of interlocking slats like a fan, and fitted inside a saucepan, standing on short legs. Later I bought a set of Chinese bamboo steamer baskets for their looks rather than to cook with, but once I did, the lidded tiers sitting on a metal frame that slotted inside a saucepan or wok, I used them so much they eventually wore out.

For years I've been using a steamer set made in heavy duty stainless steel by Hackman, a Finnish company. The main pan holds 6 litres, and has side handles and a very thick, heavy induction base. It's a great pan, useful for anything and everything, and comes with a spacious perforated steamer basket, large enough to hold a lot of food, and a double boiler. Prior to that I was given a two-tier, usefully wide steamer made of thin enamel. I loved that too and used it continually until it melted.

Steamed food retains its vitamins and its shape. Steaming is particularly good for fish and vegetables. There are three important points about steaming: don't begin cooking until the water is boiling; cover the pan with a good fitting lid and reduce the heat slightly so the water is kept just below boiling point; check the water level regularly and top it up so the pan doesn't boil dry.

Lemon Brill with Saffron Tomato Vinaigrette

SERVES 6

Simple, stylish and delicious. Perfect for any occasion, but the vinaigrette is only worth making with ripe, strongly flavoured tomatoes. Serve it with French beans and new potatoes or arrange the fish over a pile of beans in the middle of the plate and spoon the sauce over the top.

6 fillets of brill, sea bass, cod or similar firm white fish	*For the vinaigrette:*
1 tbsp Maldon sea salt	5 ripe vine tomatoes, approx 500g
1 tbsp olive oil	a generous pinch of saffron threads
1 lemon	2 plump garlic cloves, preferably new season
500g green beans	1 tbsp red wine vinegar
	200ml best olive oil
	a handful of fresh basil leaves

Lay the fish fillets on a plate. Season both sides lightly with salt and leave for 30 minutes. Rinse, pat dry and season with a smear of olive oil and lemon juice. They can sit in the fridge now for up to 48 hours.

Boil the kettle. Cover the tomatoes with boiling water, count to 20, then drain and peel. Soften the saffron in 1 tablespoon of boiling water. Place a sieve over a mixing bowl. Halve the tomatoes, then slide off the skins while scraping the seeds into the sieve. Crush the pip juices through the sieve with the back of a spoon. Dice the flesh. Peel the garlic and slice into wafer-thin rounds. Mix together the vinegar, saffron and its water, a pinch of salt, several grinds of white pepper and the garlic in a large bowl. Add the tomato juices and chopped tomatoes to the bowl and leave to macerate for 30 minutes. Stir in the olive oil and tear or snip the basil over the top. Stir.

Boil the kettle again and use the water for the steamer. Lay the fish in the steamer basket. Steam the fish for 6–10 minutes, depending on the thickness of the fillets, until just cooked through. Top and tail the beans. Boil in salted water for 3 minutes, then drain. Serve the fish over the green beans, with the vinaigrette spooned over the top.

Traditional Christmas Pudding

MAKES 2 PUDDINGS, EACH SERVING 6–8

Compared to the palaver my mother went through with the annual ritual of making the Christmas puddings, not to mention mincemeat for mince pies and Christmas cake, it is shockingly easy to make them today. All you do is stir all the ingredients together and steam the mixture in pudding basins. The only thing that hasn't changed is the length of time they take to cook.

When I was a child, Stir Up Sunday, the last Sunday before Advent and the traditional time to make Christmas puddings, was the official start of the run-up to Christmas. It followed days of tedious preparation. The fruit had to be washed and dried and some had to be pitted as well. Candied citrus peel didn't come neatly chopped and ready for use, but in big, stiff, hard pieces. It was the days before food processors, so bread for crumbs had to be dried then rubbed through a special big round sieve with wooden sides. We lived surrounded by relatives and they all trooped in to stir the stiff, intoxicating pudding mixture and make a wish. The next day it was packed into cream-coloured china pudding bowls, covered with old torn sheet and tied with strips torn from the cloth. My dad was dispatched to borrow a multi-tiered steamer from his family home and the puddings steamed away all day, misting up the windows and filling the house with the smell of Christmas coming.

I went for years without making my own puddings, relying instead on a stockpile of my mother's. When she died, I feared the family recipe had gone with her to the grave but one cousin, it turned out, had salvaged a book of her mother's handwritten recipes. It went with her when she emigrated to Queensland, where she began a tradition of making Christmas puddings to give away as prizes at her husband's ballroom dancing classes. Many of the cakes and puddings, particularly Christmas recipes, will have been handed down through the generations of our mothers' family. The pudding is very dark and very fruity yet light and succulent, with a rich, mellow flavour and spicy back notes. It is far superior to any Christmas pudding I have ever eaten. My mother served it with brandy butter, custard and cream. Magically, or so it seemed, everyone got a lucky silver sixpence in their portion. My father used to slip the sixpences in as he served the pudding but a beady-eyed cousin says theirs were dispersed through the mixture in a fold of greaseproof paper.

The quantities given make two family-size puddings. The second is a splendid Christmas gift for some lucky person or can be tucked away for next year. It is tempting to make several little puddings and solve many Christmas present problems in one fell swoop.

Leftover pudding, wrapped in waxed paper then in foil, will keep for months. It freezes perfectly, but why bother when it keeps so well? When I was about eight, one of my cousins taught me how to fry a slice of Christmas pudding in butter and eat it slathered with cream. It's still one of my favourite treats of Christmas, but I recommend hoarding a slice or two to lift the spirits on a cold and miserable February afternoon.

225g raisins
225g currants
225g sultanas
200g cut mixed peel
225g shredded suet/Atora
500g dark muscovado unrefined
   cane sugar
225g fresh breadcrumbs, from
   day-old bread
75g plain flour
1 level tsp freshly grated nutmeg or
   ground cinnamon
½ level tsp ground cloves

¼ tsp salt
50g blanched almonds, chopped
1 carrot
1 Bramley cooking apple
2 lemons
3 large eggs
150ml brandy, whisky or rum
a large knob of soft butter
You will also need: 2 x 1.2 litre
   pudding basins, greaseproof
   paper or baking parchment, foil
   and kitchen string

Tip the raisins, currants, sultanas and mixed peel into a very large mixing bowl. Add the suet, sugar and breadcrumbs. Sift the flour, nutmeg and cloves into the bowl. Add the salt and chopped almonds; I prefer to do the almonds by hand, but use the pulse button if you do it by machine. Trim and scrape the carrot and grate into the bowl. Quarter

the apple, cut out the core and remove the peel. Grate over the carrot. Grate the lemon zest over the top, using the smallest hole of the grater, and squeeze the juice through a sieve into the bowl. Whisk the eggs with a fork until smooth, with half the brandy. Add to the bowl. Stir thoroughly with a wooden spoon.

Lavishly butter two 1.2 litre capacity pudding basins. Fill them with the mixture and cover with a disc of greaseproof paper. Pleat a large piece of foil and place loosely over the top. Tie securely, going round twice, with string under the rim of the basin, then loop a handle across the top, allowing room for the pudding to rise. Repeat with the second pudding. Stand the puddings on a trivet in a large saucepan with a well-fitting lid. Add sufficient boiling water to come two-thirds of the way up the basin, fit the lid and boil for 5 hours. Check every hour or so and keep topped up with boiling water. Leave the puddings to go cold.

Remove the foil and paper disc. Spoon on the remaining brandy. Re-cover with a fresh disc of greaseproof paper and wrap the entire pudding in greaseproof, then in foil. Store in a cool, dark place for at least a month to mature.

Remove foil and greaseproof, then re-cover with a greaseproof disc and foil as before. Steam for a further 2 hours. To serve, place a hot plate over the uncovered pudding, quickly invert and decorate with a sprig of holly. To flame with brandy, heat about 3 tablespoons of brandy in a ladle or small pan, pour over the pudding and ignite in the kitchen (if it isn't too far away).

⊤ Tagine

While my sons were growing up there was a long period when they wouldn't eat anything called stew. Give the dish a foreign name like Moroccan *tagine* or Spanish *cocida* and serve it with couscous, rice or polenta instead of mashed potatoes and they'd wolf it down. At the time I didn't own a tagine, the distinctive cooking pot that gives Moroccan stews their name, but I made an awful lot of these stews.

The first time I went to Morocco, I remember standing transfixed in front of a makeshift kitchen in the medina in Marrakech where a row of tiny, one-person tagines steamed away, the tall conical lids looking like a row of witches' hats. On another occasion I spent a morning in the all-women kitchens of La Mamounia, the grande dame of Marrakech hotels. They too had one-person tagines but theirs relied on some deft *mise-en-place*, so the stew had only to be heated before it was served. The real point of the pointy tagine lid is providing a cold surface where steam condenses and drips back into the food, negating the need for much liquid.

I'm embarrassed to admit that the tagine I carefully lugged back from Morocco some years ago is now in the garden. Almost the first time I used it, the earthenware bowl cracked so I still cook most of my tagines in a regular, lidded casserole and they are none the worse for it. I also own a bright red cast-iron tagine made by Le Creuset, and although it's quite a large dish, it's too small for the tagines I tend to make, for at least four if not more people. Next time I go to Morocco I shall buy another and try again.

Lamb Tagine with Green Olives and Preserved Lemon

SERVES 4

It's easy to buy the specialized ingredients needed for a pretty authentic Moroccan tagine. Even ras al hanout, *the Moroccan spice mix, and salt-preserved lemons are now stocked by most supermarkets, although the latter come in off-puttingly large jars. Once the jar has been opened it has to be stored in the fridge, taking up valuable space. So what else can be done with them? It is the peel that gets eaten; the lemons end up a bit like Seville oranges start out, all pips and no body. The peel, though, is rendered relatively soft. Though salty, it has a special tangy flavour that makes tagines like this one so delicious. I add it to all sorts of dishes, particularly couscous salads, other stews and sweet sour vegetable dishes like fennel with capers and green olives. Serve this very brown tagine with couscous; you will need 250g, hydrated in 400ml of boiling water or stock with a squeeze of lemon and a splash of olive oil. Rice or green beans and crusty bread are good alternatives.*

2 large onions, approx 500g	700–900g lamb shoulder
2 tbsp olive oil	½ chicken stock cube
10g butter	4 Belazu preserved lemons
4 large garlic cloves	70g pitted green olives
a generous pinch of saffron threads	80g bunch coriander
4 tsp *ras al hanout* (Moroccan spice mix)	1 lemon

Peel, halve and chop the onions. Heat the oil in a spacious, heavy-bottomed lidded pan (or tagine). Melt the butter in the oil and stir in the chopped onions. Stir occasionally for about 20 minutes, until juicy and glassy. Peel and chop the garlic and crush to a paste with a pinch of salt. Sprinkle the saffron over the onions, stirring as it bleeds colour into the hot juices. Stir in the garlic, followed by the *ras al hanout*, stir-frying for a couple of minutes.

Cut the lamb into double-bite-size chunks. Fold the lamb through the onions until all the pieces change colour, then add the half stock cube dissolved in 300ml of boiling water. Quarter the preserved lemons, scrape away the seeds and flesh, and slice the peel. Stir the lemon peel and olives into the stew.

Chop the coriander, slicing the stalks finely. Add the stalk half of the bunch to the pot. Establish a gentle simmer, cover and cook for 45 minutes. Check that the meat is very tender – if not, cook on a bit longer. Adjust the seasoning with salt, pepper and lemon juice. Stir in the remaining coriander and serve with couscous.

T Tart Tins

The only tarts my mother ever made were mincemeat or marmalade, occasionally jam. They happened when she had leftover pastry from making a pie, which she did at least once a week. She only ever made shortcrust pastry and she used all lard or lard with a small amount of butter. When I left home it was years before I attempted to make pastry and when I did, I found I had absorbed Mum's measures as if by osmosis – one tablespoon equalled one ounce and roughly half fat to flour mixed with very cold water. I mention it because it set me in good stead for making endless pies and tarts, particularly tarts and flans.

If you opened the cupboard door where I keep my tart tins, you'd be shocked by how many I own. Small ones, fluted ones, round ones, oblong ones, long thin ones, medium ones, huge ones, a catering size tin for tarte Tatin, heart-shaped tins and several identical pairs. Some, not many, have a non-stick surface. Most are flan rings with interchangeable bases and I always rub them with butter then dust the butter with flour, tapping out the excess, to make them reliably non-stick. To release the ring, just stand the tart on a tin.

Fig and Serrano Ham Tart

SERVES 4–6

It's hard to beat the time-honoured match of perfectly ripe figs with Parma or Serrano ham. This sublime combination of honeyed, juicy fruit with sheets of even pinker soft, salty ham was the inspiration for this tart. The creamy filling is flavoured with Parmesan and the surface is dredged with more cheese that cooks to a thin, golden crust. Perfect for any occasion.

For the pastry:
200g plain flour, plus a little extra
75g butter, plus a little extra
50g lard
3–6 tbsp ice-cold water

For the filling:
3 large eggs
250ml soured cream
75g grated Parmesan
280g ripe figs
7 slices of Serrano ham

Heat the oven to 200°C/gas mark 6. Sift the flour into a mixing bowl. Cut the fat in chunks directly into the flour. Rub the fat into the flour with your fingertips until it resembles breadcrumbs. Add 3 tablespoons of cold water and quickly work into the flour, adding more water if necessary, so you can form a soft ball. Cover and chill f or 30 minutes.

Rub the extra knob of butter over a 23cm flan tin with a removable base. Dust with flour, rolling the tin round in your hands to completely cover. Tip out any excess flour. This, incidentally, makes it non-stick. Roll out the pastry to fit, pressing it down gently into the base edges. Leave a decent overhang in case of shrinkage. Place on a baking sheet and loosely cover with foil. Cover the base with baking beans or rice (to stop the pastry rising) and bake for 10 minutes. Remove the foil and cook for a further 10 minutes, until light golden.

Whisk the eggs in a mixing bowl, then stir in the cream and 50g of grated Parmesan. Quarter the figs lengthways. Arrange the figs in the pastry case. Tear the ham into 5 or 6 pieces a sheet and drape between the figs. Season lightly with salt and pepper and pour over the egg custard. Sprinkle the remaining cheese over the top. Bake for 25–35 minutes, until the custard is almost set and the Parmesan is crusty and golden. Use a knife to cut away excess pastry, then stand on a tin to remove the collar. Slip on to a plate and serve hot, warm or cold.

Pear Custard Tart

SERVES 6

It matters little which type of pear you choose for this lovely tart, it's far more important the fruit is very ripe so it ends up succulent against soft, creamy custard and a crisp yet flaky pastry base. Rather than rich, sweetened pâte sucrée, *this tart is made with shortcrust pastry, rolled thinly and giving the tart a buttery taste but crisp finish. The pears are sliced in big long pieces and spread over the baked pastry case so the custard swells between the fruit. A triumphant recipe, rich enough for an elegant dinner, easy enough for a midweek treat and simple enough to please the youngest child at Sunday lunch.*

200g plain flour
75g butter, plus an extra knob
25g lard
4–6 tbsp cold water
4 large ripe pears

1 tbsp lemon juice
3 medium egg yolks
300ml double cream
1 tbsp caster sugar

Sift the flour into a mixing bowl. Chop 75g of butter and the lard into small pieces into the flour. Either use your fingertips to quickly rub the fat into the flour or pulse in the food processor. Stir or briefly pulse 2 tablespoons of cold water into the mixture, continuing tentatively until it clings together. Form into a ball; dust with flour if it seems too wet, adding extra water if it seems too dry. Clingfilm and chill for 30 minutes.

Heat the oven to 220°C/gas mark 7. Choose a 25–27cm tart tin with a removable base. Smear with butter and dust with flour, shaking out excess. Place on a baking sheet. Flour a work surface and roll out the pastry to fit the tin, leaving a 1cm overhang. Cover with foil and fill with baking beans. Bake for 10 minutes, then remove the foil and bake for 5 minutes until lightly coloured.

Peel, halve, core and thickly slice the pears into a bowl with the lemon juice. Arrange the lemony slices in the tart case. Beat the yolks into the cream and pour over the top. Sprinkle with the sugar. Place in the oven. Reduce the heat to 190°C/gas mark 5. Bake for 35–45 minutes, until set but wobbly in the middle. Cool slightly, shave off the pastry overhang, remove the collar and serve warm or cold.

T Terrines

Terrines are straight-sided clay or porcelain dishes with lids for making chunky pâtés in, usually called terrines, with minced or puréed fish, fowl or meat. Some, the posh ones, are elaborately decorated, sometimes with the head of a game bird or rabbit, both of which are often used to make a terrine. They are usually oblong-shaped, sometimes long and slim, like the beautiful orange cast-iron Le Creuset pan that stayed with my husband when we parted company.

I have two dishes I use when I want to make terrine or meatloaf. One is the real McCoy, made by Apilco of thick, chunky porcelain. The other, a rough and ready version, is oval-shaped with a slightly dodgy lid. Terrines and meatloaf are useful fridge food for packed lunches and sandwiches, or on toast when you come in starving at the end of the day. They keep safely in the fridge for a couple of weeks, so are a useful backstop for meals with baked potatoes and salad, and perfect for a party, picnic or Jacob's Join/bring-a-dish.

A terrine doesn't have to be made with expensive meat or game, in fact almost anything goes and it is a good way of using inexpensive fatty cuts minced by you or your butcher with a small amount of lean. Plenty of sloppily cooked onion keeps it moist, with breadcrumbs to soften the flavour and texture.

I like taking the seasoning away from Europe to the Middle East and Asia, particularly with chicken and pork, using coriander instead of parsley, chilli and ginger, even water chestnuts and bamboo shoots. These terrines-cum-meatloaves go with Thai sweet chilli sauce and salads, finely sliced pickled garlic or cucumber, and quickly made mint and coriander salsas, instead of the more usual onion marmalade and cornichons.

The way to cook a terrine is slowly, at a low temperature in the oven, standing in a pan of hot water known as a bain-marie. It is cooled in the water, then kept in the fridge for at least 24 hours, although several days is better, for the flavours to mature. It is served in thick slices from the dish; any jelly will be delicious pure meat juice.

Leek Terrine with Crayfish Tails and Lemon Vinaigrette

SERVES 8

This is leeks vinaigrette in a different form and just as simple to make. It's a lovely show-off dinner party dish. A slice of the pretty green and white chequerboard terrine is served eighties throw-back style surrounded by a few crayfish tails, prettily dressed with a swirl of lemon vinaigrette and a sprinkling of chives. Alternatively and just as stunning, surround it with slivers of black truffle. The terrine is inspired by a refined version I ate years ago when Pierre Koffmann presided over La Tante Claire on Royal Hospital Road (now Gordon Ramsay), and again more recently, when he cooked at a pop-up restaurant on the roof of Selfridges.

1.5kg similar-thickness leeks
180g crayfish tails in brine or 1 preserved black truffle
1 lemon
a small bunch of chives

For the vinaigrette:
1 tsp runny honey
50ml fresh lemon juice
1 tsp Maille Dijon mustard
freshly ground black pepper
150ml extra virgin olive oil
You will need a 24 x 7 x 7cm deep terrine tin or something comparable, and some clingfilm

Trim the leeks and leave to soak in a bowl of water to draw out any dirt trapped between the layers. Steam until tender. Line the terrine with a sheet of clingfilm large enough to fold over and securely cover the leeks. Pack the leeks into the terrine, trimming where necessary to line them up snugly and piling them high in the tin. Fold over the clingfilm. Place on a small roasting tin to catch the inevitable overspill. It's the sticky juice that squeezes out of the compressed leeks that acts as glue to hold them together. Hunt down a piece of wood or cut a thick piece of card to fit the top of the tin, pop it into a plastic bag or wrap in clingfilm to avoid it getting sodden, and pile with weights, heavy cans or similar. The card distributes the weight so the leeks are evenly compressed. Cool, then chill for at least 24 hours and up to 48.

To make the vinaigrette, dissolve the honey and a pinch of salt in the lemon juice. Stir in the mustard, season with black pepper and whisk in the olive oil, adding it in a trickle, to make a thick, glossy, yellow vinaigrette. Thin with a little water if it seems too thick.

Remove the weights just before serving. Lift the terrine out of the tin with the help of the unfurled clingfilm, cover with a chopping board and invert. Have 8 plates, the drained crayfish tossed with lemon juice or thinly sliced truffle and the vinaigrette ready. Slice the terrine with a sharp, thin-bladed knife, using a fish slice to deftly lift the slices and quickly transfer them to a plate. Continue thus, then scatter 5 or 6 crayfish or truffle slices around the terrine and spoon over the vinaigrette, serving the rest in a bowl or jug for top-ups. Garnish with snipped chives.

T Tin Opener

When I was about ten, a friend and I ran away. We took a loaf of bread, the bread knife, some cheese and fruit, a few hoarded tins and Granny's tin opener. Granny lived next door and I knew she wouldn't notice if it went missing. It was a pathetic effort because we just went down the lane to one of our favourite picnic spots, sat under a tree and started to eat the food. We'd forgotten to bring a drink and neither of us wanted to be the one to use the tin opener. It was the type where you had to stab the top of the tin and force it with jerking movements to cut its way round. It left a scary jagged edge. I can't remember if we left a note or why we ran away in the first place but our mothers were on to us in double quick time. All I can remember about the aftermath was my mother telling my friend's mother that we would have soon got hungry because I wouldn't have been able to cut straight slices of bread. I still think it's a strange response, but I used my own money to buy Granny a new tin opener.

Tin openers are tricky bits of kit. The best ones work effortlessly, sliding round the tin and leaving no jagged edges. I like the butterfly-handled openers that clamp on to the side or top edge of the tin, requiring a quick reverse turn to release. We had a wall-mounted tin opener in the matrimonial home and it was a godsend, highly recommended even if you don't use that many tins. It held the tin by the rim even when the top was removed. I have a drawer full of tin openers but my newest is my favourite. Its bright red rubber-dipped steel batwing handles (8 x 5cm) mean it's easy to spot in the gadget drawer and the super-smooth action makes it a joy to use. Called Super Kim, I found it at Labour and Wait, a delightful East End shop specializing in everyday hardware and kitchen classics that mellow and improve with age (see page 275).

Spanish Chickpea Soup with Caramelized Onion and *Albondigas*

SERVES 4

Who'd have thought that a couple of tins of chickpeas could be turned into a wonderful soup? It is desperately simple to make, doesn't require stock and is ready within minutes. Describing it as liquid hummus gives you an idea of what to expect, but it has a noticeable garlicky kick and the creamy, mealy chickpeas liquidize with a cappuccino finish, the flavours sharpened with lemon juice. It is great as it is but can be jazzed up with a garnish of thinly sliced, crisp-fried chorizo and freshly chopped coriander, although the original – sopa de panela – calls for masses of chopped mint and flat-leaf parsley. Another idea is to add a spoonful of slippery soft, dark brown caramelized onion, giving each mouthful a pleasing sweet yet bitter finish enriched by a swirl of olive oil. Another more fulsome addition is albondigas, meatballs made with highly seasoned lamb. They turn the soup into a meal and are good with or without the caramelized onion.

This way of cooking meatballs means they could also be reheated later (kept, covered, in the fridge) in, say, tomato sauce or stock to serve as part of a tapas/picnic spread, in curls of crisp lettuce with hummus or mixed with cooked peas and chopped mint.

2 x 400g tins of chickpeas
3 large garlic cloves
6 tbsp fruity olive oil
1 large lemon
Onion garnish:
1 medium-large onion
1 tbsp olive oil
extra virgin olive oil, to serve

For the albondigas:
50g fresh breadcrumbs
1 tbsp sheep's yoghurt
1 egg
500g organic minced lamb
1 heaped tsp ground cumin
¼ tsp chilli flakes
2 garlic cloves
25g bunch flat-leaf parsley
1 tbsp vegetable oil

Begin by preparing the onion garnish. Halve, peel and finely slice the onion. Heat 1 tablespoon of olive oil in a frying pan, stir in the onion and cook briskly, stirring often, as it glistens and browns. Reduce the heat and cook, stirring occasionally, until soft, dark and withered, but still juicy. Remove from the heat.

To make the *albondigas*, mix the breadcrumbs into the yoghurt in a saucer. Crack the egg into a mixing bowl and whisk smooth. Crumble the meat over the top and sprinkle with the cumin and chilli flakes, ½ teaspoon of salt and a generous seasoning of pepper. Crumble the yoghurt crumbs over the meat.

Peel and finely chop the garlic then crush to a paste with the flat of a knife. Pick the leaves off the parsley stalks and finely chop them. Add both to the bowl. Use a fork to mix thoroughly, then form into a ball. Divide into quarters.

Heat the oven to 200°C/gas mark 6. Pinch off a small amount of mixture and roll between your hands to make a meatball somewhere between a cherry tomato and a walnut in size. Expect to make 10-12 balls from each quarter. Smear a sheet of foil with oil and arrange on a baking sheet. Add the meatballs. Roast for 15 minutes. Cool on the sheet.

To make the soup, drain the liquid from the chickpeas into a measuring jug and make the amount up to 900ml. Peel and coarsely chop the garlic. You will probably need to liquidize the soup in two or three batches and the mixture of chickpeas, liquid, garlic, 6 tablespoons of olive oil and 2 tablespoons of lemon juice, with ½ teaspoon of salt and a generous seasoning of freshly grated black pepper, needs to blitz for several minutes until smooth and fluffy.

Pour into a pan and simmer for 5 or 6 minutes. Taste and adjust the seasoning with salt, pepper and lemon juice. If adding the cooled meatballs, simmer for a further 6-8 minutes. Serve with a swirl of your best olive oil and a spoonful of caramelized onion (or not).

Store Cupboard Banoffi Pies

SERVES 6

Banoffee is an amalgam of banana, toffee and coffee, and refers to a pudding invented at the Hungry Monk at Jevington in Sussex in 1972. They christened it Banoffi Pie, often wrongly called Banoffee Pie, but it's a tart, not a pie, made with a shortcrust pastry base, not digestive biscuit crumbs as most recipes would have it. The original was made by simmering two *unopened cans of Nestlé's condensed milk – the tin totally immersed – for* five hours *to turn it into dark, gooey caramel known by its Spanish name,* dulce de leche. *It's now easy to buy dulce de leche in a jar, but it's far cheaper to make your own. Why not boil several tins, as they'll keep indefinitely, while you're at it, so you can whip up this 'marvellous emergency pudding'?*

For this recipe the entire pudding is a cheat, using individual ready-made pastry cases or a 20cm all-butter shortcrust case. To make your own pastry for a 23cm flan tin or 6 individual pies, you will need 200g of plain flour, 75g of butter and 25g of lard. Follow the recipe for blind baking instructions given for Fig and Serrano Ham Tart on page 229.

6 all-butter ready-made individual tart cases or 1 x 20cm all-butter ready-made tart case
For the filling:
400g tin of condensed milk or 450g jar of Merchant Gourmet Dulce de Leche

4–6 under-ripe bananas
300ml whipping or double cream
½ tsp powdered instant coffee
2 tsp caster sugar
a generous pinch of fine, ground coffee

If using condensed milk, place the tin or tins in a pan and cover with water. Boil, semi-covered, checking regularly that the tins are completely immersed, for at least 2 hours. Leave to cool, then chill before opening. Thickly spread the *dulce de leche* in the pastry cases – you may not need it all. Peel the bananas, slice thickly and nudge up closely over the caramel to entirely cover. If making a tart, slice the banana lengthways. Whip the cream with the instant coffee and sugar until firm but floppy. Spoon, then smooth or pipe it over the bananas. Dust with the ground coffee and chill until required.

T Toaster

Getting toast right is a serious business. Some people like what I regard as hot bread whereas I'm a burnt toast girl. When I was a child it wasn't usual to own a toaster, there wasn't the need. Toast was made once a day for breakfast, several slices cooked together under the grill, and served in a toast rack. It was invariably on the table some time before we were, so was always cold and bendy, never uniformly toasted and rarely living up to the tempting smells that lured us from our beds. It wasn't until I left home and shared a flat with people who demolished a loaf's worth of toast, made slice after slice from a *sliced* loaf and eaten hot from the grill, that I realized toast should be eaten hot.

I don't remember my first toaster but I've owned an indecent number over the years. I've set several on fire, nearly burnt down two kitchens and stunk the house out on numerous occasions. Most problems have been caused by inexperience. As a child I noticed that brown bread toasted differently from white, never as well, and it took longer, but every loaf brings toast anxiety. The time required doesn't necessarily relate to the density of the crumb. Ciabatta, for example, with its big gaping holes and loose texture, always catches me out. You'd think it would be a quick toast but it's quite the reverse. Sourdough is the most difficult to gauge, but if you push it too far, the crust burns to a cinder. The irritating thing is that using a toaster is supposed to remove all the risk involved in toast-making. You aren't supposed to have to watch it constantly, adjusting the knobs to get the right result.

The best toaster I've ever owned is an inexpensive French device called Grille Pain Panor, recommended by Elizabeth David. I bought it before our predilection for griddle pans, which also make superb toast (particularly if the bread is spread first on both sides with butter or olive oil, stopping it going soggy like regular toast, therefore excellent for scrambled eggs or devilled kidneys), and like the griddle it sits over direct heat. Unlike that indestructible pan, this quirky toaster is made of thin metal and constructed like a large empty sandwich with a long flimsy handle. The bottom layer, which sits over the flame, is a punctured square of metal with a grooved circular saucer-like middle, but the top, where the toast goes, is punched with holes like a Damien Hirst spotty painting. They leave a pretty imprint on the toast. Once heated up, it toasts the bread incredibly quickly and that is its downfall. Over time the wall of the circular inner base has split, creating a

moon-shaped slash. As the toaster heats up, it grins a big gaping smile where the flames can leap through and burn the toast. One day I'll find a replacement but until then, I rather enjoy its toast tension. I love the crackly sound the bread makes when it's laid on the hot, holey mat. If I stand and watch, waiting to turn the slice, nothing happens. The moment I turn my back, a corner will be burnt. It's tense.

Hotels offering a buffet-style breakfast are a good place to spot weird toasting apparatus. Most operate like a revolving conveyor belt but the most Heath Robinson version, built like a wire cage with the element revealed, was in a fairly posh hotel in Mauritius. The toaster had an entrance where it was fed with bread on a conveyor belt with heating panels placed above and below, toasting the bread as it passed through. It shuddered, often stopped completely, often burnt the toast and, worst of all, regularly set it on fire.

Many more weird and wonderful toasters that chart the history of toaster design can be seen at the virtual toaster museum (see page 275).

When we moved into this house, I treated myself to one of those big, catering-style toasters with slots wide enough to hold crumpets. The British-made Dualit toaster was quite a novelty at the time and mine is still going strong, although I'm not so keen on the toast it makes with the latest hotplate replacement design. It's definitely moody now, my toaster, fickle and not reliably keen on toasting bread evenly. I'll stick with it, though, until it dies on me or I set it on fire, because it has certainly served my family well.

Pitta Pockets with Chicken Kofte, Hummus and Pickled Cucumber

My father-in-law Edwin John introduced me to toasted pitta bread. He liked it for breakfast with marmalade and would lightly toast the pitta, then carefully slit it open – it traps a lot of steam – toasting each half until crusty. I often do the same with brown pitta.

For as long as I can remember, I have made hummus regularly, at least once a week when the boys were growing up. They liked it in their packed lunch sandwiches – a constant source of intrigue to their friends, I discovered years later – and we ate it for supper with chicken and kebabs instead of potatoes. When people came for drinks they sliced toasted pitta into strips (kept warm in a folded napkin) to swipe through hummus to eat with black olives. Sometimes I would, and still do, decorate the hummus with dukkah or toasted sesame seeds, or glistening pomegranate seeds. When the boys were rushing off out and wanted supper on the hoof, kofte or chicken kebabs stuffed into toasted pitta envelopes with hummus and salad was top favourite, easy to eat roller-blading.

Kofte is another name for large, slightly flattened meatballs or small patties and this recipe, highly seasoned with mint and coriander, is one of many versions. They are good with tzatziki (see page 138) or tomato sauce (see page 198) but this is a Fraser Street special: stuffed into toasted pitta envelopes with garlicky hummus and crunchy pickled cucumber with a lemon wedge to squeeze over the top.

pitta bread
lemon wedges, to serve
For the kofte:
50g crustless bread
2 large garlic cloves
2 shallots
15g mint leaves
25g bunch coriander
500g minced chicken
1 egg
1 tsp ground cumin
2 tbsp natural yoghurt
2–4 tbsp vegetable oil

For the hummus:
400g tin of chickpeas
3 new season garlic cloves
1 large, juicy lemon
¼ tsp ground cumin
1 tbsp tahini (optional)
a shake of Tabasco
approx 150ml olive oil
For the pickled cucumber:
4 Lebanese/small cucumbers
1 tbsp salt
½ tsp sugar
2 tbsp white wine vinegar
1 tbsp chopped dill

Begin with the pickled cucumber. Use a mandoline or the slicing attachment of your food processor to slice the cucumber very thinly (as if making crisps). Spread out in a basin, sprinkle with 1 tablespoon of salt and leave for 20 minutes. Gather up, rinse, squeeze dry, pile into a clean tea towel and squeeze dry again. Dissolve the sugar in the vinegar and stir in the cucumber, then the dill. Cover and chill until required.

Tear the bread into small pieces and blitz to make crumbs with 2 peeled garlic cloves. Trim, halve and finely chop the shallots. Add to the bowl and blitz again with most of the mint and coarsely chopped coriander. Add the minced chicken, egg, cumin, ½ teaspoon of salt and 2 tablespoons of yoghurt and pulse briefly a few times until blended. Turn into a mixing bowl. Rinse your hands in cold water – this helps prevent the mixture sticking to your hands – and form into large walnut-sized balls. Flatten the balls slightly as you transfer them to a plate. Cover with clingfilm and chill to firm while you make the hummus.

Drain the chickpeas in a sieve or colander. Rinse with cold water and shake dry. If you want to make the smoothest, creamiest hummus ever, you have to remove the chickpea husks. This is messy and a fiddle. Rub the chickpeas briskly between your hands or in the fold of a tea towel. You'll be amazed how the little skins multiply. Place the chickpeas in the food processor bowl with the peeled and crushed garlic, the juice from the lemon, the cumin, a generous seasoning of salt and black pepper, the tahini, if using, the Tabasco and 2 tablespoons of olive oil. Blitz to roughly chop, scraping down inside the bowl a couple of times, then, with the motor running, add the remaining olive oil in a steady stream. Continue until very smooth, adding extra olive oil or lemon juice and water for the texture you favour; I like it thick but creamy. Taste and fine-tune the seasoning.

To finish the dish, heat the vegetable oil in a frying pan and fry the kofte in batches, turning after a couple of minutes as they form delicious crusty edges. Rest on a fold of kitchen paper and continue with the rest. Cut the pitta in half across the middle, to make two envelopes. Toast as if making normal toast, so the pocket opens and the bread is lightly toasted. Serve everything for people to help themselves or fill and serve with a lemon wedge.

Pea, Watercress and Brown Shrimp on Toast

SERVES 4

This looks so pretty, a thick green purée of peas and watercress thickly spread over buttered sourdough toast, topped with little brown shrimps. It makes a lovely summery starter or snack before, say, roast tomato soup followed by Orange and Apple Crumble (page 111).

200g frozen petits pois

50g watercress

1 tsp Maille Dijon mustard

1 tbsp white wine vinegar

3 tbsp olive oil

4 slices of sourdough bread

a knob of butter, plus extra for toast

100g brown/grey shrimps

lemon wedges, to serve

Cook the peas in boiling salted water. Drain and tip into the bowl of a food processor. Add the watercress, mustard, vinegar and oil and blitz for several minutes, scraping down the inside walls as necessary, to make a thick herb sauce similar to pesto. Toast the bread and spread generously with butter. Spread thickly with the green paste and top with a tumble of shrimps. Serve with a lemon wedge to squeeze over the top.

T Trifle Bowl

I sometimes wonder if I would make trifle as often as I do if I didn't own my mother's scalloped, cut glass trifle bowl. Once upon a time I had two, but I'm ashamed to recall that I broke the other one making jelly with boiling water. The trifles of my childhood were the sort made with jelly from a packet, tinned mandarin oranges and thick Bird's custard that set hard and made a skin, but my love affair was cruelly dashed at the Lord Mayor's Fancy Dress Party. I must have been eight, my brother ten, me done up as Little Miss Muffet, complete with an enormous black velvet spider with long pipe cleaner legs dangling from my waist, and he as the Knave of Hearts. I still have *his* hat, an old-fashioned beret with a row of red felt hearts lined up round the edge. The entertainment was spectacular but the highlight, as far as I was concerned, was the food. I queued for trifle (extra large, please) but it was a rude awakening: at the Mansion House, the trifle was tipsy with booze.

Childhood trifles were for birthdays and Boxing Day, always Boxing Day, the predictable pudding for the annual Christmas leftovers lunch at the cousins' house in Westcliff-on-Sea. Eight children and five adults – while Great-Aunt Meg was alive – would be squashed round a long table in the playroom and afterwards there would be the inevitable squabble over who could read what from the cousins' collection of the *Broons* and *Oor Wullie* annuals. I still remember one story, where the dog jumped on to a bench and started patting the man's head, fed up with being petted himself.

Trifle is a wonderful dish for a party and endlessly variable. It can be made with store cupboard ingredients like dried apricots plumped with orange juice, the top decorated with silver balls. Or with any tinned fruit you care to mention, from mandarin oranges or cling peaches to more exotic fruit like lychees and figs, although seasonal fresh fruit trifles are very special. My Christmas trifle is more likely to be made with frozen raspberries saved from the allotment, proper vanilla custard and very boozy syllabub instead of sugary whipped cream. The top can be decorated with raspberries and angelica to look like surreal sprigs of holly.

Trifle basics are sugary oblong trifle sponges, Swiss rolls or boudoir biscuits, soaked in sherry or other strong booze to soften them. Jam or fruit purée, or stewed or macerated fruit makes the next layer, topped with custard and whipped cream. The cream can be flavoured with yet more alcohol and turned into syllabub. Trifle can be quickly whipped up, everyone loves it, and it looks charming, particularly if you are lucky enough to own a crystal trifle bowl or a large glass dish to show off the layers. Alternatively, and this is a good tip if you want to make non-alcoholic versions of tipsy trifle for small children, make theirs in individual glasses using fruit juice instead of sherry and whipped cream instead of syllabub.

Trifles by Helen Saberi (Prospect Books, 2009) makes fascinating reading, tracing the history and giving many intriguing recipes for one of our favourite nursery puddings.

Raspberry Jelly Trifle

SERVES 6–8

A gentle update on the jelly trifles of my childhood. A little gelatine instead of fruit jelly to set fresh raspberry purée, with extra raspberries for decoration. I have made this with Bird's custard and 'fresh' supermarket custard and both are delicious; the latter is fluffier and unlikely to set firm. The trifle will reach another level of deliciousness if it is made with fresh vanilla custard.

8 trifle sponges
5 tbsp sherry
750g fresh raspberries
2 tbsp caster sugar
a squeeze of lemon juice
4 sheets of gelatine

750ml Bird's or luxury thick and
    creamy 'fresh' custard, or fresh
    vanilla custard (see page 245)
300ml whipping cream
1 tbsp icing sugar
additional extras: angelica and
    silver balls   (*cont.*)

For the vanilla custard:
600ml milk
½ vanilla pod

6 egg yolks
1 egg
75g caster sugar

Place the trifle sponges in a glass bowl and dredge with the sherry. Set aside 12 perfect raspberries. Place the rest in a small pan with the caster sugar and lemon juice. Cook briefly, stirring as the sugar dissolves, just long enough for the raspberries to soften and turn very juicy. Place a sieve over a bowl and tip the raspberries into the sieve, forcing as much through as possible with the back of a wooden spoon. Scrape underneath so nothing is wasted, aiming to leave only pips in the sieve. Return the raspberry juice to the pan.

Soften the gelatine in a little water. Lift the wobbly gelatine into the raspberry juice and gently heat, stirring as it melts. Do not let it boil. Cool slightly, then pour the raspberry jelly over the soggy trifle sponges. Cover with clingfilm and chill for about an hour, possibly longer, until set.

To make the vanilla custard, scald the milk with the split vanilla pod, giving it a few prods with a wooden spoon to disperse the vanilla seeds. Beat the egg yolks with the whole egg and sugar. Strain the vanilla-flavoured milk over the egg and stir to mix before pouring back into the pan. Cook very gently over a low flame, beating with a wooden spoon regularly to disperse hot spots, continuing until very thick with a slight wobble to the texture. Pour the custard into a bowl and suspend over another bowl of iced water to chill the custard quickly. Stir occasionally. When tepid, spoon the custard over the jellied trifle sponges, or add the slightly cooled Bird's custard or 'fresh' custard from the carton.

Whip the cream by hand with the icing sugar until it just holds peaks. Spoon or pipe the cream over the custard. Decorate with the reserved raspberries and slivers of angelica; add the silver balls just before serving. Cover with a tight stretch of clingfilm and chill until required.

Lychee, Mango and Pineapple Fruit Salad with Lime

SERVES 4

A glass bowl is what you need to show off this subtly colour-coded fruit salad that goes through shades of cream to deep, dark orange yellow, all offset by the dark, edible seeds of the passion fruit. It smells so fantastic as you slice, the sweet but fresh zing of pineapple mingling with lime and the deep, honeyed richness of mango. All these gorgeous flavours are brought together with the sweet sour juices from the passion fruit. The salad is a treat by any standards.

1 small pineapple

425g tin lychees or 300g fresh

1 large ripe mango or 2 small ones

2 limes

4 large passion fruit

Slice the skin off the pineapple, cutting out any hairy 'eyes' that remain. You will notice that the eyes line up radiating round the fruit; just follow the line, making a shallow trench with a sharp knife. Slice the flesh into thin rounds about the thickness of a £1 coin, then cut into small wedges, discarding the woody central core. Transfer the fruit and any juices to a glass bowl.

Slice the 'cheeks' off the mango and score the flesh to make chunky dice. Make the dice stand out by pressing the skin to invert the flesh and give a hedgehog effect. Slice the dice into the bowl. Cut any remaining flesh from the wide, flat stone. Halve the passion fruit round their middles and scrape the juices, seeds and all, over the top. Drain tinned lychees and tear into 2 or 3 pieces into the bowl. If using fresh, peel them by making a crack in the brittle shell then carefully peeling it away. Tear the lychees off their stones in big pieces directly into the bowl.

Squeeze the lime over the fruit and use your hands or a spoon to mix thoroughly. Let the salad sit for at least 10 minutes, preferably longer, for the flavours to mix and mingle. Cream is not needed.

U *Ulek-ulek* and Other Pestles and Mortars

I think I was about twelve when my mum decided to add curry to her repertoire of what-to-do-with-Sunday-roast-leftovers. At the time there was one Indian restaurant in the village, and Vesta 'just add water' curry was the inspiration for someone like Mum who didn't know anything about Indian food. She didn't reach for the pestle and mortar and start pounding spices but sought help from the village general store, ending up with curry powder in a pale blue tin. All Mum's curries tasted the same, the meat floating in thin, vaguely curried gravy with a few sultanas and cashew nuts and sloppy rice. The smell, rather than the taste, was exceedingly fragrant and aromatic, or maybe my memory is playing tricks because it was shocking to smell curry in our house on any night, particularly on a Monday.

I bought my first pestle and mortar in the market at Camden Lock. It was very heavy, made of pale stone and very cheap. The mortar was shallow and wide, the pestle a curious shape, more like a flattened, bent pipe than a large carrot. I didn't discover until years later, and long after it had been lost between moves, that I'd bought an Indonesian pestle and mortar, known as *cobek* or *ulek-ulek*, its distinctive shape crucial for slide-pounding chilli-hot sambals.

My favourite pestle and mortar is made of dark grey granite and comes from Thailand, bought in a Thai shop but available online (see page 275) through various outlets in various sizes. Jamie Oliver popularized them when he launched himself as the Naked Chef, and they are now part of his range of cookware. I bought two, one for Zach and one for me, and it is deep (12.5cm) and chunky, big enough (600ml capacity) to make mayonnaise in, or pesto and salsa verde, which I do, very occasionally. It is indestructible, so there's never any anxiety about giving something a good pounding. The other great point is that it being so deep, spices rarely jump out, as they often do in small mortars.

I also own three small ceramic pestles and mortars. One is designed for grinding paints but is useful for garlic and dried or fresh chilli. The most recent is a clever double-ended mortar – 10cm diameter one end and 5cm the other – just large enough for a single garlic. It's made by Vacu Vin, more famous for their handy chill-sleeves for wine, and available online (see page 275).

Sri Lankan Ginger and Lime Chicken Curry with Coriander Relish

SERVES 6

I'm reluctant to call this a Sri Lankan curry but it was inspired by ingredients listed on the back of a packet of curry powder Zach brought back from holiday. It is, though, fragrant and aromatic, a subtly spiced curry seasoned with pounded cardamom, coriander, black pepper and cloves. With onions and garlic and quite a lot of ginger, it thickens into a voluptuous brown gravy that stains the chicken so it looks like lamb. Young leaf spinach melts into swirls of green and the curry is served with a scoop of creamy yoghurt and a vibrant coriander relish-cum-sambal. This is quickly liquidized in a blender, the coriander, bird's-eye chillies, lime juice and garlic pulled together with a little creamed coconut.

Without the relish, the curry is subtle and elegant with rice, yoghurt and mango chutney, but I love its extra zing. It must, though, be made at the last minute so the bright green doesn't get a chance to fade. Chapattis, for scooping or rolling, make a good alternative to rice.

50g fresh ginger

1kg chicken thigh fillets

juice of 3 limes

2 large red onions, approx 350g

2 garlic cloves

25g butter

1 tsp vegetable oil

1 tsp cardamom pods

1 tsp coriander seeds

1 tsp black peppercorns

1 tsp cloves

½ tsp turmeric

165ml tin of coconut cream

250ml chicken stock

100g young spinach leaves

250ml thick natural yoghurt

For the relish:

60g bunch coriander

1 large garlic clove

2 red bird's-eye chillies

50ml lime juice

¼ tsp sugar

15g creamed coconut

Peel and finely grate the ginger. Slice the chicken fillets into 3 or 4 strips. Mix the ginger, chicken and lime juice, then cover and chill. Peel, halve and finely slice the onions. Peel and chop the garlic. Heat the butter and oil in a spacious frying pan and gently soften the onion and garlic, stirring occasionally, for about 15 minutes, until wilted. Crack the cardamoms, extract the seeds and grind to a powder with the coriander seeds, peppercorns and cloves. Sprinkle the powder over the wilting onions and cook for a couple more minutes. Add the chicken and its marinade, turning as the pieces firm and colour. Mix together the turmeric, coconut cream and stock and add to the pan. Simmer, stirring occasionally, for 35–45 minutes, until thick, dark and creamy. Taste for salt; I needed 1 teaspoon.

Just before serving, place the spinach in a bowl, cover with boiling water and leave for 30 seconds. Drain and stir into the curry. Serve with a dollop of yoghurt topped with relish. To make the relish, coarsely chop the coriander bunch, peeled garlic and seeded chillies. Blitz smooth with the lime juice, 1 tablespoon of water, sugar and crumbled creamed coconut.

Massaman Thai Duck Curry with Toasted Cashew Nuts

SERVES 4

When my nephew got married on Koh Samui and the entire family gathered for an extended hooley, we all agreed that the best curries were from stalls by the side of the road. One exception, good wherever we tried it, was fragrant Massaman curry with chunks of intensely delicious potato. It's a good curry to make with just-dug little new potatoes or tiny Jersey Royal potatoes. In fact any new potato with a dense yet creamy texture, very thin skin and noticeable flavour is perfect. Although I've made it with duck, this recipe adapts to chicken (thigh fillet), lamb (shoulder) or shin of beef. If you are making this ahead, and it could be made 24 hours in advance, don't add the beans – or coriander – until the last minute, so they remain crunchy with fresh flavour and vibrant colour. Serve with rice and a garnish of toasted crushed cashew nuts. Did you know, by the way, that the reason cashews are always sold shelled, peeled and roasted, is because the skin contains allergenic resin and oil similar to that in poison ivy? And they're a seed, not a nut.

500g baby Jersey Royal or other small new potatoes
200g green beans
4 duck breast fillets, approx 750–900g
1 large garlic clove
15g fresh ginger
1 tbsp vegetable oil
4 shallots, approx 75g

35g sachet or 2 tbsp Massaman curry paste
165g tin of coconut cream
1 tbsp Thai fish sauce (nam pla)
50g salted, roasted cashew nuts
a few sprigs of coriander
2 limes
rice, to serve

Boil the scrubbed potatoes in salted water until tender. Trim the green beans, snap in half and boil for 1 minute in salted water. Drain, but reserve 8 tablespoons of the cooking water. Slice diagonally down the duck fillets, cutting into large bite-size strips, approx 5 × 2cm. Peel and chop the garlic and ginger and liquidize with 3 tablespoons of cooking water.

Heat the oil in a spacious, heavy-bottomed, lidded pan and gently soften the peeled and chopped shallots, allowing about 8 minutes, until soft and golden. Push to the sides, increase the heat and quickly brown the duck. Stir back the shallots and add the garlic and ginger and the curry paste. Let it bubble up for a couple of minutes, then add 2 tablespoons of coconut cream and stir thoroughly for 2 more minutes. Add the rest of the coconut cream, the fish sauce and reserved bean water. Establish a steady simmer over a low heat, cover and cook for 10 minutes before adding the potatoes and beans. Stir well, cover again and cook for a further 30 minutes, or until thick and creamy and the duck is tender. Taste and adjust the seasoning with lime juice. Place the cashews in a plastic bag. Use the pestle lightly but firmly to coarsely crush. Garnish the curry with cashews and coriander, and serve with rice and a lime wedge.

V Very Large Saucepan

Every kitchen needs a very large saucepan with a well-fitting lid. It might not get used that often but it is essential for certain things like cooking a ham, making marmalade or jam and cooking mussels. Mine holds 10 litres, so it's useful too when I get the urge to make stock for the freezer or stew for a party.

I got by without one for years, borrowing a pan from a chef friend, but when the requests starting getting too regular, I bit the bullet and bought my own. It comes from Ikea and cost about fifty quid. It's made of good-quality stainless steel, with a thick heavy base, handles on the tall, straight sides and a heavy lid. Where to keep the bugger is its only downside.

Steamed Mussels with Thyme and Crème Fraîche

SERVES 2–4

It's hard to beat the Belgian way of eating mussels with chips, mayo and a cold beer, but French moules marinière seasoned with thyme and a dollop of crème fraîche in the soup pips it at the post for me. Whenever I make it, and it's still a treat worthy of the best unsalted Normandy butter for the obligatory crusty bread, and authentic crème fraîche for the sauce, I remember my first tentative foray. It was in Brittany, at a pretty basic seaside café. As we chucked our shells into a discard bucket, I watched bemused as a lone gentleman grazed through a huge portion, easily as much as our meal for two. He neatly lined up his empty shells as he ate, tucking them snugly together, making a long black-blue coil. The next time, and forever after, I copied that man. I also picked up on his neat way of using the first empty shell as tweezers for the rest of the mussels. My husband, a greedy, fast eater, used to pick out all his mussels in double-quick time into the juices at the bottom of the bowl, then smugly wolf everything down soup-style. You can tell a lot by how someone tackles moules marinière.

Two kilos – actually more like 1.75 – is the standard net of mussels sold in fishmongers. They will feed four as a hearty starter and two as a very generous main course.

2kg mussels
1 large garlic clove
2 large shallots
a handful of flat-leaf parsley
50g unsalted French butter
a sprig of thyme

1 bay leaf
150ml dry cider or white wine
2 heaped tbsp crème fraîche
crusty bread and unsalted French
  butter, to serve

If necessary, scrub the mussels and rinse in several changes of cold water. Pull off the 'beards', scrape away barnacles and discard any broken or open mussels that don't close after a sharp tap. Drain thoroughly in a colander. Crack the garlic with your fist, flake away the skin and finely chop. Peel and finely chop the shallots. Coarsely chop the parsley leaves.

Melt the butter in a large pan (or use two pans, dividing all the ingredients; you want the mussels to no more than three-quarters fill the pan) and gently soften the shallot and garlic with the thyme and bay. Add the cider or wine, letting it bubble up for a moment or two, then add the mussels. Clamp on the lid, give the pan a couple of shakes to disperse the mussels, cooking at full steam for 3–5 minutes, until all the mussels have opened. Scoop about half the mussels into a large, warmed serving bowl, add the crème fraîche and most of the chopped parsley to the cooking pan, stir to mix thoroughly, then pour the contents of the pan over the mussels. Add the last of the parsley and serve with crusty bread and unsalted butter, and a bottle of chilled Muscadet or decent cider.

Singapore Chicken Rice

SERVES 6–8

It's all about the skin, my Singaporean friend Eddie Lim said, preparing me for the first time I tasted chicken rice at the long-gone Equatorial in Soho's Chinatown, where they made it every Saturday lunchtime. He, like most Chinese, loves skin and gelatinous bits, and soliloquized about the blubbery, rubbery texture of the chicken skin in this dish. But don't let that put you off.

The traditional way of preparing the bird, plunging it alternately into hot and cold water, and then minimal cooking with long soaking, also results in unusually silky, moist meat. The rice, too, is incredibly good. It is briefly stir-fried in rendered chicken fat with garlic and ginger before it's cooked in chicken stock with pandan (screw pine) leaves. These lend a piney, resinous flavour. They look like long tulip leaves and can be frozen. You'll find them in the chill cabinet of all Thai stores. Should you ever need to know, they repel cockroaches.

I learnt to make this delicious dish from Eddie and his wife Miranda, taking on board their refinements for maximum flavour and to suit the anglicized palate of their friends. Eddie bothers, for example, to cook the bird in stock rather than water, takes care to remove the seeds from the accompanying chilli sauce and brings down the heat with sugar. The jointed bird is piled over chunky pieces of peeled cucumber. They soak up the chicken juices and the soy sauce and toasted sesame oil poured over the top. Sprigs of coriander and slivers of tomato give a decorative finish.

No Singaporean would want chicken rice without ketjap *or* kecap manis. *This is a thick, syrupy sweet soy sauce from Indonesia, a sort of oriental balsamic vinegar found in the oriental section of large supermarkets or in Thai stores.*

Hainanese or Singapore chicken rice is a great party dish, perfect for Sunday lunch, and because the chicken is served at room temperature, all the preparations can be done in advance. Only finalizing the rice, and reheating the broth to be sipped with the meal, need be done at the last minute.

1.5–2kg chicken or 2 smaller birds

3 x 50g knobs of fresh ginger

2 tbsp sea salt

7 garlic cloves

5 spring onions

about 2 litres chicken stock or water

1 chicken stock cube

2 pandan leaves

6 coriander roots or 10g bunch
   coriander

5 Lebanese/small cucumbers

800g long-grain rice

soy sauce

toasted sesame oil

ketjap/kecap manis

For the chilli sauce:

10 mild red chillies, about 12cm
   long

50ml stock from the chicken

½ tsp salt

2 tbsp lime juice

sugar

For the ginger sauce:

50g fresh ginger

50ml hot chicken stock

½ tsp sugar

For the garnish:

2 vine tomatoes

10g bunch coriander

Put your hand inside the chicken cavity and remove any nuggets of white fat. Set aside. Rinse the chicken inside and out. Smash one 50g knob of ginger with a rolling pin or similar and rub it all over the chicken with the salt. Place the smashed ginger inside the cavity with 2 crushed garlic cloves and 2 trimmed spring onions, folded in half to fit. Choose a large lidded pan that can comfortably hold the chicken thoroughly when immersed in water or stock. Place 1 pandan leaf, 3 trimmed spring onions, a second 50g knob of ginger, sliced but unpeeled, 3 crushed garlic cloves, the coriander roots or bunch in the pan with the stock or water. Bring to the boil.

Immerse the back of the chicken in the boiling stock and allow the stock to come back to the boil. After 2 minutes of boiling, use tongs to turn the chicken, returning it breast down to the stock. Return to the boil and, depending on the size of the chicken, boil for 4–6 minutes. Turn off the heat, cover the pan and leave the chicken to soak in the stock for at least 45 minutes. Use tongs to carefully remove the chicken, emptying any stock back into the pan. Run the chicken under cold water; this gives the skin the rubbery, jellyfish texture. I don't bother to do this, as I always discard all the skin from my serving. Leave the chicken on a chopping board to cool.

While the chicken cools, prepare everything else. To make the chilli sauce, split the chillies, discard the stalks and scrape away the seeds. Coarsely chop, then pulse in a small liquidizer/food processor with the stock, salt and lime juice until finely chopped and sauce-like. Watch out for a whoosh of chilli when you remove the lid, taste tentatively, then bring down the heat with sugar. To make the ginger sauce, peel and very finely grate the ginger. Add the 50ml of hot chicken stock and season with salt and sugar. Peel the cucumbers and slice quite chunkily on the diagonal. Pack the cucumber in a gratin-style serving dish or dishes or on a large platter. Cover with clingfilm.

Wash the rice until the water runs clean. Strain and measure off 1 litre of stock into a small pan. Measure the remaining stock and if necessary make it up to 1.2 litres with a stock cube and water. Smash the last knob of ginger and peel and chop the remaining 2 garlic cloves. In a suitable lidded pan, render the chicken fat and stir in the ginger and garlic. Add the rice and another pandan leaf and cook, stirring often, for 5 minutes. The rice can be prepared until this stage and finished 30 minutes before it is required. Add the 1.2 litres of stock and bring to the boil. Reduce the heat, cover the pan and cook very gently for 10 minutes. Turn off the heat. Leave for 10 minutes without removing the lid. Fork up and turn out into a warm serving dish.

To prepare the garnish for the soup, quarter the tomatoes and scrape away the seeds. Slice the tomatoes into strips and then into dice. Place in a bowl and cover with clingfilm. Coarsely chop 2 tablespoons of coriander. Place in a bowl and cover with clingfilm.

When the chicken has cooled, chop it into chunky pieces and arrange them, skin side up, over the cucumber. Do this by removing the legs first. Joint then chop the thigh in half across the bone. Use kitchen scissors to remove the two breasts attached to the ribcage (if preferred, slip the whole breast off the bone) and cut across the width to make 5 or 6 pieces from each one. Moisten the pieces with a ladle of hot stock (from the soup broth), splash with soy sauce and glisten with sesame oil. Decorate with sprigs of coriander and a few pieces of the tomato prepared for the soup. Serve the chicken and rice for people to help themselves, putting the ginger and chilli sauces and *ketjap/kecap manis* on the table.

Finally, bring the soup stock to the boil, pour into Chinese-style soup bowls, decorate with the prepared tomatoes and coriander and serve piping hot alongside each placing.

W Whisks

There is something very appealing about the distant sound of a whisk at
work in someone else's kitchen. I always imagine an omelette in the
making and I've been known to down tools and make one myself. It's
quite rare to hear the rhythmic beat of a globe whisk coming from my
kitchen because my favourite whisk is silenced with silicone. Instead of
the loops scratching across the pan or bowl as they work, a silicone-
covered whisk thuds in a muffled way with the extra bonus that non-stick
pans are safe from scratches. Mine is a balloon whisk, shaped like a wide,
elongated peardrop, anchored in a heavy stainless steel handle. The
curved edges of the loops are harmonious with the shape of a mixing
bowl. I have various similar, larger classic whisks like the favourite but
without silicone and they are used when it's in the dishwasher. Very small
versions, with a wire coil instead of a solid handle, are useful for whisking
a single egg or a small amount of cream, or milk for cappuccino; in fact
one lives in my sponge bag specially for my friend Tessa's breakfast
coffee when we are on holiday in Lemnos. Even better for all these jobs is
the so-called Roux whisk, a loop of steel piping encased in a thin, light
handle, the end covered with a loose spring or tight twist. Its clever design
makes it ideal for whisking in shallow vessels but I find it clogs up if used
to smooth a thick, flour-based sauce.

Aeration is the main function of a whisk, turning egg white and
cream fluffy and light. Sometimes a hand-held whisk is a better option
than an electric one because it gives more control. Hand whisks are also
invaluable for smoothing a sauce and removing lumps in gravy.

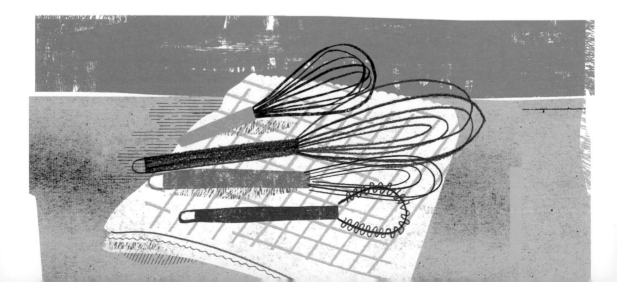

Fresh Pineapple Custard with Chilli

SERVES 4–6

Serving pineapple with chilli is an idea I picked up in Mauritius and the combination has wow factor appeal in this egg custard cooked in a shallow dish. The chilli heat is softened by the sweetness of the pineapple but the flavours, though subtle, and not immediately obvious, deliver the occasional hit of mild chilli. The pineapple is sliced into small, quite thin pieces and baked on its own before the custard is added, making it incredibly juicy and tender. The pudding is ready when the edges are puffy and golden and the top has souffléd into a pineapple patchwork, but it is best eaten lukewarm and slightly deflated.

1 small red chilli	2 medium egg yolks
300ml milk	100ml full-fat crème fraîche
1 medium-sized ripe pineapple	50g caster sugar
a knob of butter	1 tbsp flour
2 medium eggs	

Heat the oven to 200°C/gas mark 6. Trim, split, deseed and finely chop the chilli. Place in a pan with the milk and a pinch of salt. Simmer gently for 3 minutes. Turn off the heat. Cover and leave while you prepare everything else. Trim the pineapple, stand it on one end and slice off the rind. Remove all the hairy 'eyes'. Quarter the pineapple cylinder lengthways, then lengthways halve the pieces. Slice off the pithy core and cut into 1cm thick triangles. You want about 400g of pineapple.

Smear a 5cm deep, 2 litre capacity gratin-style ceramic dish with butter and pile in the pineapple, smoothing the surface. Bake the pineapple for 10 minutes. Rest for 5 minutes. Place the eggs, egg yolks, crème fraîche, caster sugar and sifted flour in a mixing bowl. Whisk only until smooth and fluffy. Gradually whisk in the warm milk. Pour the custard over the pineapple. Bake for 40–45 minutes, until golden and puffy, just set and firm to a flat hand. Cool before serving at room temperature.

W White Bowls

Most people who cook for pleasure enjoy serving their food on white china. It is the obvious choice. I am always adding to my collection but I have a particular weakness for large white bowls. Some girls like Louboutins, I like white bowls. My main pile is stacked in a deep shelf above the oven. The oldest survivor – many bowls have come and gone – is Italian (ARM Ceramica). It started out white but has developed a pleasing network of fine lines similar to crackleware. It's the perfect family bowl, measuring 26 x 14cm high with a nipped in 11cm base. It has a pretty rolled lip with a border marked on the inside under which it curves and tapers to a narrow base with a deep indent on the underside. There must be reasons for these details but I don't know what they are. It is reminiscent of a wider, squatter, heavier, thicker, whiter and glossier Pillivuyt French porcelain bowl of a similar size. The latter gets used for gazpacho and other cold soups, and hot dishes like chili or a stew, while the Italian bowl is favourite for potato salad, lentil salads and pasta dishes, particularly tomato-based sauces and meatballs.

A squatter, wider bowl with a pronounced curve to its base is favourite for stewed fruit and pea salads with tomatoes and white cheese; I love this combination. A larger version of that bowl (another ARM Ceramica), with a base almost as wide as its diameter, cries out for figs and Parma ham, stuffed tomatoes and peppers, courgettes and aubergine lasagne, and curls of lettuce covered with a tumble of tabbouleh or Thai-style minced pork with sweet chilli sauce. The *pièce de résistance* of my white bowls, also made by ARM Ceramica, has a pretty scalloped edge. This bowl is always centre stage when there's a party. It looks stunning filled with a colourful couscous salad, or stuffed vine leaves, or a humungous fruit salad. It was a gift from my friend Tessa.

The simplest way to warm a large white bowl, incidentally, is with boiling water from the kettle.

The Favourite Potato Salad

SERVES 4

I always make potato salad in the same bowl: the big, deep white one with a slight crackle effect that I've loved for years. I make it all year round. Sometimes I add scraps of crisp bacon or chopped black olives, or sliced red onion wilted first in boiling water then lime juice. Sometimes I add grated hard-boiled egg and ring the changes with different herbs; it might be flat-leaf parsley with a little shallot mixed into the dressing, or dill if I'm serving it with fish, but my all-time favourite is chives. I love the simplicity of this recipe. The background hint of mint and the fresh onion tang from the chives goes with everything and anything, from roast peppers and burrata or mozzarella, to lamb or chicken kebabs.

There are two important points about making potato salad. One is to peel the potatoes and the other is to add the dressing while the potatoes are still hot. The first means you won't get potato skin interfering with the creamy textures and the second means the dressing flavours the potatoes rather than sitting on top of them.

750g small new potatoes	1 tbsp red wine vinegar
2 sprigs of mint	150ml/6 tbsp sunflower or
1 tbsp Hellmann's mayonnaise	groundnut oil
1 tbsp smooth Dijon mustard	a bunch of chives

Boil the washed but unpeeled potatoes in salted water with the mint until just tender. Drain. Return to the pan and refill with cold water, leaving the tap running for a minute or so. Drain again; the potatoes will still be hot but cool enough to remove the skin without too much discomfort.

While the potatoes boil, make the dressing in your chosen bowl. Put in the mayo and stir in the mustard, pushing it to the side. Add the vinegar in a puddle next to the mayo mix. Season with a generous twist of Maldon sea salt and a few grinds of black pepper, stirring to dissolve the salt. Now mix the two together. Add the oil gradually, whisking it in with a globe whisk until smooth and creamy. Add the hot potatoes and mix thoroughly with a rubber spatula. Snip the chives over the top – you want at least 3 tablespoons – and mix them in just before serving. I like the salad still warm.

Crab with Black Spaghetti

SERVES 4

One of my favourite convenience treats is a 100g carton of white Cornish crab, freshly picked in Newlyn (see page 276). The silky white meat is perfect for this simple yet classy pasta supper. The glistening strands of silky crab look stunning against black spaghetti, but ordinary spaghetti gives similarly delicious results.

The crab is mixed with finely chopped red chilli, its heat softened slightly by olive oil, lemon juice and lots of coriander. This lovely South East Asian inspired combination of flavours is wonderful on thick slabs of hot, buttered crusty toast or piled into curls of lettuce heart, but when mixed with peeled and seeded, finely sliced cucumber, preferably so-called little Lebanese cucumbers, it makes the perfect summery salad-sauce for spaghetti and can be served hot or cold.

1 red bird's-eye chilli	50g fresh coriander
4 tbsp best olive oil	1 Lebanese cucumber or a 14cm
300g black or regular spaghetti	piece of cucumber
2 x 100g tubs of fresh white crabmeat	1 lemon

Put a full kettle on to boil. Trim the chilli and split lengthways. Scrape away the seeds, and slice first into thin strips and then into tiny dice. Place in a ramekin, or similar, and cover with 3 tablespoons of olive oil.

Cook the spaghetti in a large pan in lavishly salted boiling water from the kettle. Drain and return to the pan with the remaining 1 tablespoon of olive oil. Toss and cover to keep hot.

Place the crab in a mixing bowl. Finely chop the coriander. Use a potato peeler to peel the cucumber. Split lengthways and use a teaspoon to scrape out the seeds. Slice into very thin half-moons. Stir the cucumber into the spaghetti. Stir the chilli and its oil into the crab with the chopped coriander. Season with lemon juice, a little salt and plenty of freshly grated black pepper. Fold the spaghetti into the crab and tip into a warmed white bowl to serve.

W Wok

My wok hangs unloved and forgotten for months on end, then something sets me off and I want to use it for everything. It is an incredibly versatile pan for cooking over a flame, suitable for frying, obviously, but also for steaming, poaching, braising, even smoking. It becomes more versatile with a lid. Its shape is extremely clever, curved so that liquid collects in the bottom but with a wide diameter that means there is plenty of room for tossing ingredients, enabling large quantities of finely sliced or chopped food to be cooked at the same time. Once food is cooked, it can be kept on hold, as it were, away from direct heat at the edge of the pan.

My wok is huge, family-size, with a chunky wooden handle that never gets hot so negates the need to have an oven glove at the ready. I bought it years ago in London's Chinatown for a pittance. After years of loving care the carbon steel has blackened to a perfect non-stick surface but it is easy to find a wok with a ready-made non-stick surface, although it will eventually wear out. Many woks come with a lid and a special metal ring or collar to set over the flame to support the rounded base that is otherwise unstable. When I bought my hob, I was very keen on stir-frying and bought one with a double-burner wok ring.

Chinese woks like mine are made of thin carbon steel to absorb the heat quickly and evenly, so food has to be kept on the move to avoid burning. This is done with a long, wooden-handled, flat metal spoon-cum-spatula that shovels up the food and makes tossing and moving it extremely pleasurable.

Carbon steel woks have to be initially 'seasoned' by heating them up with salt and beaten egg then rubbing with oil. There is a palaver attached to owning such a wok. To avoid rusting, it has to be washed up fairly immediately after use, dried with kitchen paper and smeared with a little oil. This does, though, build the non-stick surface. When my sons went off to college, I bought them both smaller woks like mine. Judging by the state of one I came across recently, my advice about how to look after it obviously fell on deaf ears.

The golden rules of wok cooking are to prepare all the food, even measuring out the sauces and seasonings, in advance, and have everything lined up ready to hit the hot pan as needed and in the right order. Always place the wok over the burner and allow it to get very hot before adding a little oil. This is swirled round the wok before the food is added. Keep the food moving all the time, tossing constantly so nothing burns and nothing ends up raw.

Stir-fried Sprouts with Nutmeg

SERVES 6–8

This is now my family's preferred way of cooking sprouts at Christmas. It sounds odd, but briefly stir-frying shredded sprouts with an awful lot of nutmeg crumblings rather than gratings is really delicious. The preparation can be done in advance and then the cooking is fast and furious and very last-minute. The idea was inspired by Jeremy Round, in his book The Independent Cook. *He did something similar with caraway seed.*

750g Brussels sprouts	4 tbsp vegetable oil
2 whole nutmegs	

Trim the sprouts. Cut into quarters lengthways, then halve the quarters lengthways. Use a small, sharp knife to shave the nutmeg into crumbly scraps. Heat the oil in a wok over a very high heat. Add the sprouts, toss a few times, then add the nutmeg shavings. Continue stir-frying for 2–3 minutes, no more.

Prawn Egg-fried Rice with Chilli and Coriander

SERVES 3

Egg-fried rice is excellent fridge tidy food. Those leftover peas, the pickings from the roast chicken or the single egg can be the beginnings of Chinese-style egg-fried rice. It was one of the first things my son Henry learnt to cook. When he was about six or seven, he loved going to Chinatown and wandering round the shops; a dim sum lunch was his idea of heaven. I kept a supply of cooked rice in the fridge specially, so he could make 'fri ri' with whatever else was in need of eating up. 'What must be avoided,' says legendary Chinese expert Kenneth Lo in his book Chinese Vegetable and Vegetarian Cooking, *'is a fried rice that is so mixed-up that it borders on a mess.' Ah so.*

200g basmati rice
100g frozen peas
150g raw, peeled prawns
1 garlic clove
8 spring onions

25g bunch coriander
2 eggs
3 tbsp vegetable oil
3 tbsp sweet chilli sauce
2 tbsp soy sauce

Rinse the rice until the water runs clean. Place in a pan with 350ml water, bring to the boil, then reduce the heat very low, cover and cook for 10 minutes. Turn off the heat and leave covered for 10 minutes. Fork up the rice and spread out on a plate to cool. Cook the peas in boiling water. Drain. Uncurl the prawns and halve lengthways. Wipe away the thin black vein. Peel and finely chop the garlic and crush to a paste with the flat of a knife. Trim and finely slice the spring onions. Finely chop the coriander.

Beat the eggs with a fork with ½ tablespoon of oil, 1 tablespoon of chilli sauce and half the chopped coriander. Mix the remaining chilli and the soy sauce in a ramekin. Get a wok very hot, add the remaining oil and quickly swirl it round. Add the spring onions and stir-fry continuously for 30 seconds. Add the prawns and garlic and keep the food moving, continuing as the prawns change colour. Add the rice, peas, chilli and soy sauce. Toss thoroughly for a few seconds until hot, then add the egg, stirring vigorously, mixing it through the rice. Add the last of the coriander and serve with the chilli and soy sauce bottles.

W Wooden Spoons

On the window ledge above my kitchen sink is a large blue and white striped Cornish Ware jug full of wooden spoons and spatulas and wooden-handled pastry brushes. My favourite spoon is always right at the front, instantly recognizable and seeming to push itself forward to be chosen for action. It generally is my first choice and has been for an incredible thirty-odd years. I bought it in Tabarka, on the north-west coast of Tunisia, when I worked there at an Arts Festival. Every few days a dusty space on the edge of town filled with people selling their wares and I bought a lot wooden spoons, many of which I gave away as presents when I got back. They all look obviously hand-carved,

but the favourite feels smooth and slippery in my hand and has worn to fit nicely into the corners of my pans and bowls as I stir and beat.

Two other survivors are far smaller, almost like teaspoons but with nearly flat, elongated bowls and disproportionately long handles. I use them when I want to be dainty. Then there is a spoon made of light, pale wood, its bowl mirroring the shape of an egg. And that's what I use it for, lowering breakfast eggs into boiling water and fishing them out again a few minutes later.

I have two neatly carved, rather elegant, pointed spoons made, I think, from bamboo. One lives in the salt jar at the other end of the window ledge, the other is useful for stirring creamy sauces and maybe scrambled eggs for one or two. Another favourite is the corgi of wooden spoons, with a big, flattish bowl and curiously short handle. It is my first choice when I'm making a cheese sauce, because it feels so connected with the food as I stir. There is another similarly short spoon with an endearingly curved handle that I single out when I'm making custard.

The rest of my spoons, and there are about ten of them, are in various states of wear and tear and have less specific roles. Although all are old and distinctive, they are not in the same league as the favourites. I've forgotten to mention my two long spoons. One is carved from dark, mottled wood like walnut and its very long handle means it avoids splashback when stirring polenta. The other long spoon is chunky and about two feet long and is my jam-making spoon.

And finally, a spoon for extracting pickled onions. It's a bit like a pipe, beautifully turned, but the bowl has holes drilled all over it, and there is dainty detail on the handle. I automatically set it out with the pickled onions but it rarely gets used because it's far easier to pick them out with your fingers.

My wooden spatulas are equally distinctive. I have five, all made from different wood so quite different to handle. I tend to use them with non-stick frying pans but I find the wood too thick to work deftly like my beloved fish slice. The one I like the most is the smallest and most idiosyncratic. I think the wood is oak because it feels sturdy and strong but is light and thin, beautifully smooth and neatly tapered at the end to give a thin finish. It would be ideal for scooping up eggs and turning fish and is obviously made by someone who understands the finer details of spatulas. That person was Ben, my ex-husband, who got into wood-turning in a big way in his later years. It was made specially for me, a last gift given to me after he had died. It's silly, I know, but I keep it on my desk in my study and have never used it.

I would be lost without my wooden spoons. I use them every day, stirring this, beating that and flipping something else. They get mentioned time over time in the recipes in this book, so it seems a bit unfair to single out one recipe. So I won't.

Y Yorkshire Pudding Tray

The first time individual Yorkshire puddings made a serious impression on me was in the early days of Bibendum when Simon Hopkinson was chef. Big, crisp Yorkshire puddings came with a traditional roast beef Sunday lunch. The recipe, he said, was Delia's but he liked to add fizzy mineral water instead of tap, believing it made a difference. That was enough for me, so I went out and bought two Yorkshire pudding trays and the Delia-via-Simon batter is what I always make.

Yorkshire pudding can, of course, be made in any sturdy, metal baking tin or bun tray, but a so-called Yorkshire pudding tray has four shallow, wide indentations to make just the right sized individual puddings. It is also known as a 4-cup tin, or muffin tin in the States. The tray is likely to have a non-stick coating and the straight sides and flat base of the indentations encourage the puddings to rise and crisp quickly and evenly.

The pudding mixture is actually a thick pancake batter, but proportions of egg to flour, milk and water, and seasoning, vary from cook to cook. Elaine Lemm, author of an exhaustive little book on the subject, *The Great Book of Yorkshire Pudding* (Great Northern Books, 2010), says the secret is to weigh the eggs and then mix them with an equal weight of seasoned flour and milk, adding a splash of cold water after resting for a minimum 30 minutes. She likes to whisk the eggs and milk together and then add the flour. Also crucial is pouring the batter into a small amount of very hot fat and cooking the Yorkshires at a very high temperature. In my experience, the batter performs differently every time and puddings never rise evenly. This wonky aspect adds to their charm.

Part of the pleasure of Yorkshire pudding is a certain amount of gooey middle, and the proportion of goo to crisp is greater if it's made, as my mother always did, in a roasting tin. We only ever had Yorkshire pudding with roast beef but in Yorkshire it's a course on its own, often with onion gravy, sometimes with stewed fruit and custard. Toad-in-the-hole, though, which is basically stuffed Yorkshire pudding, was a regular weekday supper.

Leftover batter can be thinned with extra milk or water to make pancakes. Adding sugar to the mix will turn individual Yorkshire puddings into popovers. These are delicious hot from the oven, slathered with thick cream and cold stewed fruit.

Mushroom Toad with Caramelized Onion, Red Wine Gravy and Poached Eggs

SERVES 2–4

One of these makes a good snack or first course, two will satisfy most appetites and is a great weekend brunch with crisp bacon on the side. There is sufficient batter for eight puddings.

For the batter:	1 tbsp olive oil
150g plain flour	a small sprig of fresh rosemary
2 medium eggs	1 tbsp thick balsamic vinegar
150ml milk	2 tbsp flour
dripping or lard	250ml red wine
4 tbsp fizzy water	2–4 eggs
For the filling:	1 tbsp red wine vinegar
200g button mushrooms	1 tsp snipped chives
1 medium onion	

Sift the flour into a mixing bowl with a generous pinch of salt. Add the eggs and milk and whisk smooth. Leave to rest for 30 minutes. Heat the oven to 220°C/gas mark 7.

Smear the base and sides of two 4-hole non-stick Yorkshire pudding trays with dripping or lard. Place in the oven until the fat is smoking. Add the fizzy water to the batter and give it a final stir. One-third fill the indentations with batter and quickly return the pan to the oven. Cook for 25 minutes, or until the puddings are puffy and golden.

Wipe the mushrooms clean and cut in half. Halve, peel and finely chop the onion. Heat the olive oil in a spacious frying pan and gently soften the onion, allowing 10–15 minutes.

Chop the rosemary to dust and stir into the onion. Increase the heat slightly and add the mushrooms. Stir constantly – at first they will seem dry but they will quickly turn shiny. At this point season with salt and pepper and add the balsamic vinegar. Stir as it bubbles up into the mushrooms and virtually disappears. Sift the flour over the top, stirring it into the juices, then add the wine gradually, continuing to stir to make a smooth sauce. Simmer until the liquid reduces by half and the mushrooms have shrunk and darkened. If it turns very thick, add a little water. Remove from the heat.

Crack the eggs, one at a time, into a cup and slip, one after the other, into a pan of simmering water acidulated with the vinegar. Simmer for 2–3 minutes, until the egg white is set but the yolk still soft. Place one or more Yorkshires on a plate, fill with the quickly reheated mushroom mixture, top with an egg and sprinkle with chives. Yum.

Individual Potato Gratins

SERVES 4

I'm crazy about this way of cooking potatoes. I tried it first when I wanted something quick but special to go with steak, and it was so good, so crusty yet creamy, that I make them to go with everything from egg and bacon to roast chicken.

It is basically deconstructed pommes Dauphinoise *but these gratins end up drier and crisper – just over a centimetre thick – and comparatively healthy, as the cream quota is far lower.*

a knob of butter
600g medium-sized potatoes
Maldon sea salt
4 tbsp full-fat crème fraîche

2 tbsp milk
Optional extras:
1 garlic clove and 1 tsp finely
  chopped thyme

For a background hint of garlic, cut the garlic in half and rub vigorously over the tins. Smear the base and sides of 2 × 4-hole non-stick Yorkshire pudding trays with butter. Scrub or scrape the potatoes and slice finely, as if making thick crisps, on a mandoline or the appropriate attachment of your food processor. Place them, un-rinsed, in a mixing bowl. Add a generous pinch of salt, and mix with your hands. Heat together the crème fraîche and milk, and add the thyme if liked, stirring to melt the cream. Immediately remove from the heat and spoon 4 tablespoons of milky cream into the potatoes. Mix thoroughly, using a wooden spoon or, better still, your hands, so all the slices are smeared with cream.

Pile the slices into the prepared tins and finish with a neat round slice in the middle. Heat the oven to 200°C/gas mark 6 and bake for 40 minutes, checking after 30, until the potato pile is tender and the top golden. Remove from the oven and rest for a couple of minutes before running a metal spatula under and around the gratins so they lift out neatly. They reheat very successfully on foil in a hot oven for 10 minutes.

Z Zester

I'm pretty certain that my mother didn't own a zester and it's only relatively recently that I have. For years I used a swivel-head potato peeler to remove the zest from lemons or other citrus fruit, then a sharp paring knife to remove any white, then chopped it into whatever sized pieces I wanted for my recipe. I have been known to chop it to dust, sometimes with rosemary, to make an intense seasoning for stews or to flavour breadcrumbs for escalopes or gratins.

The first zester I bought is a stumpy little stainless steel tool, with a heavy round handle set with a squared, slightly hooked blade. A row of five small holes is punched in the end, cut to create a sharp raised edge. The blade is dragged firmly across the surface of the lemon, orange or other citrus fruit, and the holes remove tiny strings of zest.

These can be used as they are or chopped smaller. There is a larger hole on the side of the blade for single strings of zest.

My latest and current favourite zester-cum-grater (made by Edgeware) is long and thin, with tiny perforations-cum-blades covered with a non-stick ceramic coating. This ensures that zest, or anything else for that matter, doesn't stick. It also has a sliding chamber to collect whatever has been grated, and a protective cover for safe storage. Also see Graters (page 81).

Cauliflower and Lemon Soup

SERVES 4

St Piran is the patron saint of Cornwall and, along with pasties, cream teas and clotted cream, crab, new potatoes and fish, I particularly associate cauliflower with Cornwall and have got into the habit of making this soup on St Piran's Day, 5 March. Lemon zest and a hint of chilli, with mascarpone – or clotted cream – and quite a lot of Parmesan, work wonders on what Mark Twain described as cabbage with a college education. The soup gets an extra upgrade if you serve it with bruschetta or another garlic bread.

1 medium onion	1 unwaxed lemon
1 large garlic clove	1½ chicken stock cubes
1 tbsp olive oil	2 tbsp mascarpone or clotted cream
a generous pinch of chilli flakes	4 tbsp grated Parmesan
1 medium-sized cauliflower	

Boil the kettle. Peel, halve and finely chop the onion and garlic. Heat the olive oil over a medium-low heat in a pan that can accommodate the soup. Stir in the onion, garlic, chilli and ½ teaspoon of salt. Cover and cook, stirring once, for 15 minutes, adjusting the heat so the vegetables sweat and soften rather than brown.

Meanwhile, remove the green cauliflower leaves, quarter the cauli and chop each quarter into 4 or 5 pieces. Remove the zest from the lemon. Dissolve the stock cubes in 1 litre of water from the kettle. Add the stock, cauliflower and lemon zest to the pan. Bring to the boil, reduce the heat to a simmer, cover with a tilted lid and cook until tender. Liquidize in batches, return to a clean pan, stir in the mascarpone and Parmesan, taste and adjust the seasoning with lemon juice.

Lemon and Honey Madeleines

I love these pretty little cakes warm from the oven. If you don't own a special madeleine baking tray, use a tart tray. They erupt, Vesuvius-like, as they bake but it is the ridged underside that gives them their distinctive puppy paw look. Eat them as they are, or dusted with icing sugar. These madeleines look very pretty smeared with a lemon glaze, made by mixing 75g of icing sugar with 2 teaspoons of lemon juice and a smidgin of water. Another idea is to dip one end in melted chocolate. Delicious with a cuppa or a cappuccino, they also go with jelly, milk puddings and ice cream.

75g butter, plus an extra knob
1 unwaxed lemon
2 eggs
50g caster sugar

3 tbsp runny honey
100g plain flour, plus a little extra
½ tsp baking powder
a pinch of salt

Melt the butter. Finely grate 1 teaspoon of lemon zest. Stir the zest into the melted butter and leave for 10 minutes. Using an electric mixer, beat the eggs and caster sugar until pale, thick and fluffy. Add the honey and beat for a further couple of minutes. Sift the flour, baking powder and salt into a bowl. Gently fold the dry ingredients into the wet ones, followed by the lemon butter, to make a thick, smooth batter. Stretch a sheet of clingfilm over the bowl, sagging to skim the batter, and chill for an hour, after which the mixture will have thickened and turned spongy.

Heat the oven to 200°C/gas mark 6. If using a metal mould, butter 12 indentations, dust with flour and shake out the excess. If using a silicone mould, this shouldn't be necessary. Put a spoonful of mix into each mould so they are three-quarters full. Place on a middle shelf of the oven and bake for 10-14 minutes, until golden, swollen in the middle and the tops spring back when lightly pressed. If using a tin mould, tap on the side to loosen the cakes before turning out on to a cake rack to cool. A silicone mould should peel away.

Recommended Suppliers/ Stockists/Useful Information

EQUIPMENT

Burger press
Lakeland (**www.lakeland. co.uk**) sell the Quarter Pounder Burger Press.

Cake tins
Amazon (**www.amazon.co.uk**). John Lewis (**www. johnlewis.com**). Lakeland (**www.lakeland. co.uk**), especially their PushPan range.

Casserole pans
Le Creuset (**www.lecreuset.co.uk**).

Charlotte moulds
Alan Silverwood (**www. alansilverwood.co.uk**) make excellent inexpensive aluminium moulds.

Chicken bricks
www.habitat.co.uk sell one that holds a large chicken, and **www. internetgardener.co.uk** sell one that is large enough to hold a small turkey.

Crab crackers
Denny & Sons (**www. dennyandsons.co.uk**) for pink ones.

Dariole moulds
Silicone dariole moulds, sold singly or joined in sets, are available through **www. siliconemoulds.com**.

Fish kettle
www.fishkettle.co.uk gives a consumer guide to what's available.

Fondue
www.fondueBits.com is devoted to fondue and offers a helpful consumer guide, with reviews of all types of fondue sets, including cast iron and electric. **www.cookoo. co.uk** is a good place to look for Swiss sets. Hilaire Walden, *Fantastic Fondues*, (Piatkus, 1998).

Food processor
Magimix: spares for all models can be bought through **www.magimix-spares.co.uk**. BBS Ltd, the family business who run the online store, are always available for advice (tel. 01252 727755, or visit their Farnham showroom: Unit B, Grovebell Industrial Estate, Wrecclesham Road, Farnham, Surrey GU10 4PL).

Frying pan
For a tarte Tatin pan, Alan Silverwood (**www. alansilverwood.co.uk**).

Funnels
For your nearest stockist of the Architec funnel, telephone 0151 647 1748.

Griddle
The Swift griddle is available from Lakeland (**www.lakeland.co.uk**).

Glass jars
Lakeland (**www.lakeland. co.uk**) is an inexpensive source of Le Parfait preserving jars and they also sell the rubber seals separately.

Gratin dishes
To see the Form 1382 and Tric range from Arzberg, visit **www.rmhall.com.au**, a fabulous site for anyone interested in fine ceramics, and buy them through **www.kitchenshop.com**. Le Creuset (**www. lecreuset.com**).

Griddle pan
Grillit range from Le Creuset (**www.lecreuset.com**). For tongs to use on the griddle, see opposite.

Jelly moulds
www.kitchencraft.co.uk for a wide range of replica Victorian shapes made in

inexpensive plastic.
Sam Bompas and Harry
Parr (**www.jellymongers.
co.uk**).
Jelly with Bompas & Parr
(Pavilion, 2010);
Peter Brears, *Jellies & Their
Moulds* (Prospect Books,
2010).

Knives
www.cooks-knives.co.uk
and **www.chefsknifestore.
co.uk**.
Henckels, Opinel, **www.
pamperedchef.co.uk** and
www.johnlewis.com sell
various block sets of knives
that afford good value.

Nutcracker
For my Italian
Schiaccianoci nutcracker,
see **www.premax.it**.
For the Mono Pico
walnut opener, **www.
designathome.co.uk**.

Paella kit and pans
The Paella Company sell
various kits and numerous
pans of different sizes
and finishes (**www.
thepaellacompany.co.uk**).
Alberto Herraiz, *Paella*
(Phaidon, 2011).

Parchment-lined foil
Lakeland (**www.lakeland.
co.uk**).

Pestle and mortar
Thai style granite pestle
and mortar (**www.
hartsofstur.com**).
Double-ended mortar by
Vacu Vin, available through
www.amazon.co.uk.

Pie funnel
To see Clarice Cliff,
Nutbrown and other
pie funnels, visit **www.
homethingspast.com**.
For Stuart Bass pottery,
see **www.squidoo.com/
pie-bird**.
June Tyler, *Collecting Stuart
Bass Pie Funnels*, (2010)
(**www.pie-funnels.co.uk**).

Piping bag
For the Lékué Decomax,
shaped like a bowl with a
spout, see **www.lekue.es**.

Plastic boxes
Large quantities: catering
supplier **www.cater4you.
co.uk** sell boxes in sets
of 50. Boxes in smaller
quantities: I get mine
from Del's Housewares
in Shepherd's Bush (125
Askew Rd, London W12
9AU, tel. 020 8743 4949).
And from
www.whiskcooking.co.uk.

Potato masher
For the traditional Tala
potato masher, **www.
picup.co.uk**.
For the German-made
stainless steel masher,
www.wmf.com.

Potato peeler
For the Fissler potato
peeler, suitable for left- and
right-handed users, **www.
finestkitchenware.co.uk**.

Pudding basins
For vintage Mason
Cash basins, see **www.
robertopiecollection.com**.

For modern Mason Cash
basins, including sets of six,
see **www.supaprice.co.uk**.

Roasting tins
Alan Silverwood (**www.
alansilverwood.co.uk**).
Lakeland (**www.lakeland.
co.uk**).

Salad bowls
For Guzzini bowls, **www.
madeindesign.com**.
For Zuperzozial bowls,
www.formahouse.co.uk.

Saucepans
For Le Pentole pans, **www.
davidmellordesign.com**.
Pans sometimes come up
on eBay (**www.ebay.co.uk**),
and 'bargain' sets can be
bought through **www.
cookoo.co.uk**.
For the Stellar Eazi pan set,
see **www.lakeland.co.uk**.
For budget pans, see **www.
ikea.com**.

Steamer
Hackman steamers, see
www.hackman.fi.

Tin opener
Super Kim tin opener,
from **www.labourandwait.
co.uk**.

Toaster
Virtual toaster museum
(**www.toaster.org**).

Tongs
24cm tongs are available
from **www.cookware.
co.uk**, and 24cm, 30cm and
40cm tongs from **www.
divertimenti.co.uk**.

Black garlic
www.blackgarlic.co.uk.

Crabmeat
Waitrose sell packs of white and brown handpicked Cornish crab from **www.seafoodandeatit. co.uk**, and you can also order it through **www. crabmeat.co.uk** and **www. fishforthought.co.uk**.

Duck
See **www.gressingham foods.co.uk**, for full details of how to carve a duck.

Fish
Turners, Newlyn (**www.jhturner.co.uk**), my favourite fish shop. For information about eco-friendly fish, **www.fishonline.org**.

For overnight delivery, **www.fishforthought.co.uk**.

Limoncello
For tips on making limoncello, check out **www.limoncelloquest. com**.

Nuts
The Nut Tree (**www.thenuttree.co.uk**) – a brilliant website.

Scallops
For fine Isle of Man queen scallops, vacuum-packed, go to **www.manxkippers. com**. For overnight delivery of diver-caught scallops on the half shell, **www.fishforthought.co.uk**. They also sell scallop shells. Greater quantities and different sized shells can be bought through

shell specialist **www. scallopshells.net**. For details of the annual scallop week in Rye, see **www.ryebayscallops.co.uk**.

Suet pastry
If you have leftover suet pastry, it is superb for pasties. For recipes, see Lindsey Bareham, *Pasties*, (Mabecron Books, 2008).

Vegetables
In London, Andreas Chiswick and Andreas Chelsea (**www.andreasveg.co.uk**), who supply the River Café.

Wagyu beef
Buy it through **www. freedownfood.co.uk/ wagyubeef.aspx**, or your butcher may be able to order it for you.

Acknowledgements

Writing this book has been a roller coaster of memories. Once I started, it became obvious that food is far more of a repository of emotion than we give it credit for, easily on a par with music and clothes. Those memories came thick and fast as I began to write, and while most centre round my childhood, many relate to this house and my two sons.

In no particular order, I especially want to thank my cousin Liz Bailey and her daughter Frances Lee, who tracked down the Sanderson Christmas pudding recipe and filled me in on family history. I also want to thank Andrew Payne, Roger Margrave, Roger de Freitas, Eddie Lim, my sons Zach and Henry, my agent Andrew Gordon, and Rebecca Wright, my editor, who saw the potential in this project and made it happen. Thank you, too, to Chris Terry and his evocative photography and to Lawrence Morton for interpreting the mood of the book so well.

The person most crucial to this book is Tessa de Mestre, my dear friend who is very much part of my kitchen. She even has her own ashtray here. Thank you, dear Tess.

Index